After the Flood

The Early post-Flood History of Europe

Bill Cooper

New Wine Press

New Wine Press
PO Box 17
Chichester
West Sussex PO20 6YB
England

ISBN: 1 874367 40 X

Typeset by CRB Associates, Reepham, Norfolk
Printed in the United States of America

'When all men were of one language, some of them built a high tower, as if they would thereby ascend up to heaven; but the gods sent storms of wind and overthrew the tower, and gave everyone his peculiar language; and for this reason it was that the city was called Babylon.... After this they were dispersed abroad, on account of their languages, and went out by colonies everywhere; and each colony took possession of that land which they lighted upon, and unto which God led them; so that the whole continent was filled with them, both the inland and maritime countries. There were some also who passed over the sea in ships, and inhabited the islands; and some of these nations do still retain the names which were given to them by their first founders; but some also have lost them...'

The Sybil (Josephus. Antiq. i. 5.)

for
Eileen
my wife

Acknowledgements

My special thanks must go to Dr David and Joan Rosevear whose active encouragement and support over the years in the face of bitter disappointments and setbacks, have ensured that this book has reached completion and may now, at long last, reach the public. My thanks must also go to Andrew Yeuille of Reading, a CSM member whose freely offered skills produced the excellent OHP slides without which my lectures on the Table of Nations would have been that much less successful. To Dr Andrew Snelling who published articles of mine on this subject in the Creation Ex Nihilo Technical Journal, and to Laurel Hemmings his very able assistant. To those numberless librarians up and down the land whose burrowings produced so much material over the years, and who freely opened their priceless archives to me. And finally, but by no means least, to my wife Eileen, to whom this book is dedicated, and whose patience and understanding over the years ensured my release from all those domestic chores which otherwise would have diverted my time away from my researches. Thank you all.

Contents

Appendices

AFTER THE FLOOD

The Early post-Flood History of Europe

Introduction

In the Beginning

It is commonly thought in this present age that nothing is worthy of our belief unless first it can be scientifically demonstrated and observed to be true. This idea, known today as empiricism, has been around since the 1920s, and says basically that nothing is to be taken on trust, and that anything which lacks direct corroboration must be discarded from mankind's fund of knowledge as simply not worth the knowing. Not surprisingly, a special case was made by those who had thought of the idea for including the Bible in this great process of deselection, and it was assumed without further enquiry that nothing in especially the earlier portions of the biblical record could be demonstrated to be true and factual. This applied particularly to the book of Genesis. There all was relegated, by modernist scholars at least, to the realms of myth and fiction, with very little of its contents being said to bear any relevance at all for 20th-century man. Not even a moral relevance was granted. In other words, we were solemnly assured in the light of modern wisdom that, historically speaking, the book of Genesis was simply not worth the paper it was written on.

When I first came across this problem some thirty years ago, I found it most perplexing. On the one hand I had the Bible itself claiming to be the very Word of God, and on the other I was presented with numerous commentaries that spoke with one voice in telling me that the Bible was nothing of the kind. It was merely a hotch-potch collection of middle- eastern myths and fables that sought to explain the world in primitive terms, whose parts had been patched together by a series of later editors. Modern scientific man need have nothing whatever to do with it.

Now, it simply was not possible for both these claims to be valid. Only one of them could be right, and I saw it as my duty, to myself at least, to find out which was the true account and which was the false. So it was then that I decided to select a certain portion of Genesis and submit it to a test which, if applied to any ordinary historical document, would be considered a test of the most unreasonable severity. And I would continue that test until either the book of Genesis revealed itself to be a false account, or it would be shown to be utterly reliable in its historical statements. Either way, I would discover once and for all whether the biblical record was worthy of my trust or not. It seemed a little irreverent to treat a book that claimed to be the very Word of God in such a fashion. But if truth has any substance at all, then that book would surely be able to bear such a test. If Genesis contained any falsehood, error or misleading statement of fact, then a severe testing would reveal it and I would be the first to add my own voice to those of all the other scholars who declared the book of Genesis to be little more than fable.

With any ordinary historical document, of course, a simple error or even a small series of errors, would not necessarily disqualify it from being regarded as an historical account, or one that could at least be made use of by historians. But Genesis is no ordinary record. No ordinary document would claim inerrancy in its statements, and any document which did make such a claim for itself could expect a thorough and severe drubbing at the hands of scholars. But, if Genesis was indeed a true account of what had happened all those years ago, if it was indeed everything that it claimed itself to be, then the truth that it proclaimed could not be destroyed by any amount of testing. It could only be vindicated. In that regard at least, truth is indestructible.

What I had not expected at the time was the fact that the task was to engage my attention and energies for more than twenty-five years. Nor had I expected the astonishing degree to which Genesis, particularly the tenth and eleventh chapters, was to be vindicated. These chapters are conveniently known to scholars as the Table of Nations, and the sheer breadth and depth of the historical evidence that was available for their study astonished me. It bore very little relation indeed to what I had been led to expect. But that was not the only surprise in store.

The test that I devised was a simple one. If the names of the individuals, families, peoples and tribes listed in the Table of Nations were genuine, then those same names should appear also in the records of other nations of the Middle East. Archaeology should also reveal that those same families and peoples are listed in Genesis (or not as the case may be) in their correct ethnological, geographical and linguistic relationships. I allowed for the fact that a good proportion of these names would not appear. Either the records that once contained them had long since perished, or the diversity of language and dialect had rendered them unrecognisable. Some would be lost in obscurity. It simply was not realistic to expect that every name would have been recorded in the annals of the ancient Middle East and would also have survived to the present day. I therefore would have been content to have found say 40% of the list vindicated. In fact that would have been a very high achievement given the sheer antiquity of the Table of Nations itself and the reported sparsity of the surviving extra-biblical records from those ancient times. But when, over my twenty-five years of research, that confirmatory evidence grew past 40% to 50%, and then 60% and beyond, it soon became apparent that modern wisdom in this matter was wide of the mark. Very wide of the mark indeed. Today I can say that the names so far vindicated in the Table of Nations make up over 99% of the list, and I shall make no further comment on that other than to say that no other ancient historical document of purely human authorship could be expected to yield such a level of corroboration as that! And I will add further that modern biblical commentators must make of it what they will.

But the test didn't stop there. I had determined at the very beginning that the test was to be one of unreasonable severity, so even the astonishing level of vindication so far achieved did not fully satisfy the requirements of the test. The reason for this was simple. The Table of Nations was written in the Middle East. But all the records consulted by me in investigating that Table were also written in the Middle East. I therefore decided that the test should continue beyond those geographical bounds, and I carried the search into the records of the early peoples of Europe. I wanted to see firstly whether the same patriarchs mentioned in Genesis were evident in the most ancient genealogies and chronicles of the peoples of Europe, and I wanted also to assess the level at which these early peoples were aware of other events mentioned in Genesis. The important part of this test was that the documents and records consulted by me had to date from before the time that any given European nation was converted to Christianity. That was because it is too often alleged by certain scholars that the early Christian church, particularly the monastic community, was given to forgery and invention. So only documents that predated the coming of Christianity and its forging monks to a particular nation whose records I was consulting would be considered. This part of the test was crucial and was to yield as great a level of vindication for the tenth and eleventh chapters of Genesis as the first part of the test.

What follows is a summary of all that evidence. I will not pretend that this book has been easy to write. It hasn't. Although I have aimed for readability, most of the evidence that I uncovered over the years consisted merely of lists of names, innumerable cross-references, royal genealogies, king-lists and old chronicles. So if I have failed in any way to make all that a rattling good read, then please blame all those skeletal documents that ancient officialdom has left us rather than the present writer, whose self-appointed and lonely task has been to make sense of them all! Any student who wishes to pursue matters further will find copious references to help him or her in further study. The rest, as they say, is history.

Bill Cooper
Ashford
Middlesex

March 1995

Chapter 1

The Knowledge of God amongst the early Pagans

So that we may bring the subject we are about to study into its proper perspective, we must first allow that many of our preconceptions regarding ancient man are mistaken. It is commonly supposed, for example, that the nations of the world became aware of the God of Genesis only after they were evangelised by Christian missionaries. Only since the translation of the scriptures into their own language, it is assumed, did they become conscious of the Creation and the God who created it. It is further supposed that early pagan man can have had no concept of a divinity higher than that of an idol, because it is impossible to come to a knowledge of the one true God without that knowledge being given through the direct revelation of His Word, and so on. Popular thought seems never to have considered the possibility that pagan man was indeed aware of God and of His attributes and power, and that this awareness had existed and flourished for centuries without any recourse at all to the scriptures. So it is with something of a surprise that we meet with exactly that, a profound knowledge and appreciation of an eternal and almighty Creator God, His fatherhood of the human race and His infinite attributes in the writings of various historians in the ancient world and amongst the teachings of the earliest philosophers. It is of the utmost importance that we familiarise ourselves with this truth as we begin our investigations into the

Table of Nations itself and the knowledge amongst the pagan nations of those patriarchs and events that are so familiar to us from the Genesis record.

So profound was the concept and knowledge of God amongst certain pagan peoples in the ancient world, and in particular the Greek and Roman worlds, that a controversy eventually arose and was to rage for many centuries between those who propagated and preserved that knowledge of God as the Creator, and those who sought to destroy it by attributing the creation of the universe to purely natural forces. The marked similarity between that pagan controversy and the controversy that rages today between creationists and evolutionists is surprising and we shall be examining that controversy in this chapter. But first we must understand something of the sheer profundity of the pagan philosophical concept of the one true God. We meet with it in places as distant from each other as the world is wide, and among cultures as socially and politically diverse as those of ancient Greece and China. For example, it is from the writings of the Taoist *Lao-tzu*, who flourished in the China of the 6th century BC, that the following profound statement concerning the existence and some of the attributes of God is taken:

> 'Before time, and throughout time, there has been a self-existing being, eternal, infinite, complete, omnipresent ... Outside this being, before the beginning, there was nothing.' [1]

It was clearly from no copy of Genesis that *Lao-tzu* could possibly have derived such an awareness of God. But then as other pagan philosophers from different cultures altogether were to add their convictions to that of the Chinese sage *Lao-tzu*, (and that takes no account of all those who lived before him), it becomes immediately obvious that no such copy was necessary. It would seem that, contrary to most of the assumptions of modern psychology on the matter, the knowledge of God is in fact and indeed innate within the human soul. It is a built-in awareness that may well be awakened and perfected with the reception of God's Word, but it is certainly something that exists quite independently of a knowledge of scripture. That is not to say that it was admitted to or proclaimed equally by all men in the ancient world. Many, of course, denied it just as they deny it today, for alongside every *Lao-tzu* who proclaimed the existence of God in the world of ancient China, there was a *Kuo-Hsiang* ready to dispute it:

> 'I venture to ask whether the creator is or is not. If he is not, how can he create things? . . . The creating of things has no Lord; everything creates itself.' [2]

But such exceptions gloriously prove the rule. For the existence of the Creator to be denied by one philosopher, it first has to be expounded by another, and the question that interests us here is where did that knowledge come from? If not from scripture, which was unknown to these peoples, then from where? If not from Christian missionary teachers who did not yet exist, then from whom? For, imperfect as the concept of God may have been among the early pagans, it was nevertheless very real, often profound, and can only have been founded upon a body of knowledge that had been preserved amongst the early races from a particular point in history. What that point in history was may become evident as our study proceeds and as we meet with the families of humankind dispersing from a single point around the globe. But that it was profound and in many ways inspiring, can hardly be denied, as the following ancient text from Heliopolis in Egypt testifies:

> 'I am the creator of all things that exist . . . that came forth from my mouth. Heaven and earth did not exist, nor had been created the herbs of the ground nor the creeping things. I raised them out of the primeval abyss from a state of non-being . . .' [3]

It would not be overstating the case to say that the Egyptian concept of a divine creation of the universe was so strongly held that throughout Egypt it governed every sphere of thought and action, political, educational, philosophical and so on. And it is also noteworthy to consider that there is no record anywhere amongst the vast amount of literature to be recovered from ancient Egypt, that suggests that this view was ever challenged. Nowhere in all the long history of Egypt do we find that a philosopher arose who was prepared to propagate the notion that the universe came into being through the agency of non-divine forces and processes. There were indeed other types of heretic and dissident, notably the pharoah Akhnaten who sought to bring all Egypt under the persuasion that there was but one god instead of the many that the Egyptians worshipped, but this was hardly atheism or a materialist concept that denied the place and reality of the Creator. [4] On the contrary, it was an effort, albeit an unsuccessful effort ultimately, on the part of Akhnaten to clear away much of the theological dross and debris that had obscured by his day the purity of the concept of such a Creator.

Curiously, we meet with the same lack of challenge to the creationist view almost throughout the ancient literate world. For example, we encounter this same absence of atheism or materialism in both Mesopotamia and early Israel, where records make no mention at all of any materialist thinker even by way of condemnation or refutation, save perhaps the solitary biblical observation that, 'the fool hath said in his heart, there is no God'. [5] This, of course, presupposes the existence of such fools at the time the statement was written, ca 1000 BC, yet not a shadow of a controversy has come down to us that so much as hints that the prevailing creationist view was ever challenged or even questioned in the ancient Middle East, so strongly was it held to in that region of the earth at least. And that is a notable fact that no one, to my knowledge, has ever sought to examine. [6] Indeed, in every major culture throughout the ancient world of which we have any record, the overwhelming consensus was that the universe had been created by often a single and usually supreme divine being (even in notoriously polytheistic cultures). But more remarkably, each culture was capable of expressing a view of the Creator that was not always perverse even though it flourished in the midst of an aggressive and thoroughly perverse paganism. For example, amongst the early Greeks we have in the **Theogony** of Hesiod (8th century BC) an account of the creation of the world that bears unmistakeable and remarkably close similarities with the Genesis account:

> 'First of all the Void came into being ... next Earth ... Out of the Void came darkness ... and out of the Night came Light and Day ...'[7]

And yet it is immediately obvious upon reading the whole of the **Theogony** that Hesiod did not get his information from the book of Genesis. This is evident from his debased view of the Creator alone. But even though Hesiod's debased view may have been typical, and indeed understandable, for one who lived in a thoroughly pagan society, it was by no means a view that was shared by all his fellow pagans. Xenophanes, for example, who lived some two centuries after Hesiod, held an altogether loftier view of the Creator and in a most inspiring passage sought to redress the theological balance:

> 'Homer and Hesiod attributed to the gods all the things which among men are shameful and blameworthy – theft and adultery and mutual deception...[But] there is one God, greatest among gods and men, similar to mortals neither in shape nor in thought ... he sees as a whole, he thinks as a whole, he hears as a whole ... Always he remains in the same state, changing not at all ... But far from toil he governs everything with his mind.'[8]

Xenophanes, typically, would have known the names of all the Greek gods as well as the multitude of functions that they were thought to serve. Yet, significantly, and it is a **most** significant point, he did not attempt to name or identify the God of whom he now spoke and whom he clearly admired. This God was not a Zeus or a Hermes. This God was ineffable, and His ineffability was a concept that was to persist in Greek thought for as long as Greek philosophy itself was to persist. The concept of this ineffable Creator God permeated the thought of Plato, for example, who sought to replace Hesiod's perverse concepts of the Creation with a more reasonable one, based no doubt upon philosophical concepts far more ancient than Hesiod's and certainly far more profound:

> 'Let us therefore state the reason why the framer of this universe of change framed it at all. He was good, and what is good has no particle of envy in it; being therefore without envy, he wished all things to be as like himself as possible. This is as valid a principle for the origin of the world of change as we shall discover from the wisdom of men . . .'[9]

Note the echo from Genesis: *'And God saw that it was good.'* We may also note here that Plato had discovered this concept from the wisdom of philosophers who had gone before him, and that it was therefore not something that originated in Plato's thought alone. We can say though that, with the advent of Plato's refined and carefully reasoned model of the Creation together with his (and Xenophanes') higher concept of the Creator, it would seem that the classical Greek model of origins was changed for all time. Never again was it to revert to the divine capriciousness of the many Hesiodic gods for an explanation of the universe. The creationist concept of the ancient world was rather to become, under Plato's inspiration and that of his pupils, more 'scientifically' and logically based, with its firm belief in a single and almighty Creator. However, in its wake, something far more serious than the earlier Hesiodic misconception was to occur.

It is with some irony that whilst the philosophically nurtured concept of the Creator was undergoing in ancient Greece such a profound shift towards a greater appreciation of His nature and attributes, there was taking place at the same time and in the same land the birth of another and hitherto unheard of concept amongst the Greeks, atheism. We simply do not know how atheism came to be born in ancient Greece, for, as we have seen, it was virtually an unheard of concept even in the most pagan cultures of the ancient world. But given the timing of its advent along with that of a higher concept of the Creator, which is of an equally mysterious source historically speaking, it would seem that the atheism of ancient Greece was conceived to directly oppose the burgeoning concept amongst the philosophers of a single supreme and omnipotent Deity. It is significant, no doubt, that no such concept as atheism arose earlier to deny the lesser pagan gods of Hesiod's philosophy. But with its advent we see the first beginnings of the great controversy that was to rage for centuries between those who held to the now reasonably argued belief in a Creator, and those who utterly denied it.

Thales of Miletus (ca 625–545 BC) is usually credited with having been the first materialist philosopher among the Greeks. But it is very doubtful that Thales was a materialist at all. All that we know of Thales comes to us through later writers, Aristotle the most notable amongst them, and he simply described him as the 'founder of natural philosophy'. [10] It is upon little more than the strength of this one remark by Aristotle that the case against Thales rests. But against that must be set the aphorisms that are attributed by others to Thales, such as: 'Of existing things, God is the oldest – for he is ungenerated. The world is the most beautiful, for it is God's creation ... Mind is the swiftest, for it runs through everything ...', [11] and so on. All of which are classic creationist sentiments.

But Thales did have a pupil named Anaximander (ca 610–540 BC), and it is to him that we must look for the first **recorded** challenge to creationism from the materialist school. We must be careful, though, in assuming Anaximander to have been the very first materialist thinker amongst the Greeks, for the view held by Anaximander was nothing less than a fully developed theory of evolution. From Plutarch's pen we hear Anaximander propounding that, '... originally, humans were born from animals of a different kind ...', [12] and so on, the creative principle that brought the universe into existence being held to be entirely impersonal and 'natural'. This argument, of course, has a somewhat familiar ring to it in our own century, but we must ask ourselves whether it is likely that such a fully fledged evolutionary model of origins can have sprung from a single mind and in such a mature state, especially from a thinker who was an immediate disciple of the creationist Thales. Or is it more likely that, for many years prior to Anaximander, there was at least some kind of materialist challenge developing perhaps even underground amongst certain thinkers in Greece, and that Anaximander simply plucked the baton from an unknown predecessor's hand? The laws of the time suggest strongly that such was the case, and our knowledge of just how the modern concept of evolution was nurtured and developed by a succession of thinkers across several centuries, virtually demands that we assume a similarly prolonged development in Greek materialist thought.

The evidence, such as it is, that is contained in the laws of ancient Greece against blasphemy and impiety, makes it certain that there were blasphemers and impious men to be legislated against, and such laws invariably prescribed death as the penalty for such a crime, the famous Socrates himself having finally fallen foul of such laws. And Plato, who was later to discuss in depth exactly how he thought the impious might be more effectively legislated against in the ideal city-state,[13] paints for us a picture of the condition of things in his own day, but speaks of the materialists as if they were an unlikely new breed of thinkers who had only just arrived on the scene:

> 'Some people, I believe, account for all things which have come to exist, all things which are coming into existence now, and all things which will do so in the future, by attributing them either to nature, art, or chance.'[14]

...going on to tell us how these thinkers define the gods as 'artificial concepts' and 'legal fictions'. He names the trend for what he thought it to be, a 'pernicious doctrine' that 'must be the ruin of the younger generation, both in the state at large and in private families'.[15] Unfortunately, Plato declines to name the thinkers who were responsible for this state of affairs and against whom he is contending. But this in turn only adds strength to the suggestion that atheism as an idea was more generally and anciently held, and more widespread amongst Plato's own contemporaries, than either the records of the time or Plato himself would lead us to believe. But whoever they were, Plato was to offer them a mightily effective challenge through his own refined creationist model of origins, for whatever the materialists proposed, Plato's model was of a higher concept altogether. For him, the Creator turned chaos into order simply because it was His good nature, and His good pleasure, so to do. He loved order rather than chaos, and to ensure the maintenance of that order everything He created was made according to an eternal and flawless pattern, Plato's justly famous Theory of Forms. But the real importance of Plato's model of origins for our enquiry is that it effectively silenced the materialist school for the next fifty years or so, that is until the time when Epicurus was to lay down his own counter-challenge to the creationist model. Aristotle had evidently already attempted to find some middle ground between the idealist Plato and his materialist opponents, but this did little or nothing to modify the scale of the philosophical provocation of what Plato had proposed.

Epicurus felt bound to oppose it, and he laid down his challenge around the close of the 4th century BC with a cosmology whose effects were to reverberate throughout the coming Roman world for many centuries to come. Indeed, it still survives in the elements of several modern philosophies.

The challenge issued by Plato's model of origins was met by Epicurus at every point, even on those more mundane matters that had merely to do with the city-state and jurisprudence. But in particular, Epicurus argued that it was insufficient to contend for the divine creation of the universe, as Plato did, from the assumption of a well-ordered cosmos, simply because the cosmos, in Epicurus's eyes, was not well-ordered.[16] It had culminated from a long, perhaps infinite, series of accidents resulting from the random jostling of atoms. But then, ever the sophist, Epicurus shrewdly shifted the ground a little so that any rebuttal from the creationist camp would need to take on board an added complication and consequently be more difficult to propound, for in spite of his unabashed materialism, Epicurus was careful to acknowledge the existence of the gods! He relegated them to a place of complete ineffectuality and disinterest in the cosmos, but he avoided an outright denial of their existence. Apart from the fact that he had to beware of the still-standing laws of the time against impiety and blasphemy, Epicurus knew that outright atheism is easily refuted by any philosopher with an eye for controversy, and the fact that few men in any age are outright atheists anyway would ensure scant support for his views. But, if the existence of the gods is acknowledged at the same time in which the divine creation of the universe is denied, then the arguments against the Epicurean view become infinitely more complex, affording the materialist with the subsequent ability to change ground at will. Such sophistry, of course, was entirely in keeping with the character of Epicurus who was roundly criticised for it on more than one occasion:

> 'Epicurus himself used to do the same thing. For instance, he saw that if those atoms of his were always falling downwards by their own weight, their motion would be fixed and predetermined, and there would be no room for free will in the world. So casting about for a way to avoid this determinism, which Democritus had apparently overlooked, he said that the atoms, as they fell, just **swerved** a little!'[17]

However, the acknowledgement of the existence of the gods did have the virtue of imparting to Epicurus control of the field and the ability to state the terms under which the ensuing controversy was to be fought. Or so he vainly hoped, for far from seeing creationism off the proverbial field, Epicureanism merely served to rally the creationist camp towards a better definition of its views, and the school of thought which raised itself to meet the challenge of Epicurean materialism was the Stoic school, founded by Zeno in ca 308 BC.

As events were to prove, Stoicism was to become a very effective challenge indeed in the pagan world against materialism in any guise or form, and that challenge was brought about by a most significant development. This development began with a far more profound concept of the Creator than had hitherto prevailed in Greek thought, whether that of Hesiod, of Xenophanes or even of Plato. Indeed, the incipient and lightly veiled atheism of Epicurus's philosophy was now answered by the Stoics in the most compelling terms, with Chrysippus giving it perhaps its most persuasive voice:

> 'If there is anything in nature which the human mind, which human intelligence, energy and power could not create, then the creator of such things must be a being superior to man. But the heavenly bodies in their eternal orbits could not be created by man. They must therefore be created by a being greater than man ... Only an arrogant fool would imagine that there was nothing in the whole world greater than himself. Therefore there must be something greater than man. And that something must be God.'[18]

This may be a good place to briefly reflect upon the somewhat mysterious source of such endearingly plain logic, a plainness of logic indeed that is quite uncharacteristic of Greek philosophy. What processes of thought can conceivably have led from the grotesque parodies of human corruption that one sees in the older Hesiodic creation model of the Greeks amongst beings that passed for 'gods', to the majestic and undeniably sublime concept of a supreme and omnipotent Deity that was now being voiced by Chrysippus and his colleagues?[19] The Christian faith had yet to be born, its influence on Greek thought still lying some centuries into the future. So could it perhaps have been through the agency of the recently Hellenised Jews who, albeit they horrified the orthodox of their faith by mingling much of Judaism with Greek thought and practices, unwittingly carried with them into the Greek camp an inherent knowledge of the God of

Genesis in a kind of theological Trojan horse? The answer is no, for apart from the fact that one can hardly claim that Jewish philosophical thought was any less complex and sophistic than that of the Greeks, there are also strong historical and chronological grounds for denying Jewish influence in the sphere of Greek philosophy at this particular point in history.

The Greeks, it appears, first made contact with Judaism as early as the year 587 BC, when Greek mercenaries assisted the armies of Nebuchadnezzar of Babylon in the investing and destruction of Jerusalem. Along with the mercenaries, of course, would have been a smaller army of civil servants, spies and so on, many of whom during the long and enforced hours of leisure doubtless spent their time in philosophical discussion. But to suggest that this would have included the taking on board of Jewish thought is quite beyond the realms of probability. The Jews were invariably viewed with a poorly disguised contempt by the Greeks throughout their centuries of contact with one another, to the extent that many Jews found it politic to become Greek, or Hellenised, in order to survive at all.[20] The persecution of the Jews under Antiochus IV Epiphanes (175–163 BC), and his determined attempt to expunge the Jewish faith altogether, is perhaps the most telling episode regarding the often mutual hostility that existed between the orthodox of either side. It has to be admitted, of course, that the Jewish Torah, which naturally included the book of Genesis, was translated into Greek in the year 250 BC, some seventeen years before Chrysippus became head of the Stoic school in 233 BC. But even the remarkable translation of Genesis into Greek did not take place until fifty-eight years after the foundation of the Stoic school by Zeno in 308 BC. So clearly Stoicism as a philosophy owed nothing to the book of Genesis, and the philosophical path that the Stoics trod in order to arrive at their conclusions must therefore remain a mystery to us.

However, apart from the new and lofty concept voiced by Xenophanes, Plato and Chrysippus of the Creator of the universe, another concept was to follow which, in the hands of Chrysippus and his colleagues, was to lend the voice of the

Stoic school an almost irresistible authority. It was the concept of 'evidence from design', an argument for that divinely inspired intent and purpose which was observable throughout the universe and which convinced the Stoic, as it convinces the creationist of today, of the scientific and philosophical correctness of his model. Refined and brilliantly expressed by Paley at the beginning of the last century, the importance of evidence from design was not lost on earlier classical theorists who were quick to give it its permanent setting in the idea of creationism. A later Stoic, the Roman Cicero, was to give the concept perhaps its highest expression in pre-Christian times, and his words are worth quoting at a little length:

> 'When you see a sundial or a water-clock, you see that it tells the time by design and not by chance. How then can you imagine that the universe as a whole is devoid of purpose and intelligence when it embraces everything, including these artifacts themselves and their artificers? Our friend Posidonius as you know has recently made a globe which in its revolution shows the movements of the sun and stars and planets, by day and night, just as they appear in the sky. Now if someone were to take this globe and show it to the people of Britain or Scythia would a single one of those barbarians fail to see that it was the product of a conscious intelligence?'[21]

With these beautifully simple words, Cicero gives voice to an idea which even today is the most difficult for the materialist to refute, for it is nigh impossible to explain away convincingly, say, the indescribable complexity of living organisms, or even merely parts thereof, as the product of blind chance or accident. But Cicero was not just giving voice to one of creationism's most forceful ideas for its own sake. He was doing so by way of refuting the Epicurean notions of Lucretius, the Roman materialist poet and a contemporary of his, whose book[22] Cicero mentions in a letter to his brother Quintus in February 54 BC, and which he says was written 'with many highlights of genius, but with much art'.[23] Cicero's own dialogue, *On the Nature of the Gods*, was written some ten years later in ca 44 BC specifically as a rebuttal of Lucretius, and it is between Cicero and Lucretius that the controversy rages, with both sides using arguments which are still very familiar to us today.

One of those arguments concerned the trustworthiness or otherwise of the senses when it comes to deducing the validity of evidence from design. How, for example, can we be sure that we interpret that evidence correctly through our senses? This, for the Stoic, was the fatal weakness in the Epicurean argument which, as Lucretius stated it, runs:

> The nature of phenomena cannot be understood by the eyes.'[24]

Lucretius said this not because he believed the eyes themselves to be at fault, but because it was a failing of the mind to perceive things correctly or accurately through the senses. In fairness to Lucretius, he did go on to qualify this statement, recognising that this dictum, though it appeared to answer the creationist on a philosophical level, could not usefully be translated into everyday experience, for:

> 'This is to attack belief at its very roots – to tear up the entire foundation on which the maintainance of life is built. If you did not dare trust your senses so as to keep clear of precipices and other such things to be avoided and make for their opposites, there would be a speedy end to life itself.'[25]

But such sophistry was to cut no ice at all with the Stoic Cicero. It smacked too much of that special pleading for which Cicero, as an advocate in law, had little patience. For if our reasoning powers could be trusted to interpret what our senses were telling us on a day to day basis when it came to such vital matters as personal safety and survival, then they could surely be trusted to interpret less vital phenomena such as evidence from design in the universe around us, which spoke so eloquently and forcefully of the universe having been created by an infinite and omnipotent intelligence. As a creationist, the Stoic Cicero simply could not appreciate the Epicurean viewpoint of Lucretius:

> 'In the heavens there is nothing accidental, nothing arbitrary, nothing out of order, nothing erratic. Everywhere is order, truth, reason, constancy ... I cannot understand this regularity in the stars, this harmony of time and motion in their various orbits through all eternity, except as the expression of reason, mind and purpose ... Their constant and eternal motion, wonderful and mysterious in its regularity, declares the indwelling power of a divine intelligence. If any man cannot feel the power of God when he looks upon the stars, then I doubt whether he is capable of any feeling at all.'[26]

To Cicero's mind, it was the greatest irony that a thinker like Lucretius who bleated most about his unshakeable faith in the innate powers of matter to create itself and arrange itself into a meaningful and purposeful order without any outside aid or influence, found himself unable to trust that same matter when it came to perceiving or even explaining this fact! It matters not, it seems, how eloquently one may fulminate against creationism, charging it with every superstition under the sun, if one then declares that the reasoning powers of him who so fulminates cannot be trusted. Whether expressed in ancient times or in modern, it is still a case of shooting oneself in the philosophical foot, and it has effectively disarmed the materialist cause at every turn. It bedevilled the 18th century Enlightenment philosopher David Hume, whose philosophy in a nutshell stated that it was only reasonable to believe in God. But as we know that God does not exist, then our reasoning powers cannot be trusted. What Hume, along with every other materialist philosopher, was really trying to say, of course, was that no one's reasoning powers could be trusted but his own, thus making himself the only sure point of reference in the universe. But such was the philosophical mess into which this led him, that Kant, the inheritor of Hume's mantle, once painfully lamented the fact that:

> '...it remains a scandal to philosophy and to human reason in general that the existence of things outside us ... must be accepted merely on faith, and that if anyone thinks good to doubt their existence, we are unable to counter his doubts by any satisfactory proof.'[27]

No creationist could have expressed the materialist's dilemma more concisely, and Kant has highlighted a phenomenon that has not only ensured throughout history that creationism would always hold the higher ground when it came to the expression of simple logic, but which also led out of sheer frustration to the birth and rigours of the empiricist school of thought in the 1920s. But there is another element in the controversy that has also persisted down the ages concerning the part that chance might have played in the successful arrangement of matter whether animate or inanimate. The pagan Greeks had taken the argument down to the atomic level, and instead of the desperately sought-after simplicity of arrangement that was so necessary to the materialist's cause, they found only a greater and more mind-boggling complexity, which again only added to their difficulties in attempting to explain the allegedly accidental creation and mindless existence of the universe. Again, we turn to Cicero for a judgment on the scene:

> 'Is it not a wonder that anyone can bring himself to believe that a number of solid and separate particles by their chance collisions and moved only by the force of their own weight could bring into being so marvellous and beautiful a world? If anybody thinks that this is possible, I do not see why he should not think that if an infinite number of examples of the twenty-one letters of the alphabet, made of gold or what you will, were shaken together and poured out on the ground it would be

> possible for them to fall so as to spell out, say, the whole text of the *Annals* of Ennius. In fact I doubt whether chance would permit them to spell out a single verse!'[28]

Now where have we heard **that** analogy before? This argument, which was the Roman equivalent of today's monkeys and typewriters tapping out the works of Shakespeare, has endured simply because it has always proved to be unanswerable by the materialist in any but the most strained and unlikely terms. Though even this argument was hardly new in Cicero's day, but seems to have been merely part and parcel of the already ancient creationist armoury of vexing philosophical questions that the materialist could never satisfactorily answer.

The Epicurean school, through Lucretius, did attempt to wreak a vengeance of sorts, for Lucretius went on to specify an idea that threatened to provide a stumbling-block to classical (i.e. pagan) creationism. Conceding the fact that the materialist's perception of the universe was marred somewhat by the alleged inability of human reason to perceive correctly the nature of the physical universe, Lucretius claimed that creationism likewise had a chink in its philosophical armour when it came to explaining the earth's place in the universe. The classical perception of the universe amongst the Greeks was that it was geocentric, the stars, planets and everything else revolving around a fixed and immoveable earth. And Lucretius assumed, wrongly, that this was crucial to the creationist view. It gave a fixed point of reference to the universe, and it was a philosophical concept that allowed the teaching of absolute values. Lucretius, therefore, attempted to introduce a more relativistic framework by claiming that the earth was not fixed at all, but moved in an infinite space that possessed no centre. This was to counter the Stoic's view of a finite universe whose outer bounds were equidistant from the earth:

> 'It is a matter of observation that one thing is limited by another. The hills are demarcated by air, and air by the

> hills. Land sets bound to sea, and sea to every land. But the universe has nothing outside to limit it.'[29]

... shrewdly going on to make his point that:

> 'There can be no centre in infinity.'[30]

With these ludicrously simple statements, Lucretius had put forward an idea that was truly revolutionary but for which he has received scant acknowledgement from historians of any hue. He did not develop the idea into that of a strictly heliocentric universe, as Copernicus was later to do, but he did depart radically even from the view of his materialist colleagues, for they too held that the earth was fixed and the universe revolved around it. Lucretius had hoped to rob the creationist camp of the finest weapon in its armoury, the argument for an ordered and hence designed universe, by introducing the concept of randomness, aimlessness and sheer relativism. But he was disappointed, for even his materialist peers were unable to follow him down that particular path. Ironically, this had nothing to do with the fact that the Greeks and Romans of the time were ignorant in any way. On the contrary, they were great observers, and the virtue of the geocentric model lay in the fact that it complied with all the **observed** facts of contemporary science. Indeed, few theories in the history of science have ever enjoyed such overwhelming and indisputable proofs as those which once graced geocentrism. And that, in this present age that virtually worships the concept of empiricism, has to be one of the greatest ironies of all.

To add to the irony, and contrary to all expectations from the materialist camp, when the Copernican revolution finally did arrive in the 16th century, it did not mean the end of creationism for a very good and simple reason. In creationist terms, it matters not a jot whether the earth revolves around the sun or the sun around the earth. For whichever model of the universe is the correct one, the question still remains – Who created it? How did it come into existence and whence came its astonishing degree of order and complexity? These are questions that have been asked by men since the beginning of time. And one of them, named Lucilius, had worked out the answer for himself without any help from either Christian or Jew, attributed the design, creation and maintenance of the universe to that Creator who:

> '. . . is, as Ennius says, "the father both of gods and men", a present and a mighty God. If anyone doubts this, then so far as I can see he might just as well doubt the existence of the sun. For the one is as plain as the other. **And if this were not clearly known and manifest to our intelligence, the faith of men would not have remained so constant, would not have deepened with the lapse of time, and taken ever firmer root throughout the ages and the generations of mankind.**'[31]
>
> (Emphasis mine)

It is Lucilius's 'generations of mankind' that now must occupy our attention, for with his profound statement this present chapter must draw to a close. But what Lucilius was referring to is the fact that alongside even the very worst aspects of paganism in the ancient world, there was preserved a definite knowledge of God. The value of this lies in the fact that this knowledge existed (and still exists) quite independently of Genesis amidst cultures that were and are entirely antagonistic towards the concept of one God, the Creator of all things. We shall now encounter this same knowledge in the early genealogies and historical records of the early pagan nations, and note that their testimony is unexpected to say the least when we consider what the modernist school has been claiming all these years.

Notes

1. Lao-tzu. *Tao-te-ching*. tr. Léon Wieger. English version by Derek Bryce. 1991. Llanerch Publishers. Lampeter. p. 13.
2. Clarke, John. 1993. *Nature in Question*. Earthscan. p. 24.

3. My paraphrase of Wallace Budge's literal translation in *The Gods of the Egyptians*. Vol. 1. Dover. New York. 1969. pp. 308–313.
4. There is a superb account of the Akhnaten heresy in: Eliade, Mircea. 1979. *A History of Religious Ideas: From the Stone Age to the Eleusinian Mysteries*. Collins. London. Vol. 1. pp. 106–109.
5. Psalm 14:1.
6. Not that such a task would be easy. One scholar, David Berman (author of *A History of Atheism in Britain*. Routledge. London. 1988), complains that atheism is hard enough to detect even when records, as for the last four centuries, are to be had in plenty. By the very nature of things, the task would be nigh hopeless when it comes to the woefully sparse, and doubtless sometimes heavily censored, records of the ancient world.
7. Hesiod. *Theogony*. (tr. Norman Brown. 1953). Bobbs-Merrill Co. New York. p. 15.
8. Barnes, Jonathan. 1987. *Early Greek Philosophy*. Penguin Classics. Harmondsworth. p. 95–97.
9. Plato. *Timaeus and Criteas*. (tr. Desmond Lee. 1965). Penguin Classics. Harmondsworth. p. 42.
10. Barnes. p. 61.
11. *ibid*. p. 68.
12. *ibid*. p. 73.
13. Plato. *The Laws*. (tr. Trevor Saunders. 1970). Penguin Classics. Harmondsworth. pp. 408–447.
14. *ibid*. p. 416.
15. *ibid*. p. 417.
16. Lund, Erik. *A History of European Ideas* C. Hurst & Co. 1976?. pp. 61–62.
17. Cicero. *On the Nature of the Gods*. (tr. Horace McGregor. 1988). Penguin Classics. Harmondsworth.
18. *ibid*. p. 130.
19. An excellent discussion of the development of (pagan) Greek theology is given in: Murray, Gilbert. 1925. *Five Stages in Greek Religion*. Oxford. – Murray traces the development of the primitive, anthropomorphic gods of Greece up to the concept of the First Cause, or Creator of the Stoics. The last chapter of the book, pp. 241–267, contains a particularly illuminating translation of Sallustius's *On the Gods and the World*.
20. This is very well documented in the apocryphal books of the Maccabees, and especially in: *Josephus*. (tr. Whiston). Pickering &

Inglis. London. 1960. pp. 250–289 and 607–636 (*Against Apion*).

21. Cicero. p. 159.
22. Lucretius. *On the Nature of the Universe.* (tr. Ronald Latham. 1951). Penguin Classics. Harmondsworth.
23. *ibid.* p. 9.
24. *ibid.* p. 142.
25. *ibid.* p. 146.
26. Cicero. pp. 144–145.
27. Stroud, Barry. 1984. *The Significance of Philosophical Scepticism.* Oxford University Press. p. 141.
28. Cicero. p. 161.
29. Lucretius. p. 56.
30. *ibid.* p. 58.
31. Cicero. p. 124.

Chapter 2

Where to Begin

History has never been so popular. The man in the street has never been so well informed about his past as he is today. And yet it is a sad and unhappy fact that for all that has been said, written and broadcast about the early and more recent history of mankind, there remains a very large body of historical evidence that is mostly passed over in silence by today's scholars. And because it is passed over by today's scholars, it never reaches today's general public. I say that this is sad because it is not as if this vast fund of knowledge is hard to get at. On the contrary, every fact that you are about to read is available to anyone who takes the trouble to look. And each fact can be obtained cheaply enough. It does not lie in obscure libraries about which no one has heard or to which none can gain access. Nor is it written in languages or scripts that cannot be deciphered. Indeed, scholars have been aware of the existence of this vast body of information for many years. So why is it passed over in such silence?

Why is it, for example, that no modern book on the early history of Britain goes back beyond the year 55 BC, the year when Julius Caesar made his first attempt to invade these islands? We may read in such books of this culture or that people, this stone age or that method of farming. But we will read of no particular individual or of any particular event before the year 55 BC. This has the unfortunate effect of causing us to believe that this is because there exists no written history for those pre-Roman times, and that when they landed in Britain the Romans encountered only a bunch of illiterate savages who had no recorded history of their own. But our conclusion would be wrong, for we will see as our study progresses that the Britons whom the Romans encountered were, on the admission of the Romans themselves, a people who could teach the Romans a thing or two about the finer arts of warfare, and who left a clear and written record of themselves dating back to the very earliest years of their existence as a nation. These records still survive, and we shall be considering them in some detail. We shall also be examining many other ancient records that various peoples have left behind them and we shall note with interest the story that is told by each one of these documents. Far more can be known about the early recorded history of mankind than is generally allowed, and what is revealed by this history is a story that is very different indeed from the one that we are used to hearing. But where to begin?

We must begin our investigations with one of the oldest historical documents in the world. This document comprises the tenth and eleventh chapters of the book of Genesis and is known to scholars as The Table of Nations. However, when I use the word 'document', it must be understood that this in no way subscribes to the erroneous view propagated by Julius Wellhausen and his colleagues in the 19th century regarding the much-vaunted but still fashionable 'documentary hypothesis' of biblical criticism. That hypothesis was designed to be destructive of any impression that the Genesis record in particular was a reliable source of historical information, whereas the objective of our present study lies in entirely the opposite direction. But it does recognise the fact that the tenth and eleventh chapters of Genesis consist of a self-contained unit of information that is complete even if read in isolation from the rest of the Genesis account. In that sense, at least, it forms a document that we may study in isolation. But how accurate is that document? Most scholars today would denounce it as unreliable, and some would dismiss it from any further discussion by attaching to it labels of 'myth' and 'pious fiction', favourite terms among modernist scholars, thus assuring their readers that its study, and especially faith in its accuracy, is a waste of time. These terms and labels will become more familiar to us as we come across a great many extra-biblical records that substantiate rather than undermine the Genesis account, but their over-use by certain scholars has left the definite impression that the modernist protests too much, and when applied as often as they are to so many historical records, they become tired and meaningless phrases that convey no information at all. There is doubtless method in this academic madness, given the question that if Genesis cannot be relied upon when it comes to stating accurately simple historical facts, then how can it be relied upon when it comes to stating higher truths? But the over-use of such labels becomes wearisome and ultimately meaningless, and is of no service whatever to healthy historical research.

When applied to the Table of Nations, this healthy historical research yields some surprising facts, surprising that is, in the light of what most commentaries go to such great lengths to assure us of, namely that Genesis is not to be trusted as accurate history. This became very clear when I first began my researches into the Table of Nations, and the nature of those researches is as follows.

Having constructed the Table of Nations into a simple genealogy, I wanted to see how many of its names were attested in the records of other nations in the Middle East, which included for my purposes all the nations of Mesopotamia, Arabia, Egypt, Turkey and even Greece. It was an obvious procedure, but one that had not, as far as I was aware, been conducted before and the results published. I had already found certain individual names that were mentioned in scattered works of varying merit, often Victorian, but the whole had never been gathered together into one cohesive study. And so my research began. Over the years, little by little, pieces of corroborative evidence came together and a picture began to build up that revealed the tenth and eleventh chapters of Genesis to be an astonishingly accurate record of events. The Table of Nations had listed all the families and tribes of mankind in their correct groupings, whether those groupings were ethnological, linguistic or geographical. All the names, without exception, were accurate, and in more than twenty-five years of searching and analysing, I uncovered not one mistake or false statement of fact in the Table of Nations.

It has to be said here that such a result could simply not be expected or obtained from any comparable historical document, especially one as ancient as this. The Table of Nations embraces a sweeping panorama of history that is not only truly vast in its content but unique. Its like simply does not exist. But as a sample, we shall here consider some of the descendants of Japheth as they are listed in the Table of Nations. For students who wish to pursue the matter in greater depth, I have set out in full the three genealogies of Shem, Ham and Japheth with accompanying historical notices and references in Appendices 1, 2 and 3 of this present study. But in this chapter, a summary of the corroborative evidence that appears in the nations of the Middle East concerning the descendants of Japheth, will suffice to show the trend of that evidence in vindicating the Genesis account. Moreover, the Japhetic line is the briefest in the Table of Nations and therefore the least wearisome for the general reader to follow, and it also forms the foundation for much else that comes after in this study.

The Japhetic list in the Table of Nations looks like this when set out as a conventional genealogy:

By way of illustration as to how contemporary records

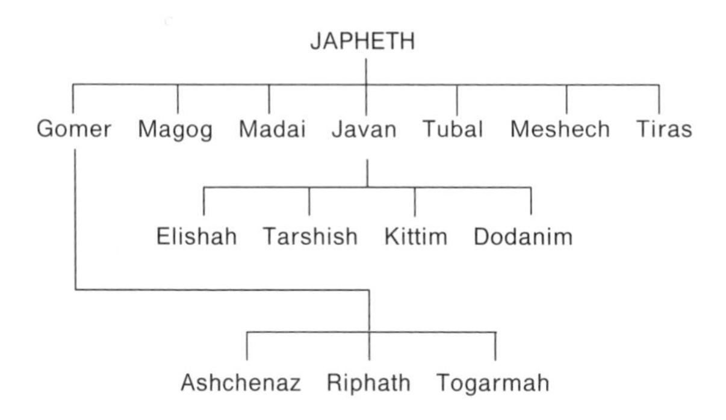

vindicate this statement of Genesis, the evidence for the historical reality of these peoples gleaned from the records of the surrounding nations is summarised as follows, although I have avoided wearying the reader by providing copious references here. Such references are to be found accompanying the historical notices provided in Appendices 1, 2 and 3, and I see no good reason for cluttering the text with footnotes at this particular stage.

Very briefly then, as we consider just a few of the names in the Japhetic list, we find that in the mythology of the old world, Japheth was regarded as the father of many peoples, particularly the Indo-European nations. The pagan Greeks perpetuated his name as Iapetos, the son of heaven and earth and again the father of many nations. We find his name in the vedas of India where it appears in Sanskrit as Pra-Japati, Father Japheth, who was deemed to be the sun and lord of creation, the source of life in other words for those descended from him. Later, the Romans were to perpetuate his name as that of Iu-Pater, Father Jove, later standardised to Jupiter (see Appendix 11). We shall see also that the early Irish Celts, the early Britons and other pagan European races traced the descent of their royal houses from Japheth, including the Saxons who knew him as Sceaf (pr. sheaf or shaif). And all these peoples, we must remember, were pagans whose knowledge or even awareness of the book of Genesis was non-existent.

Gomer, the first son of Japheth according to Genesis, founded a people known to the early Greeks as the Cimmerians who dwelt on the shores of the Caspian Sea. From here, they were later driven away by the Elamites. The prophet Ezekiel, during the time of the Captivity, referred to them as those who dwelt in the uppermost parts of the north. They appear in Assyrian records as the Gimirraya whose defeat under king Esarhaddon is duly noted. They appear also in the annals of the reign of Ashurbanipal of Assyria around 660 BC.

The people of Ashchenaz are found in earliest times in Armenia, and later Jewish writers associate them with the Germanic races (Germanic Jews to this day are called

Ashkenazim). They appear also in the 6th century BC records of Assyria as the Askuza who allied themselves with the Mannai in a revolt against Assyria, an event also mentioned in Jeremiah (51:27) whose prophecy incidentally confirms the identity of the Askuza with the Ashkenazim. This people were later known to the Greeks as the Scythai, the Scythians of Herodotus. They gave their name to the lake and harbour of Ascanius and to the land of Ascania. Through Josephus we can later trace them to the Rheginians.

The descendants of Riphath gave their name to the Riphaean mountain range, which at one time was marked by early cosmographers as the northernmost boundary of the earth. The name appears in Pliny, Melo and Solinus as Riphaei, Riphaces and Piphlataei respectively. The last of these were later called Paphlagonians, as attested by Josephus.

Togarmah's earliest descendants settled in Armenia. 14th century BC Hittite documents tell us of Tegarama, a region where they settled which lay between Carchemish and Haran and which was overrun by the 'enemy from Isuwa', that is a people from beyond the Euphrates. Sargon II and Sennacherib of Assyria both mention their later city of Til-gari-manu. This lay some thirty miles east of present-day Gürün in Turkey, and was destroyed in 695 BC. Josephus knew the descendants of Togarmah as Thrugramma.

...and so on. Thus it comes about that, throughout the entire Table of Nations, whether we talk about the descendants of Shem, Ham or Japheth, every one of their names is found in the records of the early surrounding nations of the Middle East, even the many obscure names of certain remote Arab tribes that are otherwise not evident in any modern history book of the times, and enough is available for a detailed history to be written about them. It is a phemonenon of immense implications. These records were mostly written (and then lost until their rediscovery in modern times) during the Old Testament period, during which time many of the peoples mentioned in them had vanished altogether from the historical scene or had been assimilated into other more powerful nations and cultures. Even those who retained their national or tribal identities soon lost all trace and memory of their own beginnings and went on to invent fantastic accounts of how they came to be. Indeed, the very early emergence of such mythological invention and the exceedingly rapid growth of paganism is a very telling point indeed against the modernist notion that Genesis is a late composition, for many of the names recorded with such astonishing accuracy in the Table of Nations, had disappeared from the historical scene many centuries before the time in which modernism would say that the Table of Nations was written. The Table of Nations, it thus seems, is a very ancient document indeed.

In time, of course, the true histories of several of these early nations became obscured beyond all recognition. Josephus was given good cause to complain that this had happened to the Greeks of his own day, and he lamented the fact that by obscuring their own history, they had obscured the histories of other nations also.[1] Yet by no means all of the early nations were to follow this path. We shall see that many kept an accurate record down the centuries of their beginnings and wrote down the names of their founding patriarchs, bringing the records up to date with the advent of each new generation, and it is these records that provide us with such a surprising link between the ancient post-Flood era depicted in Genesis and the history of more modern times. These lists, annals and chronicles have been preserved and transmitted from generation to generation not by the nations of the Middle East this time, but by certain European peoples from times that long pre-dated the coming of Christianity, and it is most important that we remember the pre-Christian aspect of much of the following evidence, for it is too easily and too often alleged by modernist scholars that these records are the inventions of early Christian monks and are therefore worthless. Such claims of fraud will be examined in detail, particularly with regard to the records that the early Britons have left us and which are omitted in their entirety from modern history books, the media and the classroom.

When we consider the truly vast body of evidence from the Middle East that is conveniently ignored in modernist commentaries on the book of Genesis, such wholesale omission will appear as hardly surprising. Yet perhaps the reader is unaware of the sheer scale of this omission, for the records of the early Britons, and that's not counting the Irish Celtic, Saxon and continental records which we shall also be examining, cover not just a particular phase of history, but span more than two thousand years of it. I cannot think of any other literate nation on earth that has managed to obliterate from its own history books two thousand years or more of recorded and documented history. Not even the censors of Stalinist Russia or Maoist China in their vigorous hey-day were this effective, or even needed to be this effective, in doctoring their own official accounts. So how did this extraordinary circumstance come about, and who is responsible for it?

By way of a refreshing change, we cannot lay the blame entirely at the door of those evolutionary Victorian and later educationalists and philosophers who laid the foundations of our modern curricula. They are surely to blame for much else that is amiss, but this time the story begins long before their age and influence. It begins, in fact, with the closing years of the 6th century AD and the arrival on these shores of Augustine, the Roman Catholic bishop whose job it was to bring the British Isles under the political sway of the Roman pontiff. The story is well known from Bede *et al* how the British Christians who were here to greet Augustine declined his demand that they place themselves under the Roman authority, and were later massacred for their refusal at Bangor, twelve hundred of the finest scholars and monks of their day being put to the sword. From that day on there existed an animosity between the Britons (Welsh) and the papacy that was to ferment throughout the early to late Middle Ages, only to culminate in the eventual expulsion of the papal authority from the realm of England under king Henry VIII, who was significantly himself of Welsh Tudor stock. But the early ascendancy of the Saxons meant that all recorded history of the Britons was consigned to oblivion as far as historians and chroniclers were concerned, with only Roman, Saxon and, later, Norman accounts of events being taught and promulgated in schools throughout the land. The recorded history of the early Britons was to remain in oblivion for the five hundred years that followed the massacre at Bangor. But then an incident occurred that ensured its revival and survival to the present day, even though that revival was itself to last only a matter of a further five hundred years or so.

The incident, which occurred sometime in the 1130s, was the presentation of a certain book to a British (i.e. Welsh) monk by an archdeacon of Oxford. The monk's name was Geoffrey of Monmouth, the archdeacon was Walter of Oxford, and the book was a very ancient, possibly unique, copy of the recorded history of the early Britons, written in language so archaic that it needed to be translated quickly into Latin before either the book perished or the language was forgotten. Now, one would think that such a rare event would generate great interest amongst scholars of all hues. Yet even today, in our supposedly impartial and enquiring age, the mere mention of Geoffrey of Monmouth will usually bring an academic smirk to the face of scholars. Read any article today about him and you will be sure to come across statements to the effect that his great work, *Historia Regum Britanniae*, or *History of the Kings of Britain*, is at best unreliable fiction, and that Geoffrey himself is an unscrupulous liar and forger.[2] We would do well to ask ourselves what it is that could provoke such unscholarly language.

It is often claimed, in dismissing Geoffrey's work, that it contains errors. Yet, as any historian worth his salt will tell you, if we rejected histories in general on that account, we should soon be left without any history at all. But it is then claimed that Geoffrey's supposed original book no longer exists and that therefore Geoffrey must have been lying when he claimed to have translated such a book. However, it is exceedingly rare for the original manuscript or source-material of any early historical work to have survived. In fact, I personally am not aware of one instance where this has occurred. It is further claimed, and this claim is significant inasmuch as it can at least be tested, that nothing like Geoffrey's *Historia* is to be found amongst the surviving corpus of medieval Welsh literature.[3] The surprising answer to this is that not only does the same historical material survive in Welsh from medieval times, it survives in no less that fifty eight manuscript copies. These are listed in Appendix 4, but we may note here that there are not very many medieval Welsh manuscripts in existence and fifty eight of them does constitute a rather large percentage of the surviving corpus. The claim is therefore suspicious as it is hardly likely that scholars who have made this field their life's work could have missed them or have remained for long in ignorance of their existence or contents. Indeed, the manuscripts are freely available to any who care to study them, so why is even the acknowledgement of their very existence such anathema to the modernist mind?

The answer to this lies in what these early records tell us about our past. As we shall see, it is an account that flies entirely in the face of everything that we are taught nowadays about where we come from, and it makes fascinating reading. But Geoffrey of Monmouth was not the only medieval Welsh scholar to transmit to us the historical records of the early Britons. He was preceeded by another, Nennius by name, and, because Nennius passed down to us the contents of records more ancient even than Geoffrey's chronicle, we shall begin our excursion into the history of the early Britons with him.

Notes

1. Flavius Josephus. *Against Apion.* (From *Josephus's Complete Works.* tr. William Whiston. Pickering & Inglis. 1981. pp. 607–636).
2. See for just one example amongst countless others, Marsh, H. 1987. *Dark Age Britain. Some Sources of History.* Dorset Press. New York. pp. 175–190. And Marsh is amongst the gentlest of Geoffrey's critics!
3. '... no Welsh composition exists which can be reasonably looked upon as the original, or even the groundwork, of the History of the Kings of Britain' (Lloyd, J.E. 1939). *A History of Wales from the earliest times to the Edwardian Conquest.* London. 2nd ed. p. 526. (cit. also in Thorpe. p. 15. See bibliography).

Chapter 3

Nennius and the Table of European Nations

> 'I, Nennius, pupil of the holy Elvodug,[1] have undertaken to write down some extracts that the stupidity of the British cast out; for the scholars of the island of Britain had no skill ... I have therefore made a heap of all that I have found ...'[2]

With these words, Nennius opens his great book, ***Historia Brittonum*** – the *History of the Britons*. It would be difficult to overstate the immensity of Nennius's achievement and his contribution to our understanding of ancient history. And, were we not familiar with the fashions of today, it would be equally difficult to account for the disparagement that his name has suffered amongst modernist scholars in ungrateful return for his labours. His achievement was the gathering together of all the extant records touching on the origins of the Britons that he could find and which he then set down into one book. It was a time of danger for the Britons as a nation and for the records themselves, and were it not for his labours, the immensity of which we can only guess at, records that were irreplaceable would have been lost to us forever. Morris's translation of Nennius, which opens this present chapter, implies that the British of the time were stupid in the sense of being intellectually dull. But in this context, the word *hebitudo* which Nennius used, suggesting something that has been made blunt or dull and which Morris renders 'stupidity', would perhaps better be translated as complacency or lethargy, the mood of the Britons that followed in the wake of the massacre of the monks at Bangor. The profound cultural shock of seeing their finest scholars and spiritual leaders massacred by supposedly fellow Christians at the instigation of a Roman bishop no less, would have left a very deep wound indeed, and it is this state of mind amongst the Britons or Welsh that Nennius laments and which led to the neglect and loss of many records and books. They 'had no skill' (*nullam peritiam habuerunt*), because learning had practically ceased amongst them. Hence Nennius's sudden and urgent gathering together of all that remained.

Nennius completed his work towards the very end of the 8th century AD and the sources that he gathered were many and varied. They included certain items of history that had been imparted to him by Irish scholars. Then come the *'Annals of the Romans'*, *'The Law'*, *'another explanation'*, and, lapsing into his native Welsh, he then tells us that a noble elder named Cuana had compiled a British genealogy from a certain Roman (i.e. Latin) chronicle.[3] He was happy to rely on oral history too, quite unashamedly describing one such item as being 'in the writing of the writer's mind'.[4] But one of the really important aspects of his contribution in all this, is that Nennius made no apparent attempt to edit his sources or even correct some of their obvious discrepancies. Had he done so, then it would have been difficult for us to assess the actual and original contents of the records consulted by Nennius, and distinguish these from what was Nennius's own, perhaps mistaken, ideas about them. Instead, Nennius merely copied down his sources and passed them on to us, historical warts and all, so that we could make of them what we would.

A few, but only a very few, of the records preserved by Nennius, are admittedly of doubtful quality and reliability. But amongst them is one of the most important documents from the ancient world that could have come into our possession. It is set down in chapters 17 and 18 of *Historia Brittonum* (for the Latin text of these chapters, with translation, see Appendix 5 of this book), and it records the descent of a considerable number of early European nations. On the next page it is laid out as a conventional genealogy.

It is instructive to compare Nennius's Table of European Nations (as I like to call it) with Appendix 3 of this book, the genealogy of the nations of Japheth as recorded in Genesis. Nennius's source and Genesis are in remarkable agreement with one another, yet Nennius adds details that are not included in Genesis, for the natural and obvious reason that the Genesis account is necessarily brief. Gomer (1), for example, is merely cited by Nennius as being the ancestor of the Gauls, Nennius omitting entirely the names of Gomer's three immediate descendants, Ashchenaz, Riphath and Togarmah that are included in Genesis. (Would he have omitted these if he were merely copying straight from Genesis itself?) He cites Magog (2) as the ancestor of both the Scythians and the Goths, and Madai (3) as the founder of the Medes. So far so good. But it is from this point that the document from which Nennius was working, shows one or two tell-tale signs of the (albeit remarkably little) distortion that it has suffered in transmission, whether oral or written.

For example, and as we shall note in Appendix 3, Tubal (4) was the father of a people known to the Assyrians as the Tabali, whose land, Tabal, (present-day Georgia in what used to be the USSR, whose modern capital Tblisi perpetuates the name of Tubal), lay adjacent to that of the biblical Togarmah, (Assyr. Tegarama). From Nennius, however, comes the added detail that from Tubal came the Iberian, the Spanish and the Italian races. And this receives at least partial support from Josephus, who wrote some seven hundred years before Nennius, that Tubal was the father of the Thobelites, known as Iberians in his own day.[5] And as Josephus makes no mention of either the Spanish or Italian races, nor yet the descent of the Goths from Magog, Nennius was clearly not copying from him.

Likewise, Nennius's source cites Meshech (5) as the father of the Cappadocians (see Appendix 1:10 and 2:18 – the

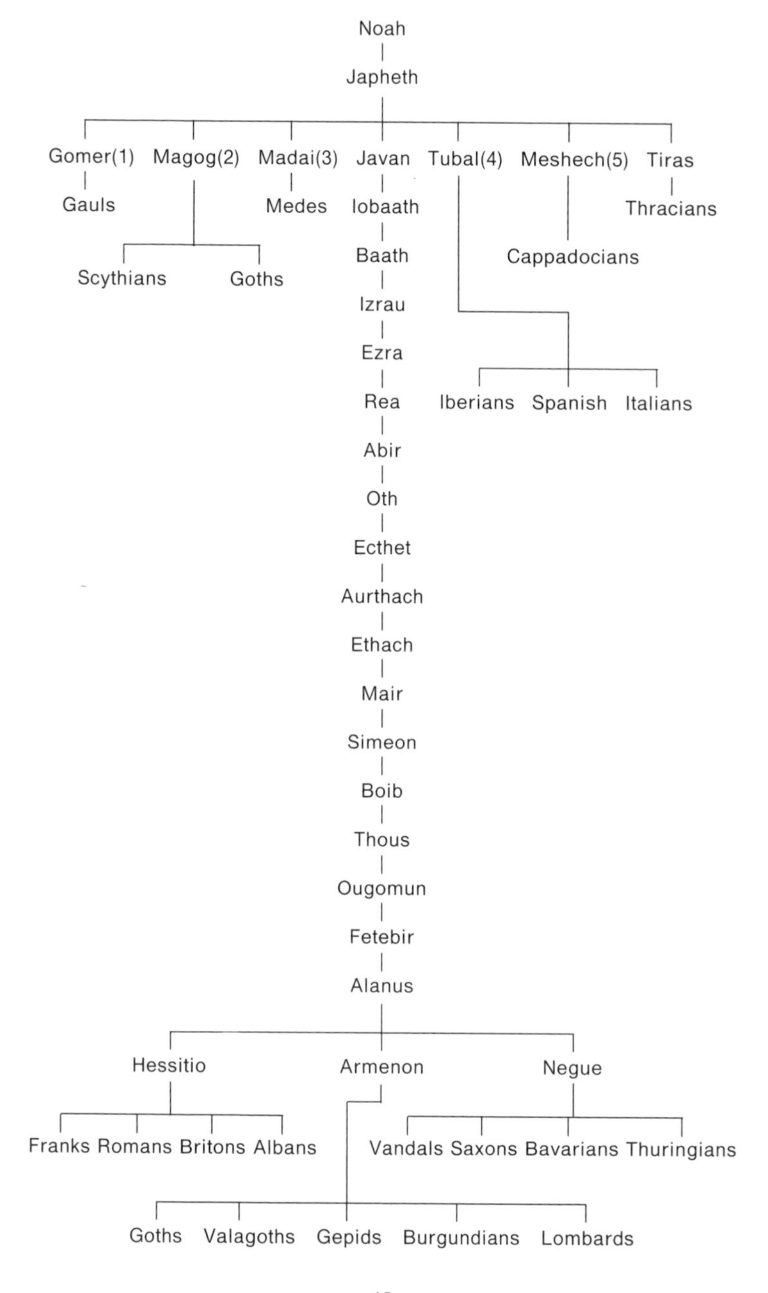
Noah
Japheth
Gomer(1)
Magog(2)
Madai(3)
Javan
Tubal(4)
Meshech(5)
Tiras
Gauls
Medes
Iobaath
Thracians
Scythians
Goths
Baath
Cappadocians
Izrau
Ezra
Rea
Iberians
Spanish
Italians
Abir
Oth
Ecthet
Aurthach
Ethach
Mair
Simeon
Boib
Thous
Ougomun
Fetebir
Alanus
Hessitio
Armenon
Negue
Franks
Romans
Britons
Albans
Vandals
Saxons
Bavarians
Thuringians
Goths
Valagoths
Gepids
Burgundians
Lombards

Caphtorim), an error that also appears in Josephus. It is doubtful though that Josephus originated these errors, simply because he was himself working from much older sources. The confusion, however, was easily brought about, for the name of the Semitic people of Mash in Genesis, is alternately rendered Meshech in 1 Chronicles. Clearly the two, the Semitic people of Meshech and the Japhetic people of Meshech, were confused with one another even in classical times, and it was upon the records of the classical world that both Josephus and Nennius relied rather than upon any mere copying of the Genesis record.

Other examples of distortion (albeit still of a minor nature) are seen in that the Goths are shown to have been descended from both Magog (2), the biblical patriarch, and from Armenon, the son of Alanus. Armenon himself is stated to have had five sons, yet only four are named. (Five nations are later shown to have descended from him.) Similarly, Negue is stated to have three sons, yet four nations derive from him. The significance of all this is that Nennius could easily have edited out or corrected these points, thereby enhancing his own credibility, yet he chose to simply leave them as they are. And it is this that, almost paradoxically, enhances his standing as a trustworthy and reliable historian, and it further assures us that we are reading these exceedingly ancient documents exactly as Nennius read them.

From Alanus onwards appears a comprehensive table of the nations of Europe. One or two of these names were archaic even in Nennius's time and would long have fallen into disuse. They are all, however, familiar to any historian today whose studies have touched upon the history of Europe at about the time of the Roman Empire. For several centuries, it seems, Europe was a seething cauldron as nation vied with nation in a bewildering array of migration, invasion and displacement. Yet not one of the names in this list of nations is historically unattested, not even that of the unlikely-sounding Gepids.

However, there is one particular aspect of this table that should be drawn emphatically to the reader's attention, because it is a matter of immense significance, a matter moreover that seems to have entirely escaped the notice of modernist scholars. It is the appearance of just four names in the early section of the genealogy. But this is not the only occasion on which we meet with them. They appear also in the patriarchal genealogy of the early Irish-Celts, and their chronological significance is just as great as their ethnic significance.

The names in the British account are: Iobaath, Baath, Izrau and Ezra.

But notice their position in the genealogy. They occupy the four generations immediately following Javan, the son of Japheth. When we later come to consider the genealogy of the Irish-Celts, which has been constructed from entirely different sources, we shall see that these same names occupy similar places, except that there they are descended from Magog, not Javan, and Baath is depicted as the elder brother, and not the son, of Iobaath.

Their names take the early Irish forms of: Jobhath, Baath, Easru and Sru, recognisably the same names as given in the British table.

However, it is the chronological position of those particular names in these ancient genealogies that provides a striking confirmation of the Genesis account. In the book of Genesis, we see that the dispersal of the nations from Babel took place during the fifth generation after the Flood. And here we are presented with the names of four successive generations of patriarchs who were common to the recorded ancestry of both the British and Irish Celts.[6] After the fifth generation, the lines of the British and Irish Celts diversify, exactly in accordance with the historical movement of the nations as depicted in Genesis. All of which is a strange occurrence in documents that are not only drawn from entirely independent ancient sources, but which the modernist school, if they cared to mention them at all, would have us believe are fictitious.

Nennius tells us that he found the above record in 'the ancient books of our elders' (*Aliud experimentum inueni . . . ex ueteribus libris ueterum nostrorum*), and we need now to establish when this ancient document was written. It is crucial to establish this, because leaving the question open would allow the familiar and by now wearisome charge to be made that it was forged by Christian monks as an act of 'pious fraud'. To settle the matter we will now examine the work of Geoffrey of Monmouth who, like Nennius, was a Welsh monk and who lived some three hundred years after him. The importance of Geoffrey's work lies in the fact that he carried the story forward from where Nennius left off, and it is the abundance of internal and external evidence from Geoffrey's book that will enable us to assess the age, and thus the authenticity, of Nennius's earlier material.

Notes

1. Elvodug, archbishop of Gwynnedd, (otherwise Elbod, Elbodogus, Elvodogus or Elfoddw), is known to us from the ***Annales Cambriae***. He was present, in AD 768, when the Britons changed their reckoning of Easter. Indeed, it was he who initially introduced the change. (*768 an. Pasca commutatur apud Brittones super dominicam diem emendante Elbodugo homine Dei.* Morris. p. 88). The second and last time he is mentioned is the entry for the year AD 809, which records his death (*809 an. Elbodug archiepiscopus Guenedotae regione migravit ad Dominum.* Morris p. 88).
2. See Morris p. 9.
3. *Is amlaid sin tugasdair ar senoir-ne uasal, i. Guanach, geinilach Breatan a cronicib na Romanach.* 'This is how our noble elder Cuanu gathered the genealogy of the British from the chronicles of the Romans.' (Morris. pp. 19 & 61).
4. *Set haec genealogia non scripta in aliquo volumine Britanniae, set in scriptione mentis scriptoris fuit.* 'But this genealogy is not written in any book of Britain, but was in the writing of the writer's mind.' (Morris. pp. 19 & 61).
5. Whiston. p. 31. See Bibliography.
6. In case some should think that the British and Irish influenced each other on a cultural level to the extent that they were willing to tamper with and falsify their own royal genealogies (and we shall ignore the inevitable death penalty that this would have incurred), they need only ask themselves why that influence should have been confined only to the four generations named,

and why there should exist such discrepancies between them both in source (Magog and Javan) and in succession of names (see chapter 9). Moreover, none of these names are those of famous figures of the past, nor yet those of mythical gods. So why should they have bothered?

Chapter 4

The Chronicles of the early Britons

> 'Yf God will, at an other apter tyme and in more apt place, marveilous agreement of the historyes of Antiquity and great unlooked for light and credit will be restored to the Originalls of Brutus . . .' (John Dee 1577. Cotton MS. Vitellius. c. vii. f 206v)

On Wednesday 7th November 1917, Flinders Petrie, a renowned archaeologist of the day, addressed the assembled members of the British Academy. He was to present a paper to them entitled *Neglected British History*,[1] in which he drew attention to the fact that a considerable body of historical documentary source-material was being overlooked if not wilfully ignored by modern historians. He drew fleeting attention to the work of Geoffrey of Monmouth and then homed in on one particular record that shed much light upon Geoffrey's too-disparaged history. The ancient book to which he drew attention was known to him as the *Tysilio Chronicle*, which is listed today as *Jesus College MS LXI* and is lodged in the Bodleian Library, Oxford. It is written in medieval Welsh, and is, as its colophon reveals,[2] a translation that was commissioned by the same Walter of Oxford who commissioned Geoffrey of Monmouth to translate a certain very ancient British book into Latin. It is, in fact, a translation from early British into medieval Welsh of the same source-material used by Geoffrey, and is an answer to all those learned critics who have stated with such emphasis over the years that Geoffrey of Monmouth was lying when he claimed to have translated such a book.

However, this is not the only light that the Welsh chronicle was to shed, for it was to address matters of far greater import and relevance than the mere vindication of Geoffrey's good name.[3] Indeed, it contains historically verifiable accounts that overturn many modernist assumptions and teachings about our past. More importantly, the material that it contains reveals an antiquity for itself that carries contemporarily recorded history back to uncomfortably early times. Uncomfortable, that is, for evolutionary and modernistic philosophy. Flinders Petrie highlights some of these points, and we shall consider these and others in this chapter.

Among the points he mentions is the account contained both in Geoffrey of Monmouth and the Welsh chronicles of the attempted invasions of these islands by Julius Caesar in 55 and 54 BC. Caesar, of course, has left us his own account of this, and it is tempting to think (and is often stated) that the Welsh chronicles (and hence Geoffrey of Monmouth) contain nothing more than a rehashed version of Caesar's account. But close examination reveals a different story. The account in Geoffrey and the Welsh chronicle turns out to be nothing less than the Julian invasion as seen through the eyes of the early Britons themselves. An eyewitness account in fact, which dates this part of the material to the middle of the 1st century BC. This, of course, is far too early for most modern scholars to accept for Celtic literacy, and it also sheds a somewhat unfavourable light upon Julius Caesar, himself the hero of many a modern book on the history of early Britain. But how, exactly, do the British and Roman accounts compare?

Caesar tells us[4] that when he initially landed on the shore of Britain, the landing was resisted in a most alarming way for the Roman troops. The British charioteers and cavalry rode into the very waves to attack the Roman soldiers as they tried to leap from their ships into the sea, and the landing was almost aborted due the unusual nature and ferocity of the attack. Moreover, Caesar had made some very serious miscalculations about the tide and weather that had almost lost him his army. But what does the British account say of all this? Nothing. Nothing whatever. There is no triumphant trumpeting about the bravery of the Celtic warriors or the Romans' difficulties in making land.

Instead, we hear only how, on first receiving news of the Roman landing, the Britons under Kasswallawn (Caesar's Cassivelaunus) gathered together at a certain fort in Kent. Caesar had clearly been resisted merely by a band of local levies of whom the Britons' intelligence reports had taken no account. But why should they? It was only to be expected (by the Britons) that the locals would meet the assault, and the opposition to the landing had been unsuccessful in any case. But perhaps the gathering of the Britons at the Kentish fort is one of the more telling aspects of the affair. The Welsh chronicle names the fort Doral, which Geoffrey of Monmouth transposes into Latin as Dorobellum.[5] It was known to later Latin writers as Durolevum, and was a fortress that stood roughly midway between Rochester and Canterbury. As Flinders Petrie points out, it would have been the ideal meeting place for an assembling army that was uncertain whether the invading force would proceed directly across the river Medway towards London, or would skirt along the coast towards Sussex and then head north to London, thus saving itself the task of having to cross the Medway. And yet Caesar never mentions this fort, for the natural reason that he would have been entirely unaware of its existence and name. A medieval monk rehashing Caesar's work would not have mentioned it either for the same reasons. Of further significance is the fact that Nennius writes in his *Historia Brittonum*:

> 'Julius Caesar ... while he was fighting with Dolabella ...'[6]

...Dolabella being mistaken in Nennius's source-document for the personal name of a British warrior rather than the fort where the warriors were gathered, thus revealing that by the end of the 8th century AD at the very latest, a serious corruption of the account of the British manouvres from which Nennius drew his own information existed. The fact that no such corruption is evident in the Welsh chronicle (or Geoffrey's Latin version) speaks volumes not only for the purity of the information contained in both the Welsh chronicle and Geoffrey, but for the antiquity and undoubted authenticity of their common source material.

Later in his account,[7] Caesar describes in detail how his cavalry came to grief when they encountered the unusual fighting tactics of the Britons. He describes these tactics in detail, remarking on their effectiveness. And yet no such description appears in the British account. One could reasonably expect that a later forger or compiler would triumphantly have mentioned how his forebears terrified and almost defeated the Romans with superior and ingenious fighting tactics, but not a contemporary Briton who was recording the same events as Caesar but from a different vantage point. But, again, why should a contemporary Briton mention tactics with which he and his intended readers would have been all too familiar?

Three further specific items in both the Welsh chronicle and Geoffrey's Latin account reveal the sometimes garbled nature of the British intelligence reports of the time that were sent over long distances, in two cases from the other side of the Channel, and the natural confusion that arose over the debriefing of warriors that returned from the front line of battle and the subsequent interviewing of eyewitnesses. The first concerns the death of a certain Roman officer. He was named as Laberius (Quintus Laberius Durus) in Caesar's account,[8] according to which Laberius died in action during the second campaign in Britain of the year 54 BC. The British account, however, states that Laberius was killed during the first campaign, and, more tellingly, it identifies the soldier concerned as Labienus[9] (Welsh Alibiens). Now, the name Labienus would earlier have been known to the Britons from reports reaching them of Caesar's second-in-command who, at the time of Caesar's second invasion and quite unknown to the native Britons, had been left behind in Gaul to administer matters there in Caesar's absence. Thus, learning from prisoners taken in battle that the dead officer's name was Laberius, they confused the names and naturally assumed that this was the Labienus of whom they had heard. It was a perfectly natural error made in wartime conditions, but not one that would have been made by a medieval forger who had Caesar's account in front of him.

Similarly, the second item concerns the garbled British report of a fortress that was erected at Caesar's command when he returned to Gaul. Caesar does not name the fort, whereas the British account reports its name as Odina.[10] Flinders Petrie points out that no such place is known, although he does mention that Caesar reports[11] the sending of troops to Lexovii (today's Lisieux), and that the river there, which again Caesar does not name but which is called Olina, suggests the origins of the British report. Again, the name Odina (which Caesar does not give) could obviously not have been borrowed from Caesar's account by any medieval hand.

The third incident concerns an inaccurate report by British scouts which led Kasswallawn's intelligence gatherers to assume that Caesar had fled Britain at a time when the Roman army was in fact firmly encamped on these shores. Caesar, having lost valuable ships during a storm, ordered that the ships be taken out of the water and dragged inland to within the Roman camp.[12] This was a prodigious feat of engineering. These ships were extremely heavy military transports, and yet the task was well within the (to us well-known) capabilities and engineering skills of the Roman sappers. However, it would not have occurred to the Britons that such a thing would be contemplated let alone possible, and so it is that when the advance scouting parties of the Britons could no longer see Caesar's ships beached upon the strand, they naturally but wrongly assumed that he had fled these shores.

There are later, touching, accounts in the early British chronicles (but on which Flinders Petrie is silent) where mention is made of British warriors fighting in this country against the armies of the kings of Syria and Lybia,[13] and which look initially like a most unlikely collection of stories. Yet, what becomes of these accounts when we view them in their correct historical perspective? The Britons were never ones to employ foreign mercenaries to do their fighting for them. They knew the dangers involved in such a policy, dangers that were unhappily demonstrated when one British king, Vortigern, invited the Saxons over to chase away the Picts. As history records, and to Vortigern's everlasting infamy as far as the Welsh are concerned, the Saxons stayed and eventually banished the Britons themselves to a rocky and inhospitable part of the island, Wales. Rather, in times of war or emergency the Britons would band together as separate tribes into one fighting force, and place their many kings under the authority of one overking for the duration of the hostilities. Thus, when the Britons encountered the Roman army, they were surprised to find not Romans only amongst the enemy's ranks (if there were any Romans at all), but separate legions made up of Syrians, Lybians and every other kind of nationality.[14] We know from the archaeological record that Syrians and others did actually make up some of the occupying legions in this country, and it is therefore not only natural that the Britons should refer to them by the names of their countries of origin, but that they should also assume that the Syrians and others were led into battle by their own petty kings as were the Britons themselves who fought them. It is an unsuspected and striking mark of authenticity that no medieval forger would have thought of.

But if this portion of the chronicle contains material that can be dated to the middle of the 1st century BC, then there is other material that goes back much further. One such item (on which again Flinders Petrie is surprisingly silent) is the account of two men named Belinus and Brennius in Geoffrey's Latin version, and Beli and Bran in the Welsh.[15] One part of the story records how Bran led an invasion of Italy and sacked Rome. Certain modernist scholars have been quick to point out that Rome has never been sacked by the Britons, and that the story is a nonsensical fiction. However, a reading of Rome's historians might have led them to a different conclusion, for the sack of Rome by the Celts is told in considerable detail by an early historian of Rome, and the early British account of the event is confirmed, and indeed expanded upon, in every point.

The Roman historian in question is Livy (Titus Livius 59 BC–17 AD), whose *History of Rome* consisted of no less than 142 books, although only 35 of these have survived to the present day. However, it is Book 5 of Livy's history that contains the rather illuminating account that follows.[16] According to Livy, the sack of Rome by the Gallic Celts occurred around the year 390 BC, and we shall see precisely how closely this accords with the chronology of events and personages that is contained in the British chronicle. It matches it exactly. But of more interest to us is the fact that Livy has preserved the names of those who were involved in the planning and carrying out of the attack.

The first name is that of the king of the Bituriges, a Gallic (Celtic) people who were to give their name to the modern city of Bourges. The king was Ambitgatus, and Livy tells us that he had two nephews, one named Bellovesus, and the other Segovesus.[17] These two names also appear in the British account where they are given as Beli in the Welsh chronicle and Belinus and Segnius (the king of the Allobroges or Burgundians) in Geoffrey of Monmouth. The Welsh chronicle mentions Segnius as the prince of the Burdundians (i.e. Byrgwin, another term for the Allobroges) but does not name him. Each name, however, must have been given in the original British source-material for them to appear in either Geoffrey or the Welsh chronicle.

It is here, however, that Livy sheds some interesting light upon the Celtic royal families of the early 4th century BC. According to both Geoffrey and the Welsh chronicle, the father and mother of Belinus and Brennius were Dunvallo Molmutius (Welsh Dyfnal Moel Myd) and Tonuuenna (Welsh Tonwen). We know from the genealogy around which both Geoffrey's and the Welsh account are built (see Appendix 7), that Dunvallo was of British descent. Which means that Tonuuenna, whose genealogy is not given, could easily have been the sister of the Gaulish king, Ambitgatus, as is implied in

Livy when he calls Bellovesus (the British Belinus and son of Tonuuenna) the nephew of Ambitgatus. There is nothing at all unlikely or improbable in such a relationship. Indeed, marriage between the British and continental Celtic royal families would have been an entirely natural and expected event.

Which brings us to the name of the leader of the Gallic sack of Rome, whom Livy names as Brennus.[18] This is practically identical to the transposition into Latin of the British name of Bran that Geoffrey gives (Brennius), and the fact that Geoffrey and Livy are such distinct and independent authorities reveals that neither of them were making up the names of their characters as they went along. That neither Geoffrey nor the Welsh chronicle are merely copies or rehashes of Livy's account is abundantly evident when one compares the British account with that of Livy. There are far too many important and fundamental differences between them to suggest that one is dependent on the other. And yet they are all clearly and independently referring to the same historical event, namely the Celtic sack of Rome in ca 390 BC, but viewing that event from different camps.

We may carry the story back another generation by referring to the laws of Dunvallo, the father of Belinus and Brennius, which were known as the Molmutine Laws and which Geoffrey tells us were still held in high esteem by the Britons (Welsh) of Geoffrey's own day.[19] However, not only were they held in high esteem in Geoffrey's day, they also have survived to the present, and they clearly reveal their pagan origins.[20] The light that they shed upon the society in which the early Britons lived is set out in Appendix 6 of this book, where Flinders Petrie tells us in his own words about the laws and their application. But the history of the early Britons can be carried back further still, much further back, to the 12th century BC in fact, the time of the very foundation of the British nation.

The story is told of how a colony once landed on these shores, a colony led by one Brutus (Bryttys in the Welsh chronicle). It was from this Brutus that the British people derived their name. The history of Brutus's descendants is set out in the following chapter, but what interests us here is how, and by which route, the colony arrived on these shores in the first place. Again, we are indebted to Flinders Petrie for bringing to our attention the following details:

> 'After leaving Greece Brutus' [and his colony] 'sails to Africa, and then passes the Philenian altars, a place called Salinae, sails between Ruscicada and the mountains of Azara in danger of pirates, passes the river Malua, arrives in Mauretania, and reaches the pillars of Hercules. On this passage the ignorant editor notes: "It is probably impossible to discover whether these names describe existing places, or are purely the invention of the author". Now all these places are known, and they are all in consecutive order. The longitudes in Ptolemy are here added, for clearness. The Philenian altars (46° 45′) were two great sand heaps, for the story of which see Sallust; they would be well known as the boundary between Carthage and Egypt, but of no importance in late Roman times. Next, Salinae are the stretch of salt lagunes (33° to 34°), which would be important to mariners for salting fish. Next, Ruscicada (27° 40′) is a headland to the south of Sardinia; Brutus sailed between this and the mountains of Azara, and Ptolemy names a mountain tribe of Sardinia as the Aisaronesioi. The prevalence of pirates noted here gives the reason for naming the Sardinian mountains, as mariners could stand well off the African coast by sighting Sardinia, which lay 120 miles north, and thus escape the pirate coast track without losing their bearings. Next is the river Malua (11° 10′), which was important as the boundary of early Mauretania. Lastly, the pillars of Hercules (6° 35′–7° 30′). The general character of these names selected is that of points well known to mariners, such as any seaman might readily give as stages of a voyage. How then do they come into the Brut legend? They cannot have been stated by any seaman after AD 700, as the Arab conquest wiped out the old names and old trade. Did a medieval writer, then, extract the names from a

> Roman author? No single author seems to contain all of them: Ptolemy omits Salinae, Pliny omits Salinae and Azara, Strabo only has the Philanae, the Antonine itinerary only Rusiccade and Malua, the Peutingerian table only Rusicade, and the Philaeni in a wrong position. When we see the medieval maps, from Cosmas on to the Mappamundi of Hereford, it is impossible to suppose a medieval writer having enough geography at hand to compile such a mariner's list of six minor places in the right order, as they stood during the Roman Empire. If this list was, then, written during the Empire, there is no reason for preferring one date to another. There is, however, internal evidence that this was written before Claudius' (i.e. 10 BC–AD 54). 'It is after passing the Malua that Brutus arrives in Mauretania. Now Mauretania was only west of the Malua originally; but in the early imperial changes the east of that river was included, and Claudius constituted two Mauretanias, Tingitana and Caesariensis, divided by the river. The geography of the Brut is, then, older than Claudius.'[21]

There is much else that Flinders Petrie could have added had he been aware of it. For example, before Brutus sailed with his colony to the African coast on their migration from the mainland of Greece, they were said to have alighted upon an island whose name is given as Legetta in the Welsh chronicle, as Leogetia in Geoffrey of Monmouth, and which was known as Leucadia amongst the classical authors of the Mediterranean world. Today, we know it as the island of Levkás. But there are certain details, important details, that the British accounts mention that could not have been gleaned by a medieval forger simply hearing of the place or seeing it on a map, even one that happened to possess an unusual degree of accuracy for medieval times. For example, although the Welsh chronicle omits the fact, Geoffrey of Monmouth's Latin version recounts the detail of the island's woodlands,[22] and we note that even today one can still see on the island 'the remnants of the oak forests which were a feature of Levkas well into the nineteenth century.'[23]

For Geoffrey of Monmouth to be aware of these woods, they must have been mentioned in the original and ancient source-material that he was translating, and we can only ask ourselves whether the presence of oak forests on this sacred island which the Britons long remembered, and the fact that the early Druids of Britain ever afterwards held the oak tree to be particularly and peculiarly sacred, are entirely unconnected. As Pliny tells us:

> 'The Druidae ... esteeme nothing more sacred in the world, than Misselto, and the tree whereupon it breedeth, so it be on Oke ... they seem well enough to be named thereupon Dryidae in Greeke, which signifieth ... Oke-priests.'[24]

However, of added interest is the fact that both Geoffrey of Monmouth and the Welsh chronicle record the presence on the island of a ruined temple that was dedicated to the goddess Diana. There then follow the descriptions of a most complex ritual performed by Brutus and the nature and attributes of the goddess Diana that could only have come from a pagan source. But there is an added aspect to all this. Diana was considered to be the personification of the moon, and although there is no apparent trace remaining today of the temple of Diana on the island, there are the ruins of a temple to Diana's theological husband, the sun god Apollo. These ruins lie on a prominence some 230 feet above the sea, and:

> '... it was from here that the priests of Apollo would hurl themselves into space, buoyed up – so it was said – by live birds and feathered wings. The relationship between the ritual and the god seems obscure, although there was an early connection between Apollo and various birds ... Ovid confirms that the virtues of the flight and the healing waters below the cliff had been known since the time of Deucalion, the Greek Noah.'[25]

Now there are definite echoes of this curious and most ancient ritual in the story of one of Brutus's not far removed descendants, king Bladud (Blaiddyd in the Welsh chronicle. See next chapter). Bladud, it is recorded, made himself pinions and wings and learned how to fly. He only had one lesson and the flight was predictably a short one, but the important detail is that Bladud was killed as he struck the temple of Apollo that once stood in the city known today as London.[26]

Yet this is not the only curious detail to emerge out of the early British record. What, for example, are we to make of the mention of Greek Fire in the story of Brutus? This appears as *tan gwyllt* in the Welsh chronicle, and as *sulphureas tedas* and *greco igne* in Geoffrey of Monmouth's account.[27] As Flinders Petrie rightly points out, Greek Fire was entirely unheard of in Europe before the time of the Crusades. Did an early medieval forger have a lucky guess? I doubt it. And what of the further detailed geographical knowledge of the ancient Greek mainland that the British accounts reveal? The region called Yssbaradings in the Welsh chronicle and Sparatinum in Geoffrey's version, was anciently known as The**sprot**ia, an area on the west coast of Greece. Archaeology tells us that the Thesprotians were the earliest inhabitants of the region, their name being perpetuated today in the modern town of Thesprotikon.[28] Moreover, the river Ystalon in the Welsh chronicle (Akalon in Geoffrey) is the Acheron that flows through the ancient region of Epirus.

Further, there is the name of the king against whom Brutus fought in order to win the freedom of his followers. His name is given as Pendrassys in the Welsh chronicle and as Pandrasus in Geoffrey.[29] I have seen no attempt whatever to identify this king, and there is now no possibility of tracing the name in the surviving records of ancient Greece, although such tracing would itself be futile. Pandrasus is not, it seems, a proper name at all but a title – *pan Doris* – meaning king of all the Dorians. Again, archaeology tells us that the Dorian Greeks overran this part of the Grecian mainland at just about the same period (12th-11th centuries BC) in which the story of Brutus begins.[30] So it is clear that the name Pandrasus belongs firmly and authentically to the times that are dealt with in the opening portions of the British account.

All of which helps us in dating not only the fascinating and undoubtedly ancient material in the Welsh chronicle and in Geoffrey's version, but also the material passed down to us by Nennius that we noted in the previous chapter and from which we were able to construct the Table of European Nations. Clearly, none of all this is attributable to the nefarious work of early Christian monks who were seeking to foist upon the world a contrived but pious history, for all the material that we have considered in this chapter pre-dates the coming of the Christian faith to the early Britons by at least a hundred years, and certainly by up to a thousand years and more. In other words, the now wearisome modernist charge of pious fraud falls flat. This will be further seen in the following chapter which summarises the contents of both Geoffrey of Monouth and the Welsh chronicles, and Appendix 7 where the genealogy of the early British kings is set out. The approximate dates of each king are also given as I have been able to calculate them from the internal evidence contained in the Welsh chronicle and in Geoffrey's Latin version,[31] and external evidence derived from other sources.

Notes

1. Published by Humphrey Milford at the Oxford University Press as part of the *Proceedings of the British Academy*. Vol. viii. pp. 1–28.
2. 'I, Walter of Oxford, translated this book from Welsh (Kymraec) into Latin, and in my old age have translated it a second time from Latin into Welsh.'
3. Happily, two English translations of this particlar Welsh chronicle already exist: Roberts, Peter. *Chronicle of the Kings*. 1811. The sole surviving copy is at the Bodleian library, shelfmark Douce T., 301. (A poorly edited 2nd edition of this was brought out by Manley Pope under the title, *A History of the Kings of Ancient Britain*. Simpkin, Marshall & Co. London. 1862. As poor as his edition is, however, [Manley Pope interpolated comments of his own without marking them as such in the text, and he makes no

acknowledgement whatever to Peter Roberts, whose translation he has clearly filched], Manley Pope does provide some very informative notes from pp. 155–216).

The second translation is by Canon Robert Ellis Jones of New York. His untitled translation is a literal rendering into English of the Welsh text, and forms part of Griscom's book (see bibliography). Canon Jones died in 1929, the year of his translation's publication.

4. Caesar. pp. 99–100. See bibliography.
5. Geoffrey of Monmouth. p. 108 and Manley Pope p. 60. See bibliography.
6. Nennius. p. 23. See bibliography.
7. Caesar. pp. 102–3.
8. Caesar. pp. 111–2.
9. Geoffrey. p. 110 and Manley Pope p. 60. As Flinders Petrie points out, while the shift in date may be due to tradition, it cannot agree with copying.
10. Geoffrey (pp. 112–3) has *Odnea*. See Manley Pope pp. 61 & 180–1.
11. Caesar. p. 87.
12. Caesar. p. 110 and Manley Pope. p. 61, *'Caesar was compelled to fly.'*
13. Geoffrey. pp. 236 & 245–6. See also Manley Pope p. 122.
14. Cottrell (pp. 63–4. See bibliography) lists Spaniards, Hungarians, Germans, Syrians, Greeks, Africans, Gauls, and so on as some of the nationalities that made up the Roman legions in Britain. Hadrian's Wall alone was manned by Spaniards, Germans, Africans and Syrians.
15. Geoffrey. pp. 90–100 and Manley Pope. pp. 38–46.
16. Livy. pp. 378–395. See bibliography.
17. Livy. p. 379. Compare Geoffrey. pp. 97–9 and Manley Pope pp. 44–5.
18. Livy. pp. 383 & 395.
19. Geoffrey. p. 89.
20. See Probert, William. *Ancient Laws of Cambria*. 1823.
21. Flinders Petrie. pp. 8–9.
22. Geoffrey. p. 64. Thorpe (p. 341. See bibliography.#alleges that the name is an invention of Geoffrey's.
23. Bradford. *Guide to the Greek Islands*. Collins. London. p. 48.
24. cit. Hawkins, Prof G. *Stonehenge Decoded*. Fontana. p. 34. Hawkins points out that as the Greek word for oak was 'drus',

then Pliny's etymology for the name Druid would appear to have been correct.

25. Bradford. p. 50.
26. Geoffrey. p. 81 and Manley Pope. pp. 28 & 167–8.
27. Geoffrey. p. 58 and Manley Pope p. 10.
28. *Webster's New Geographical Dictionary*. G & C Merriam. Massachussetts. 1977. p. 1203.
29. Geoffrey. pp. 55–64.
30. Webster's. p. 340.
31. For a technical appraisal of the chronology, see my article *The Early History of Man – Pt. 3. The Kings of the Ancient Britons: A Chronology*. CEN Tech. J., Vol. 5^2. 1991. pp. 139–142.

Chapter 5

The History of the early British Kings

What follows is a summary of the history of the kings of the early Britons as it is given in both Geoffrey of Monmouth and the Welsh chronicles. It is a recorded history that was consigned to oblivion after the massacre, at the instigation of Augustine, of the British monks at Bangor in AD 604 and was thus entirely unknown or ignored by the later Saxon and Norman chroniclers of England. Consequently, it came to be generally and unquestioningly assumed amongst English scholars by the 16th and 17th centuries that no such record had ever existed, and that works such as Geoffrey of Monmouth's or the Welsh chronicle were forgeries and fairy tales. That opinion persists today. We have seen, however, in the previous chapter how these records enjoy a great deal of historical vindication in spite of modernism's cursory and fashionable dismissal of them. But here, plain and unadorned, is the story that the chronicles themselves tell, a story that no child will have learnt at his desk in any school of this land. It spans over two thousand years, and its survival to the present day, being little short of a miracle, is a tribute to those Welsh scholars of old who recognised its importance and preserved it entire for our reading.

Amongst the ancient records that the Britons themselves left behind, there is preserved (in Nennius at least) a list of the ancestors of the early British kings as they were counted generation by generation back to Japheth, the son of Noah. But the history of the Britons as a distinct nation had its beginnings with the fall of Troy, and it is at this point that Geoffrey of Monmouth and the Welsh chronicles take up the story.

Anchises, known to us from other histories, fled with his son, Aeneas, from the burning ruins of Troy, and they made their way to the land that is nowadays called Italy, settling with their people on the banks of the river Tiber around what was later to become Rome. The indigenous population was ruled over by Latinus who received Aeneas and his people with kindness and hospitality, in return for which Aeneas defeated Latinus's foe, Turnus, king of the Rutuli. He then married the daughter of Latinus, Lavinia, from which union came Aeneas Silvius who later rose to rule over all the tribes of Italy. But it was through the line of his brother Ascanius that the royal lineage was presently to be perpetuated, and of this line was born Ascanius's son Silvius. Silvius seduced an unnamed niece of his grandfather's wife, Lavinia, and it was from their union that his son Brutus was born. The mother of Brutus died whilst giving birth to him, and when he was a lad of fifteen years, Brutus accidentally shot his father dead with an arrow whilst out hunting. For having caused the deaths of both his parents, thus fulfilling a prophecy concerning him, Brutus was exiled out of Italy, the royal line of Aeneas passing into the hands of another. And it is at this point that the history of the Britons as a distinct nation begins.

Brutus journeyed from Italy to Greece, and there he came into contact with certain slaves. These were the descendants of the soldiers who had fought against Greece in the Trojan Wars of the 13th century BC. They had been enslaved by Priam, son of Achilles, 'in vengeance for his father's death', and were subsequently to continue their slavery under Pandrasus, king of the Dorian Greeks. Learning that he was descended from their own ancient kings, the Trojans accepted Brutus into their fellowship and elected him as their leader, and under him they successfully rose against their captors. Defeating Pandrasus in battle, they set sail to look for a land in which to settle. Sailing their fleet out of the Mediterranean between the Pillars of Hercules (the Straits of Gibraltar), they came across another group of Trojans led by Corineus, who were likewise escaping abroad from their captors. They combined forces and landed in Gaul with Brutus being acclaimed as their overall king. There they fought and defeated the Picts under king Goffar (Koffarffichti – Goffar the Pict – in the Welsh). The Trojans again set sail, and came ashore at Totnes in Devon at some time in the 12th century BC. The land and its people were subsequently to derive their names from Brutus. Then Brutus founded the city of Trinovantum, or New Troy, which was later to become the city of London. Brutus, the first king of the Britons, reigned over his people in this island for twenty three years, i.e. from ca 1104–1081 BC.

Amongst the spoils that Brutus had taken from Greece was Ignoge, the daughter of Pandrasus, whom he wedded and who was to bear him three sons, Locrinus, Kamber and Albanactus. Upon the death of Brutus, Kamber and Albanactus inherited Wales (Cambria) and Scotland (Albany) respectively, and Locrinus became king of Loegria, the land named after him, which consisted of present-day England minus Cornwall. (The modern Welsh still know England as Loegria). Cornwall was ruled over by Corineus whose daughter, Gwendolen, Locrinus had married. Locrinus, however, had also taken another wife, Estrildis, whom he hid for fear of Corineus. But as soon as Corineus was dead, he made Estrildis his queen and put away Gwendolen, his lawful wife. In vengeance, Gwendolen raised an army in her father's kingdom of Cornwall, killing Locrinus in the ensuing battle. Estrildis and her daughter Habren were drowned on Gwendolen's orders, and Gwendolen herself went on to rule Loegria for the next fifteen years. Then, in ca 1056 BC, she abdicated in favour of her son Maddan and retired to her native Cornwall where she died.

Little is said of Maddan other than that he ruled the land for forty years, i.e. from ca 1056–1016 BC. His sons, on his death, contended for the throne, Malin his younger son being murdered by Mempricius, the elder. Mempricius (Membyr in the Welsh chronicle) became a noted tyrant who abandoned his wife in pursuit of unnatural vices, and he generally misruled the kingdom. Then, in the twentieth year of his reign, in about

996 BC, he was separated from his companions in a hunting party and was eaten by wolves.

He was succeeded by Ebraucus (Welsh Efrawc) who reigned for the next thirty-nine years from ca 996–957 BC. In an eventful and fondly remembered reign, Ebraucus sacked Gaul and founded the city named after him, Kaerbrauc, which the later Romans were to latinise as Eboracum, present-day York. On his death, he was succeeded by Brutus Greenshield (Bryttys darian las in the Welsh chronicle) who reigned for the next twelve years until ca 945 BC. Then Leil succeeded to the throne. He founded the city of Kaerleil which still bears his name (Carlisle), but he was a weak and vacillating king whose twenty-five year reign ended in ruin and civil-war.

His son Hudibras, (Run baladr bras in the Welsh), who came to the throne in ca 920 BC, re-established peace in the realm and went on to rule Loegria for the next thirty-nine years. A great builder, he founded the cities of Kaerreint (Canterbury), Kaerguenit (Winchester), and Paladur (Shaftesbury). He was succeeded by his son, Bladud, in ca 881 BC, who ruled the land for twenty years. During that time, he founded the city of Kaerbadum (Bath), the hot springs of which were thought to cure leprosy. At his commandment, necromancy, communicating with the dead, was practised throughout the kingdom, and he was eventually killed in a misguided attempt to fly. At his death, Leir his son took the crown, and he was to enjoy a reign of sixty years, which lasted from ca 861–801 BC. He founded the city of Kaerleir (Leicester) and lost his kingdom when he attempted to divide it amongst his three daughters. Shakespeare tells the story in his celebrated play, King Lear.

Leir's youngest daughter, Cordelia, inherited the crown on her father's death and ruled the land in peace for five years. She was then deposed by her sisters and committed suicide in prison. Marganus I (Morgan in the Welsh) then took the kingdom in the year 796 BC, sharing the kingdom with his cousin Cunedagius (Kynedda). Marganus ruled the land north of the Humber, and Cunedagius ruled the south. Marganus, during the fighting that arose between them, was pursued into

Wales by Cunedagius and slain at the place named after him, Margam near present-day Port Talbot. Cunedagius then ruled the whole kingdom for the next thirty-three years. He was succeeded in 761 BC by Rivallo (Rriallon), who reigned wisely and frugally. His reign was particularly remembered for a rain of blood, a great swarm of flies and a plague that took a heavy toll of the population. At his death in 743 BC, there followed the reigns of four kings of whom little is said save their names and their order of succession. And then, in the year 663 BC, Gorboduc (Gwrvyw in the Welsh) came to the throne. In old age he became senile, his dotage giving rise to much quarrelling over the succession between his two sons, Ferrex and Porrex. In the event, Gorboduc was to become the last king to reign over the Britons who was of the royal line of Brutus.

Gorboduc's queen, Judon was caused much grief over her quarrelling sons. On learning that Porrex had killed Ferrex, her favourite of the two, she became insane and later murdered Porrex in his sleep by hacking him to pieces. (Other accounts tell how she was tied in a sack and thrown into the Thames for the murder of her son). The land was then plunged into the political chaos of a two hundred year civil war. The outcome of the civil war was decided by a final conflict between five kings altogether, and from it all, in ca 440 BC, emerged Pinner, the king of Loegria. He was later slain in a battle by his successor but one, Dunvallo, in about the year 430 BC. Dunvallo's father, Cloten (Klydno in the Welsh), who was the king of Cornwall, ruled for ten years and was finally succeeded by his son, Dunvallo Molmutius (Dyfnal moel myd). During a forty-year reign, he codified the Molmutine Laws, a law-code which Geoffrey of Monmouth tells us was still famed and revered in his own day, and which, surprisingly, still survives. (See Probert's *Ancient Laws of Cambria.* 1823). Crimes of violence were virtually unheard of in his kingdom, such was the severity of punishment meted out to such criminals while he was on the throne. Dunvallo's eldest son, Belinus (the Great), then ruled the kingdom from ca 380–374 BC. He ruled Loegria, Cambria and Cornwall. His brother Brennius held Northumbria and Albany, and eventually led the Celtic sack of Rome in ca 390 BC. Belinus eventually defeated Brennius in battle, and so came to rule all Britain. Geoffrey tells us that Belinus was a great road-builder, and that Billingsgate in London was built by and named after him. In an eventful reign, Belinus subdued the then king of Denmark, exacting from him a great tribute.

He was succeeded by Gurguit (Gwrgant Varf Drwch), whose reign lasted from ca 374–369 BC. The son and successor of Belinus, Gurguit was renowned as a man of peace and justice. During Gurguit's reign, the king of Denmark withdrew the tribute that Belinus had exacted of him, and Gurguit promptly invaded Denmark to assert his authority there. It was during his return from Denmark that Gurguit is said to have intercepted the ships of Partholan and his fellow exiles. He is then stated to have assigned to Partholan the otherwise uninhabited land of Ireland. (This, however, leads us to a problem in chronology. A suggested solution to this is offered in a later chapter.) Gurguit died peacefully and he lies buried in the city of Caerleon-on-Usk. His son Guithelin (Kyhylyn) then held the crown from ca 369–363 BC. Guithelin was a noted and benevolent ruler. He married Marcia, a learned woman who codified the Marcian Laws, the *Lex Martiana*. Alfred the Great was later to translate the code as the Mercian Laws, believing them to have been named after the much later Saxon kingdom of Mercia.

Queen Marcia ruled Britain for about five years after Guithelin's death because of their sons' minority. But he, Sisillius (Saessyllt), came to the throne in ca 358 BC on her death, ruling for the next six years. His reign was followed by those of his sons Kinarius and Danius, and then Morvidus, his great nephew, inherited the crown. Morvidus (Morydd), who ruled from ca 341–336 BC, was the illegitimate son of Danius and Tanguesteaia, but he became king on his father's death. An otherwise heroic ruler, he was noted and feared due to the merciless cruelty that he showed towards those whom he defeated in battle. After one particular attempted invasion of his kingdom, Morvidus, against all the laws of the Celtic Britons regarding warfare, personally put to death many prisoners of war. 'When he became so exhausted that he had to give up for a time, he ordered the remainder to be skinned alive, and in this state he had them burnt'. During his reign, reports of a monstrous animal wreaking havoc in the west reached the king. (In Geoffrey of Monmouth's original Latin, the creature is called a Belua.) With typical, if hasty, bravado Morvidus fought the beast alone, but the monster killed him, and devoured his corpse 'as if he had been a tiny fish.'

Gorbonianus (Gwrviniaw) followed Morvidus in ca 336 BC. He was much renowned for his goodness as a ruler, and was succeeded by Archgallo (Arthal) who reigned from ca 330–326 BC. He was the very opposite of his elder brother, Gorbonianus, and such was his tyranny that he was eventually deposed by the nobility of the realm. His younger brother, Elidurus, was elected king in his place. He was surnamed The Dutiful because of the compassion that he showed towards his deposed elder brother. Elidurus exercised this compassion to the point of abdicating after about five years in favour of a now reformed Archgallo, whose subsequent behaviour as king was a complete reversal of his former reign. Archgallo died after about ten years, at which point Elidurus resumed the crown. However, his reign was to be interrupted once again.

His two younger brothers, Ingenius and Peredurus, rebelled and incarcerated Elidurus in a tower. Dividing the land between them, Ingenius ruled the south whilst Peredurus ruled north of the Humber. Ingenius died seven years later, and Peredurus went on to reign over the whole island for a further three years, being known as a wise and beneficent king. He died in ca 296 BC, and Elidurus came to the throne for a third time. At this point, the order of succession becomes rather complicated, with cousin succeeding cousin. Finally the succession seems to settle down to a father-son order, at least for the next thirty-one reigns, the short length of the average reign (5–6 years) indicating political turmoil for that period of one hundred and seventy years or so, until the accession of Heli (Beli Mawr in the Welsh) in about the year 113 BC. He ruled for forty years until 73 BC when his son Lud became king. Lud rebuilt the city that Brutus had founded and had named New Troy, and renamed it Kaerlud, the city of Lud, after his own name. The name of the city was later corrupted to Kaerlundein, which the Romans took up as Londinium, hence London. At his death, Lud was buried in an entrance to the city that still bears his name, Ludgate. His youngest brother, Nennius (Nynnyaw), fought hand to hand with Julius Caesar on the latter's invasion of Britain in the year 55 BC. The Romans had been trying to set up camp in the Thames estuary when the Britons fell upon them by surprise. Although Nennius was forced away from Caesar by other soldiers, he did manage to capture the emperor's sword. Escaping, Nennius died of his wounds fifteen days later and was buried beside the northern entrance to Trinovantum (modern Bishopsgate in London?). The sword that he took as spoils, and which he had named Yellow Death, was buried with him. But the man who was actually king of the Britons when Caesar landed, was Cassivelaunus (Kasswallawn) who reigned from ca 58–38 BC. Betrayed by Androgeus, his brother Lud's eldest son, Cassivelaunus was eventually starved into submission when the Romans laid siege to his fort.

He was succeeded by Tenvantius, known in other histories as Tasciovanus, who reigned from ca 38–18 BC. And then he was followed by Cymbeline (Kynvelyn who reigned ca 18 BC-AD 12). Known to the Romans as *Cunobelinus*, he was the son and heir of Tenvantius. Cymbeline had received a Roman upbringing in the Imperial household, and on his succession to the British crown, he reigned for ten years. (His reign was immortalised in Shakespeare's play, Cymbeline.) The man who succeeded him was Guiderius (Gwydr) who reigned from ca AD 12–43. On inheriting the crown, he promptly refused to pay tribute to Rome. The emperor Claudius, on his own invasion of Britain in the year AD 43, was attacked by Guiderius' forces at Portchester. During the attack, Guiderius was betrayed and killed. Arvirargus next took the crown, reigning from ca AD 43–57. Taking command of the British forces on the death of his brother Guiderius, Arviragus emerged as victor from a major skirmish with Claudius' troops. He eventually ruled Britain as the emperor's puppet-king. At his death, he was interred at Gloucester. Marius (Mayric) came next, and ruled from ca AD 57–97. Inheriting the crown from his father, Marius enjoyed friendly relations with Rome. During his reign, he defeated and killed Soderic, king of the Picts, in a great battle. The present county of Westmorland was so named in Marius' honour because of the battle, and Marius accordingly had an inscribed stone set up in the county commemorating his victory.

Coilus, his son, then ruled. He had been raised and educated as a Roman. Coilus was to rule his kingdom in peace and prosperity, being succeeded by his son Lucius. Taking up the crown on his father Coilus's death, Lucius was to send to Rome for teachers of the Christian faith. He in turn passed on the crown to Geta, a son of the Roman Severus. He was elected king of the Britons by the Roman Senate. He was eventually killed by his half-brother Bassianus who reigned from ca AD 221–256. Like Geta, he was a son of Severus, but by a British noblewoman. The Britons elected Bassianus king after he had killed his half-brother. Carausius then took the crown. After raising a fleet of ships with the blessing of the Roman Senate, Carausius invaded Britain. He compelled the Britons to proclaim him king, and killed Bassianus in the ensuing battle. He was eventually murdered by the Roman legate, Allectus, and it was during Allectus's time that a Briton once more held the throne.

Asclepiodotus (Alyssglapitwlws) reigned from ca AD 296–306. He had held the kingdom of Cornwall when he was elected overall king by the Britons. His election to the throne was an attempt by the Britons to break the tyranny of the legate Allectus. Under Allectus, Livius Gallus held the city of London. In the ensuing siege, after he had killed Allectus outside the city, Asclepiodotus promised the Romans that all the garrison would be spared if they surrendered without further resistance. This was agreed to, although the Venedoti (the men of Gwynedd in Wales), decided to put the Romans to death by beheading them all. The heads were thrown into the stream called *Nantgallum* in the British tongue after the name of Livius Gallus. The later Saxons, still perpetuating the

Roman leader's name, knew it as *Galabroc,* and today this name has been further corrupted to *Walbrook.* As an aside, in the 1860s a large number of skulls were excavated from the bed of the Walbrook before it was built over, being the remnants no doubt of this massacre. It was during the reign of Asclepiodotus that the Diocletian Persecution began in AD 303.

Asclepiodotus was finally defeated and killed by the king whose name has been immortalised in the nursery rhyme, Coel (Old King Cole), who reigned from ca AD 306–309. Known in other histories as *Coel Hen Godhebog,* Coel founded the city of Colchester that still bears his name (*Kaercolim*). His daughter, Helen, was married to Constantius, a Roman Senator, who was sent to Britain as legate. He became king on Coel's death. He in turn was succeeded by his son Constantine (I), who ruled Britain from ca AD 312–337. He went on to become the famous emperor of Rome who legalised the Christian religion. Octavius (Eydaf) took the crown in Constantine's absence at Rome, ruling during the periods of ca AD 330–335 and 335–348. He revolted whilst Constantine was in Rome, and assumed the British crown. In AD 348, he was succeeded by Maximianus (Maxen Wledic), the nephew of Coel, who held the crown by virtue of that descent. He eventually left Britain to rule in Gaul and Germany, making Caradocus (Kradawc) king of the Britons in his stead in about the year AD 362. He was later assassinated in Rome (AD 375) by one of the friends of his successor but one, Gracianus. Dionotus (unnamed in the Welsh chronicle) of the kingdom of Cornwall took the crown of Britain and ruled from ca AD 375–389. Then Gracianus reigned from ca AD 389–402. He was originally sent to Britain by Maximianus to fight off an invasion of the Picts and Huns. However, upon successfully repelling the invaders he assumed the crown and ordered the murder of Maximianus. He was later himself to suffer death at the hands of an assassin.

Constanine (II) (Kystennin) then ruled from ca AD 402–420, having invaded Britain at the request of Guithelinus, the Archbishop of London, and was crowned king at Silchester.

He was murdered by an unknown Pict. He was then succeeded by Constans (Konstant Vynarch), ca AD 420–437, Constantine II's eldest son, who had tried to avoid the perils of the crown by becoming a monk at Winchester. He was forcibly removed from the monastery and crowned by Vortigern who, however, later ordered his murder. Vortigern himself (Gwrtheyrn Gwrthenav) ruled for two periods, ca AD 437–455 and 460–480. It was Vortigern who invited the Saxon adventurers, Hengist and Horsa, to Britain to help fight the Picts. At this point, his son Vortimer took over the kingdom, expelling the Saxons after four notable battles, one of them being the battle of Aylesford in Kent where his brother Katigern was slain. Vortimer was eventually poisoned on the orders of his father's new wife, the daughter of Hengist, and Vortigern once again resumed the crown. After a disastrous reign during which the Britons began to lose their land irretrievably to the Saxons, Vortigern was burned alive in a tower by Aurelius Ambrosius. This king (Emrys Wledic in the Welsh) reigned from ca AD 480–501. Surnamed Ambrosius, he was too young at the death of Constans in AD 437 to take up the crown. He was therefore smuggled abroad, and was raised in the household of king Budicius of Britanny. Eventually declared king of Britain, Ambrosius killed Vortigern and forced the Saxons to retreat to Albany (Scotland), at the same time capturing and executing Hengist at Kaerconan, present-day Conisborough. He was eventually poisoned by Eoppa the Saxon on the orders of Paschent, the youngest son of Vortigern.

Aurelius Ambrosius was succeeded in ca AD 501 by his brother, Uther Pendragon. Named Uther at birth, he was king of the Silures. He assumed the surname pen-Dragon (son of the dragon) after the appearance of a dragon-like comet in the sky. Like his brother Aurelius, he had been smuggled abroad on the murder of Constans. Once king, however, he consorted adulterously with Ygerna (Eigr) the wife of Gorlois, duke of Cornwall. Gorlois was killed by Uther Pendragon's soldiers at Dimilioc (*Tinblot* in the Welsh chronicle) as Uther Pendragon was seducing Ygerna. But of their union was born the most famous of the British kings, Arthur, who reigned over the Britons from ca AD 521–542. Arthur succeeded his father as king at only fifteen years of age. His sister Anna married Budicius II of Britanny. The narrative is somewhat confused, but she seems later to have married Loth of Lodonesia who was later to become king of Norway.

At his death, Arthur passed the crown to Constantine (III), the son of the 'duke' of Cornwall. Constantine, whose reign lasted four years, crushed a revolt of the Saxons, but was later struck down 'by God's vengeance'. He was succeeded in AD 546 by his nephew, Aurelius Conanus (Kynan Wledic in the Welsh), who, however, only came to the throne by imprisoning his unnamed uncle, the son of Constantine, the true heir. His reign was followed in ca 549 very briefly by that of Vortiporius, who repelled an invasion from Germany. His subsequent fate is unrecorded, although he can have reigned for only a year or less. But he was followed by Malgo, whose reign lasted from ca AD 550–555. According to a speech recorded for us by Geoffrey of Monmouth, Malgo had two sons, Ennianus and Run, neither of whom succeeded him. Malgo is elsewhere known as Maelgwn Gwynedd, the king of Gwynedd who died from the Yellow Plague that was ravaging Europe during the 550s. He was succeeded by Keredic, whose origin is unrecorded, who retired into Wales after a battle, and whose reign was followed by those of three unnamed 'tyrants'.

Then, shortly after the year AD 600, came Cadvan. Known in the Welsh chronicles as Cadfan ab Iago, king of Gwynedd, he was of north Welsh descent. He began as king of the Venedoti (men of Gwynedd) and succeeded to the kingship of all the Britons by engaging in battle Ethelfrith, the Saxon king of Northumbria, who, with Ethelbert of Kent, carried out the massacre of the British monks at Bangor in AD 604. Ethelfrith and Cadvan divided the country between them, Cadvan ruling over the southern half. His reign lasted until ca AD 625. He married a Saxon noblewoman of the Gewissae. He was followed by Cadwallo who died of old age in the year AD 633. But he was succeeded by Cadwallader (Kydwaladr Vendigaid) whose reign was divided into two periods from ca

AD 633–643 and 654–664. Twelve years after he inherited the crown, Cadwallader was struck down with an unspecified illness, and during his incapacity the Britons fell to warring amongst themselves. Due to the civil war and due no doubt to the consequent neglect and destruction of the crops, the country was ravaged by a long-remembered famine that was followed by the plague. For safety's sake, Cadwallader sought refuge on the continent, entering Brittany where he was received with much kindness by king Alan II. Eleven years later, Alan persuaded Cadwallader to return to Britain and resume his reign. His stay in Brittany would thus have fallen between the years AD 643–654. He was then followed by Yvor, who, with his cousin Yni, ruled over the remaining Britons who had finally been driven into Wales. It was, indeed, during Yvor's reign that the British came to be known disparagingly as the Welsh, from an ancient Saxon word meaning a barbaric foreigner. Between them, Yvor and Yni became a persistent nuisance to the Saxons, harassing them for many years, '...but little good did it do them'!

And that, in a nutshell, is what the early chronicles tell us about the kings of the Britons. The chronicles themselves, of course, tell a much fuller story, but there is little extraordinary in any of it. Indeed, as we saw in the previous chapter, there is much of it that can be historically verified. So we are presented with the simple question as to why a two thousand year recorded history has been so pointedly ignored by modern scholars. Why is it that the history of Britain is an entirely blank page before the year 55 BC in any conventional modern history book when such an easily accessible and informative record is at hand? Could it have anything to do with the fact that the Britons traced their ancestry in these pre-Christian records back to patriarchs that are known to us from the Genesis record but of whom the Britons should have known nothing in their pre-Christian culture if what the modernists have always told us was true? This genealogy is laid out in Appendix 7 of this present book. But this is only part of the great matter that is omitted from modern reckoning and of which the public is unaware. We shall see that there is much else besides regarding the histories and genealogies of other European peoples that is also ignored but which likewise verifies the Genesis account.

Chapter 6

The Descent of the Anglo-Saxon Kings

It would not be difficult to go out and buy literally hundreds of books that deal with the history of the Saxons in England. It is a fascinating and popular subject, and the market abounds with books ranging from the seriously academic to 'coffee-table' books filled with pictures of Anglo-Saxon weaponry and other relics. Virtually all the popular works on the subject begin with the middle of the 5th century AD when the Saxons began to migrate to this country from their continental homes. Some books may even refer briefly to those continental homes in order to demonstrate to the reader that the Anglo-Saxons did not simply materialise but actually came from somewhere real. But that is virtually the only mention that is given to the pre-migration history of the Saxons. All that came before, we are left to assume, is lost in the mists of antiquity, and the pre-migration history of the Saxons is simply left as a blank page. Now why should this be? Is it because the Saxons themselves left no record of what came before? Or, as in the case of the early Britons, is it because what the Saxons did have to say about their own past, runs counter to the modernist creed?

To be fair, the Saxons do not seem to have brought over with them a detailed chronicled history of their nation like that possessed by the Britons or, indeed, the Irish Celts which we shall examine later. That is not to say that none existed, of course, just that none has survived to the present day from that pre-migration period. What has survived, however, is a

The Descent of Six Anglo-Saxon Royal Houses from Noah

(East Anglia, Kent, Lindsey, Mercia, Northumbria & Wessex)

Noah
|
Sceaf
|
Bedwig
|
Hwala
|
Hrathra
|
Itermon
|
Heremod
|
Scealdwea
|
Beaw
|
Taetwa
|
Geat
|
Godwulf
|
Fin
|
Frithuwulf
|
Freawine
|
Frealaf
|
Frithuwald
|
Woden
|

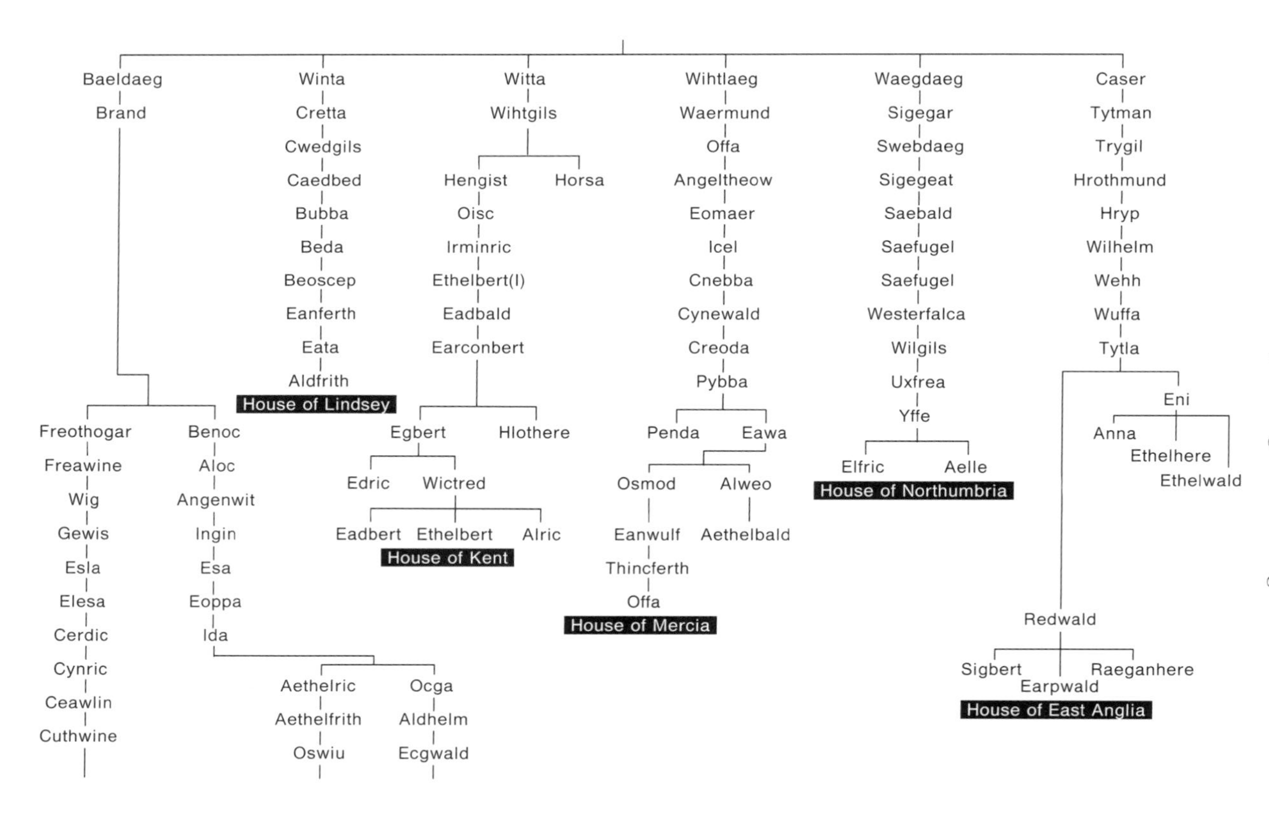
Baeldaeg
Brand
Freothogar
Freawine
Wig
Gewis
Esla
Elesa
Cerdic
Cynric
Ceawlin
Cuthwine
Benoc
Aloc
Angenwit
Ingin
Esa
Eoppa
Ida
Aethelric
Aethelfrith
Oswiu
Ocga
Aldhelm
Ecgwald
Winta
Cretta
Cwedgils
Caedbed
Bubba
Beda
Beoscep
Eanferth
Eata
Aldfrith
House of Lindsey
Witta
Wihtgils
Hengist
Horsa
Oisc
Irminric
Ethelbert(I)
Eadbald
Earconbert
Egbert
Hlothere
Edric
Wictred
Eadbert
Ethelbert
Alric
House of Kent
Wihtlaeg
Waermund
Offa
Angeltheow
Eomaer
Icel
Cnebba
Cynewald
Creoda
Pybba
Penda
Eawa
Osmod
Alweo
Eanwulf
Aethelbald
Thincferth
Offa
House of Mercia
Waegdaeg
Sigegar
Swebdaeg
Sigegeat
Saebald
Saefugel
Saefugel
Westerfalca
Wilgils
Uxfrea
Yffe
Elfric
Aelle
House of Northumbria
Caser
Tytman
Trygil
Hrothmund
Hryp
Wilhelm
Wehh
Wuffa
Tytla
Eni
Anna
Ethelhere
Ethelwald
Redwald
Sigbert
Earpwald
Raeganhere
House of East Anglia

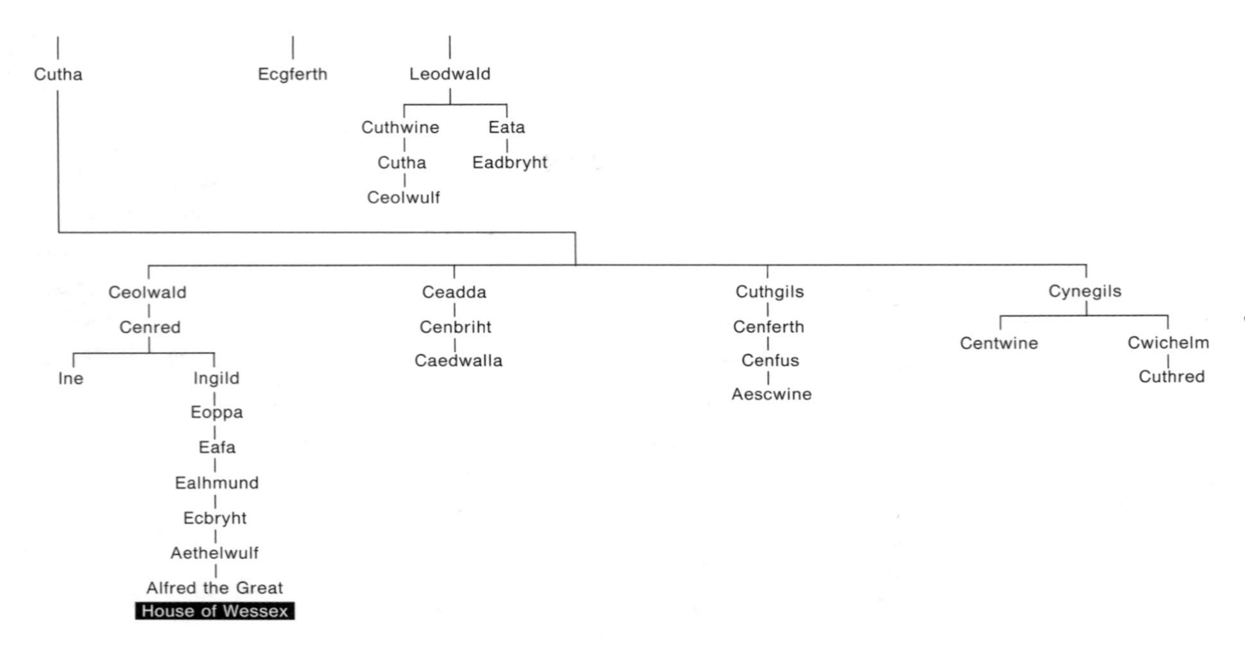

Cutha
Ecgferth
Leodwald
Cuthwine
Eata
Cutha
Eadbryht
Ceolwulf
Ceolwald
Cenred
Ine
Ingild
Eoppa
Eafa
Ealhmund
Ecbryht
Aethelwulf
Alfred the Great
House of Wessex
Ceadda
Cenbriht
Caedwalla
Cuthgils
Cenferth
Cenfus
Aescwine
Cynegils
Centwine
Cwichelm
Cuthred

detailed genealogy of the pre-migration, and hence pre-Christian, kings of the Saxons, and this enables us to take Saxon history back, generation by generation, to the earliest years after the Flood. But this is no new discovery. It was everyday knowledge to the historians of previous centuries. On Thursday 6th July 1600, for example, a certain Elizabethan tourist, Baron Waldstein, visited London's Lambeth Palace. His journal tells us that in one of the rooms there he saw:

> '. . . a splendid genealogy of all the Kings of England, and another genealogy, a historical one, which covers the whole of time and is traced down from the Beginning of the World.'[1]

Later, arriving at Richmond Palace on 28th July, he saw in the library there:

> '. . . beautifully set out on parchment, a genealogy of the kings of England which goes back to Adam.'[2]

Such genealogies were immensely popular, and as fascinating to the general public as they were to historians and other scholars. As tables of descent, they provided a continuous record of human history from the Creation, through the post-Flood era, down to modern times. But it was these very attributes that made these records unpalatable to certain scholars who delighted to call themselves Rationalists, and who sought from the 18th century onwards to replace such history with certain anti-biblical notions of their own.[3] Such was their success in this, that today hardly a scholar can be found who would dare to base his history on the truth and reliability of these records. So what is in the early Saxon records that renders them so unpalatable to modernist taste, but which might interest us in our present enquiry?

The pre-migration records that have come down to us are in the form of genealogies and king-lists, and I have assembled the table of descent which opens this chapter from each type. That table shows the (sometimes simplified) descent of six of the Anglo-Saxon royal houses of England. The houses are those of Wessex (**Occidentalium Saxonum**); of Lindsey (**Lindis fearna**); of Kent (**Cantwariorum**); of Mercia (**Merciorum**); of Northumbria (**Northa hymbrorum**); and of East Anglia (**Estanglorum**). But it is the treatment that these records have received from the hands of modernist scholars that is as fascinating, and as telling, as the records themselves, and we shall here consider the veil of confusion and obscurity that modern scholarship has thrown over them.

We are commonly asked to believe that these six royal families concocted these lists, and that the lists are thus rendered untrustworthy and false. We are asked to accept that, say, the House of Kent concocted a list of ancestral names that just happens to coincide in its earlier portions with that of, say, the House of Northumbria, in spite of the fact that the two kingdoms lay hundreds of miles apart, spoke different dialects and whose people hardly ever wandered beyond their own borders unless it was to fight. And, moreover, that this happened not between just two of the royal houses, but all six! To put it mildly, that is a lot to ask, and we shall take this opportunity to examine these records, whose earlier portions can be dated back to well before the dawning of the Christian era amongst the Saxons, so that they may speak for themselves.

During the summers of 1938 and 1939, there came to light one of the greatest archaeological discoveries of the century. It was the Sutton Hoo burial ship of one of the great kings of East Anglia. It is commonly believed to be that of Raedwald (or Redwald) who became **Bretwalda** in the year AD 616 (his name appears on the genealogy). The royal title of **Bretwalda** appears in the Anglo-Saxon Chronicle (MS. C – British Museum Cotton MS. Tiberius. B. i.) as **Bretenanwealda**, and means literally the one ruler of Britain. In other words, Raedwald was the supreme king to whom all the other provincial kings owed obeisance. Now Bede[4] tells us that Raedwald was born of the **Wuffingas**, as were all the East Anglian kings, and it is this title that tells us something of the seriousness with which the Anglo-Saxons kept their pedigrees.

Indeed, such was the veneration shown to ancestors in general that some of those ancestors who founded dynasties or who otherwise achieved distinction, were later worshipped as gods. But even if a certain ancestor was not actually deified, if he simply founded a branch from the main stock, then that branch ever after bore his name. And one such example is Raedwald's ancestor Wuffa.

Now Wuffa was not the first king of East Anglia. That honour normally goes to his father Wehh, or Wehha, who reigned in the early 6th century, and for lack of record we are left to wonder what otherwise distinguished Wuffa from his father for him to be regarded with such distinction that all his descendants named themselves after him rather than after his father, who was, after all, the very founder of the royal line of the East Anglian kings.

Wuffa, of course, was not the only Saxon to found a clan. Sceldwea, otherwise known as Scyld (pronounced 'shield') founded the **Scyldingas**. Geat, (pronounced 'geet' or 'gate'), likewise founded the **Geatingas**. Beowulf of epic fame (see chapter 12) was a Geating, and Geat himself was inevitably given a place in the Saxons' ancestral pantheon. Nennius tells us that he was one of the false gods whom the pagan Saxons worshipped, and we read the same in Assher and other sources.[5]

Most of the characters in the later part of the genealogy are well known to us. Ethelbert, for example, is famous as the king of Kent when Augustine landed here in AD 597 with instructions to bring the English under the dominion of the papacy. His (Ethelbert's) sister, Ricula, married into the East Saxon dynasty in the year AD 580 or thereabouts (see Appendix 8), thus uniting two very powerful royal dynasties. Cerdic of Wessex, who reigned from AD 519–534, is the earliest Saxon king from whom Her Majesty, Queen Elizabeth II, traces her own descent, and so on. But of great interest to us is one of the pre-migration ancestors of Cerdic, namely Gewis, who illustrates even more powerfully the veneration for ancestral names and the purity of pedigree that was considered so important to the early Saxon settlers of Britain.

Gewis founded the clan of the Gewissae who later settled in the west of England, and in the charters that have survived, the kings of Wessex are each styled *Rex Gewissorum*. However, when Alfred of Wessex translated into Old English Bede's *Historia Ecclesiasticae*, he suppressed the title *Rex Gewissorum*, and his reason for doing this was undoubtedly the blatantly pagan connotations of the name. Alfred himself, as a supposedly good and Christian king, wanted no such association of his name with that of Gewis. It would have had the same uncomfortable sound as styling himself king of the children of Woden, and this would have been anathema both to himself and to his Christian clerical ministers. And yet, and here we come to the significant point, in his own authorised biography (i.e. Asser's *Life of Alfred*), which Alfred himself undoubtedly oversaw with great care, the name of Gewis is allowed to stand proud as one of Alfred's ancestors! Alfred, whilst willing enough to drop for himself the hitherto royal but pagan title of *Rex Gewissorum*, was clearly not prepared to expunge the name of Gewis from the royal line, simply because the royal genealogies were themselves sacrosanct and inviolable. And this should be carefully considered before any further assurance is given that these royal genealogies were freely tampered with, an allegation that has been made and repeated in countless modernist works on the subject.

But it is not only alleged that these genealogies were tampered with. It is just as often stated that they were freely invented, the motive for this extraordinary act supposedly being to enhance the legal credibility of any upstart king's otherwise illegal claim to the crown. And this has led on more than one occasion to a most questionable state of affairs. Consider, for example, the case of Alfred's father, Aethelwulf, and the treatment that has been extended to his genealogy by certain scholars who should, perhaps, have known better.

Magoun [6] treats the genealogy of Aethelwulf, which appears in Asser's *Life of Alfred*, in the following way. Asser gives the line from Woden back to Noah exactly as it appears in our table, with the exception that the name Freawine is omitted. This is all well and good, because such gaps do occur and must be expected. However, Asser goes on to recite the ancestors of Noah back to Adam, and the names he gives (in ascending order) are exactly the same as those that appear in descending order in Genesis 5, the book of the Generations of Adam. Now, these same names are given exactly (except that they appear in ascending order) in Luke 3:36–38, and Magoun tries to make a case for arguing that Asser borrowed his names not from Genesis 5, but from Luke. We look in vain for any solid reason **why** Magoun should favour Luke as the source rather than Genesis, other than the fact that Luke, like Asser, lists his names in ascending order. And for want of a good reason, we are left merely with Magoun's somewhat self-assured statement, '. . . I am confident that . . .'

But now we arrive at exactly why it is that Magoun wishes to assign a Lucan origin to the names rather than an origin in Genesis. It is this:

> 'By virtue of this association (**what** association?) with Luke's genealogy of Jesus the total effect is to make Aethelwulf by accident or design, but in any case in a pointed way, a collateral relative of Our Lord.'

In other words, Magoun is alleging that this genealogy is yet another 'pious fraud' concocted by Christian monks who sought to enhance Aethelwulf's standing amongst his gullible subjects by somehow likening or relating him to Christ. But does the allegation stand up to the evidence? No! After Noah, Asser's list bears no resemblance whatever to that of Luke, and if Magoun is suggesting that by virtue of Aethelwulf's descent from Noah, Aethelwulf is thus made a collateral relative of Our Lord, then Magoun has clearly not considered the fact that as **all** men are descended from Noah, then the royal Aethelwulf would have been no better than the **common** man! A regal contradiction if ever there was one. Surely, if, as Magoun suggests, Aethelwulf had truly wished to be seen as a blood-relative of Christ, then he would have concocted a list that went back to the royal house of David, from whom Jesus was descended through His mother. But nothing of the kind is offered. Rather, Aethelwulf's line is traced through that of kings who were notorious in the early annals for their paganism, and Magoun's charge, so often quoted and so revered in modernist circles, falls flat on its proverbial face. The genealogy runs counter to all that is alleged against it.

Yet that is not the end of the folly, for Keynes and Lapidge propose the most astonishing notion of all, and it is one which draws our attention to the name of Sceaf on our genealogy, (pronounced 'sheaf' or 'shaif'). Making the most of the fact that Asser allegedly misspelt Sceaf's name as Seth in the royal genealogy, they blandly inform their readers that:

> 'Towards the end of the genealogy, Asser's "Seth", son of Noah, corresponds to Sem (i.e. Shem) of Luke iii . . .'[7]

In other words, Keynes and Lapidge are attempting the same thing as Magoun, (and they were aware of Magoun's paper for they cite it), by trying to tie in the Saxon genealogies with those of the New Testament, namely the gospel of Luke, so that the wearisome charge of 'pious fraud' could again be made. But they have merely succeeded in rendering their own argument very doubtful, for in the attempt to link Asser's list with that of Luke, they are compelled to conclude that in this case the Saxons were fraudulently trying to pass themselves off as Semites! Now, there are admittedly phases of Germanic history that are vague. But to suggest that there ever was a time when the Germanic races of all people wished to propagate the view that they were Semitic is truly extraordinary. Anti-Semitism has been an inherent feature of Germanic culture since time immemorial (it was by no means the invention of the Nazis), and to accept such a proposal we would have to fly in the face of all that we know about Saxon and Germanic culture. We would, moreover, have to ignore the fact that there exists not the slightest etymological link between the names of Seth and Shem. But was Asser's alleged misspelling of Seth for

Sceaf truly an error on Asser's part? Or did Asser know something that modernist scholars have missed?

The question, surprisingly enough, is answered in part by one of the more sceptical investigators of modern times, Sisam, who, when dealing with the identities of Seth and Sceaf, is forced to admit that:

> 'Iafeth [i.e. Japheth] was usually regarded as the ancestor of the European peoples, and the possibility that the last four letters of his name have something to do with the error Seth cannot be excluded...'[8]

To further the identity of Asser's Seth with the Sceaf of other chronicles, we have the testimony of Florence of Worcester, who wrote in AD 1118 that, '*Seth Saxonice Sceaf*', and in another of his manuscripts[9] the name of Sceaf is written over an erasure of the name Seth by a later scribe. Which shows that confusion over the names had arisen by the first half of the 12th century at the very latest, and needed to be sorted out.[10]

But after his eminently sensible observation, Sisam then went on to create problems of his own, for having written an extremely involved and in-depth study of the Anglo-Saxon royal genealogies, when it came to the lists of the various biblical patriarchs whose names appear in the earliest parts of those same pedigrees, he dismissed them thus:

> 'The Biblical names show the artificial character of this lengthened pedigree and the crudeness of the connexions that passed muster. Otherwise they need not detain us.'[11]

This rather large assumption, however, merely led him into further difficulties, for he was then led to dismiss with equal abruptness everything else that he had previously written concerning the lists of even **non**-biblical names!:

> 'Beyond Cerdic, all is fiction or error, and if the names themselves are old, they were not attached to the ancestry of the West Saxon kings by old tradition.'[12]

We could ask what they were attached by if not by old tradition, although it is more to our purpose to consider that Sisam recognised that one part of the Saxon genealogy depends very much upon the other. If one section collapses, then so do the others.

However, there are more points to consider concerning the all-important identity of Sceaf. Sisam has already pointed out that Japheth was considered by the Saxons to be the founder of the European nations. Significantly perhaps, he does not specify whether this was exclusively the belief of the later Christianised Saxons, or if it was shared by their pagan forebears. However, the Saxons themselves had something to say concerning Sceaf, and it was this:

> *Se Sceaf waes Noes sunu and he waes innan theare earce geboren.* i.e. 'This Sceaf was Noah's son, and he was born in the Ark.'[13] (My translation)

Clearly, the early Saxons identified Sceaf as a son of Noah, and not a distant descendant of his, and it is equally clear that Japheth is here being referred to. But, and here is the point of greatest significance, was Japheth known as Sceaf to the later **Christianised** Saxons? The answer is no! The later Christianised Saxons always referred to Japheth as Japheth. No later Saxon scholar knew him as Sceaf, as is witnessed in the following extract from Aelfric of Eynsham's 10th century work, *On The Beginning of Creation*:

> *... ac ic wille gehealden the aenne and thine wif and thine thrie suna Sem Cham and Iafeth.* '... and I will save thee alone and thy wife and thy three sons, Shem, Ham and Japheth.' (My translation)

This rendering of Japheth's name, Iafeth, is absolutely typical of Christianised Saxon usage, for the simple reason that it is the Latin-cum-Hebrew rendering that appears in the Vulgate and Old Latin versions of the Bible, which were the only versions known to the Christianised Saxons and copied by them. Moreover, we have to consider the remark connected with the older form of Sceaf, namely how Sceaf was not only Noah's son, but that he was born in the Ark. Now, anyone who was familiar with the Genesis account, and the book of Genesis was very much the favourite book of the Christianised Saxons,[14] would have known that Japheth helped to build the Ark. He could not have been born in it. Which brings us to the following question, namely:

If it really had been a fact that certain unscrupulous Christian monks had fraudulently invented the pre-migration Saxon genealogies, as modernists so often insist, and had it really been in their own and their present king's interests to prove that Saxon kings were royally descended from Japheth, then is it at all conceivable that they would have used a form of Japheth's name that was utterly unfamiliar to those very readers whom they hoped to convince? And surely, no educated monk would have made such a silly error over Japheth being born in the Ark when every one of his readers would have known that Japheth, far from being born in the Ark, had helped to build it! Saxon scholars were every bit as contentious as are the scholars of any age, and there were plenty of rival schools even in those days who were more than willing to bring down a scholar or two if they made a *faux pas* of this magnitude. But then, we are not here considering merely the allegedly nefarious activities of just one Christian monk, for in an altogether separate source we read:

> *Beowi Sceafing, id est filius Noe, se waes geboren on thaere Earce Noes.* i.e. 'Beaw [alias Bedwig] the son of Sceaf, that is the son of Noah, who was born on Noah's Ark.'[15]
>
> (My translation)

The pre-migration ancestral list of the Anglo-Saxon kings

would be an astonishing record even if it existed on its own. But in the next chapter we shall be considering corroborative sources from other countries altogether, which confirm the earliest parts of the Saxon genealogies in great and explicit detail. It will thus become increasingly obvious that, in spite of all modernist protests to the contrary, we are not dealing here with any attempted fraud or piece of Christian fiction. What we are dealing with is something with which we are already familiar from the chronicles of the early Britons, namely another historical account that is quite independent of the Genesis record, but which it nevertheless verifies to a considerable degree.

Notes

1. Groos, T.W. *The Diary of Baron Waldstein.* Thames & Hudson. London. p. 61.
2. Groos. p. 169.
3. For an invaluable introduction to this subject, see Bowden's *Rise of the Evolution Fraud.* pp. 7–17. (See Bibliography).
4. Bede. p. 130. See Bibliography.
5. *. . . filii Geta, qui fuit, ut aiunt, filius Dei: non ipse est Deus deorum . . . sed unus est ab idolis eorum, quod ipsi colebant.* Nennius §31. (i.e. '. . . the son of Geat, who was, they say, the son of God. But he was not the God of gods . . . but one of their idols whom they worshipped.' – My translation). Morris's translation of this sentence reads a little oddly – '. . . son of Geta, who said they were son of God . . . (sic!)' (Morris. p. 26. See Bibliography).
6. Magoun. (pp. 249–50. See Bibliography).
7. Keynes and Lapidge. (p. 229. See Bibliography).
8. *ibid.* p. 316. See Bibliography.
9. Corpus Christi College Cambridge MS XCII (Parker Library).
10. Sisam. p. 317. (See Bibliography).
11. *ibid.* p. 320.
12. *ibid.* p. 322.
13. *Reliq. Antiq.* p. 173. See Bibliography.
14. It was, for example, the sole subject of the illiterate Caedmon's songs and poetry. See Bede p. 252.
15. MS. Cotton. Otho. B. XI., cit. Magoun p. 249.

Chapter 7

The Descent of the Danish and Norwegian Kings

In the previous chapter, we took note of the genealogies of six Anglo-Saxon royal houses that traced their descent from Woden. Moreover, we noted that the lineage of Woden himself had also been preserved, and that this was traced back to Noah and Japheth, Japheth being known to the pagan Saxons as Sceaf.[1] We shall expand on this lineage in this chapter by noting the recorded descent of the pagan Danish and Norwegian kings. The royal ancestral list of Denmark and Norway is set out in the table that opens this chapter, which contains also five other ancestral lists. The source for each list is given beneath the table, but it will be noticed that three of the lists are of Anglo-Saxon origin, one early British, one Danish and the other Icelandic, i.e. six lists from four nations.

As we examine and compare the lists, we are struck by the astonishing points of similarity, and yet obvious differences, between them. Each ancestral list contains gaps, but never the same series of gaps, and each of their names is listed in at least one other of the lists (with the exceptions of ***Freawine*** and ***Fodepald***). Moreover, we should also note that the names always appear in exactly the same sequence. There is neither confusion nor discrepancy over the chronological order of each successive generation. But one thing that these lists clearly are not, and that is mere copies of the same (allegedly fraudulent) Christian source.

Patriarchal Genealogies of the Norwegians, Danes, Icelanders and English Saxons

ASS		WSC		**LAN**		ETH		EDD		NEN
Noe	=	Noe	=	**Noa**	=	?	=	?	=	?
Seth	=	Sceaf	=	**Seskef**	=	Scef	=	Seskef	=	?
Beduuig	=	Bedwig	=	**Bedvig**	=	?	=	Bethvig	=	?
Huala	=	Hwala	=	**?**	=	?	=	?	=	?
Hathra	=	Hrathra	=	**Athra**	=	?	=	Athra	=	?
Itermod	=	Itermon	=	**Itermann**	=	?	=	Ítrmann	=	?
Heremod	=	Heremod	=	**Heremotr**	=	?	=	Heremóth	=	?
Sceldwea	=	Scealdwea	=	**Scealdna**	=	Scyld	=	Skjaldun	=	?
Beauu	=	Beaw	=	**Beaf**	=	Beo	=	Bjár	=	?

Taetuua	=	Taetwa	=	**?**	=	Tetuua	=	?	=	?
Geata	=	Geata	=	**Eat**	=	Geat	=	Ját	=	Geta
Godwulf	=	Godwulf	=	**Godulfi**	=	Godfuulfe	=	Guthólfr	=	?
?	=	?	=	**?**	=	?	=	?	=	**Fodepald**
Finn	=	Finn	=	**Finn**	=	Fin	=	Finn	=	Finn
Frithuwulf	=	*Frithuwulf*	=	**?**	=	Frithouulf	=	?	=	Fredulf
?	=	**Freawine**	=	**?**	=	?	=	?	=	?
Frealaf	=	Frealaf	=	**Frealaf**	=	Frealaf	=	Frmallaf	=	Frealaf
Frithowald	=	*Frithuwald*	=	**?**	=	Frithouuald	=	?	=	?
Uuoden	=	Woden	=	**Voden**	=	Uuothen	=	Óthin	=	Woden

Niodr i Noatunum
Yngvifraeyr
Jorundr
Aun
Egill Tunnadolgr
Ottarr Vendilkraka
Athils at Uppsaulum
Eysteinn
Yngvarr
Haralldr Harfagri

The Royal House of Norway

Skjoldr
Fridleifr
Fridefrode
Frode Fraekni
Ingialdr Starkadar

The Royal House of Denmark

KEY

ASS = Asserius. **De Rebus Gestis Alfredi**. (ed. W H Stevenson. Oxford. 1904. cap I. – cit. also Klaeber. p. 254. See Bibliography.

WSC = **Brit. Mus. Cotton Ms. Tiberius. A**. fol 1–34. The names of *Frithuwulf, Freawine* and *Frithuwald* set in italics, are supplied from other mss of the Anglo-Saxon Chronicles.

LAN = **Vetustissima Regum Septentrionis Series Langfethgatal dicta**. *Scriptores Rerum Danicarum Medii Ævi*. ed. Jacobus Langebek. vol I. Hafniae. 1772. pp. 1–6. cit. also Klaeber pp. 260–1.

ETH = **Fabii Ethelwerdi Chronicorum libri quattuor**. *Monumenta Historica Britannica*. vol I. 1848. lib III. cap III. p. 512. cit. also Klaeber. p. 254.

EDD = **Prose Edda**. *Corpus Poeticum Boreale*. See Klaeber. p. 256.

NEN = **Nennius. Historia Brittonum**. §31. Harleian MS 3859. cit. Klaeber. p. 255. See Bibliography. See also *Nennius. British History and the Welsh Annals*. ed. & trans. Morris. J. Phillimore. Chichester. 1980. pp. 26 (English) & 67 (Latin).

It may be argued with conviction that Asser's list, for example, is merely a latinised version of that which appears in the Anglo-Saxon Chronicle, even though Asser includes two patriarchs that the Chronicle omits. But that cannot be argued for Ethelweard's list, since that omits no less than seven important patriarchal names. Moreover, one of those omissions concerns the name of Noah, so it cannot be argued that Ethelweard's source-document was a pious forgery, for surely the object of such forgery would be to include biblical names, and Ethelweard himself had the integrity not to add Noah's name in conformity with other lists and traditions of which he was undoubtedly aware. Unless, of course, modernism is prepared to accept that Sceaf did rank as the name of the biblical patriarch, Japheth, amongst the pagan peoples of Europe. But that would only demolish the case that modernism has built up so carefully over the years, for what knowledge could pagan Saxons *et al* have had of supposedly non-existent biblical characters under the modernist scheme of things?

Exactly the same goes for the Edda list. That too omits the name of Noah, yet accurately passes down the names of most of the other patriarchs, Sceaf or Seskef included. Further to which is the consideration that the Edda list is an Icelandic, as opposed to English or Danish, record of patriarchal descent. Allowing for obvious linguistic variations, however, each name is recognisably that of a patriarch whose name also appears in the lists of Denmark and England. The third list that omits the name of Noah, as well as other patriarchs, is that preserved in Nennius, and we shall consider this shortly for what it tells us concerning the age of his source-material.

The very diversity of the nations from which these lists emerge argues powerfully against the charge of invention, for it is safe to assume that if these various peoples were inventive enough to forge the records of their own descent, as we are assured has occurred, then they were surely inventive enough to make up their own stories and not have to copy those of other, rival, nations that were in any case difficult to get to. The various poems, sagas and fictions that have come down to us from these countries show diversity enough, and reveal in that diversity their particular national biases. That is only to be expected. But these lists, these ancestral pedigrees, show no such diversity, save that of linguistic variation and genealogical gaps, which again are only to be expected. And if it is to be argued that these lists are virtually identical because the Norse peoples shared a common heritage, then that only argues more forcefully **against** their invention and **for** the extreme antiquity of the material contained within them, for that would have to go back to the times before these nations diversified and went their separate ways, and that point in history would long predate the coming of the Christian faith.

It is a sobering thought that under any other circumstances, the historicity of these common patriarchs would be accepted unreservedly on the basis of such evidence. Indeed, they would normally be accepted on much less evidence. And yet in this case, and over each one of these lists, the cry is invariably sent up of forgery, fraud and invention, which in itself may tell us more about the real historicity of these documents than a thousand learned works on the subject. For example, Keynes's and Lapidge's assertion that the Seth in Asser's list is synonymous with the Shem of Luke's gospel (and therefore the Sceaf of all the other lists – see previous chapter) becomes laughable when seen in the context of these other lists, where it is revealed that if that is truly the case, then the Danes, Saxons and Icelanders must **all** have been claiming a Semitic descent for themselves. For if that charge is good enough to lay against the Saxons, it is also good enough to lay against the Danes and Icelanders, and few scholars, I think, would want to risk their reputations on **that** assertion!

But we should note that when charges similar to those made by Magoun, Keynes and Lapidge *et al*, are set out before the reader, they are invariably made in isolation with little or no explanatory evidence to support them. Speculation is the sole argument, and it is left merely for the uninformed reader to conclude, after a sometimes tortuous exercise in word-play, that such tables of descent must be mythical, and that no serious scholar or intelligent layman would accept these records (or the book of Genesis which they corroborate) as serious history.

But what evidence is there for the true age of the material contained in these records? For if that material, demonstrably rather than suspiciously, dates from after the time when the Saxons, (and now the Danes and Icelanders), were converted to Christianity, then it would admittedly be difficult to refute the modernist charge of Christian compilation and fraudulent use. So we will here note certain items of external and internal evidence concerning these Saxon, Icelandic and Danish patriarchs that will indicate the definitely pre-Christian origin of these ancestral lists.

We will begin our considerations with the most fragmented of the lists, that of Nennius. It is given in chapter 31 of Nennius's *Historia Brittonum*, and is a fragment from a now lost record known to scholars as the *Kentish Chronicle*. It is a near-contemporary account of the arrival of Hengist on the Isle of Thanet, and it notes the decidedly pagan ancestry that the newly-arrived Saxons claimed for themselves. But the date of this document is the most crucial point, for the landing of Hengist took place in the very middle of the 5th century, and as Morris says:

> 'There is no other sign that the text owed anything to English records; and the British knowledge of Kent cannot have lasted long beyond the 6th century, if so long.'[2]

In other words, we can be certain that at least the Woden-Geat line was in place amongst the Saxons by the mid-5th century at the very latest, long before the Christianisation of the Saxons. In fact, we would know from this that the ancestral list would itself date from much earlier times.[3] The list itself, as preserved in Nennius, displays certain internal evidences of a more extreme antiquity. For example, there is the curious appearance of the name Fodepald in Nennius's original Latin list, which Morris translates into English as Folcwald.[4] We meet with a curious corruption of this name in Henry of

Huntingdon where he renders the name Flocwald.[5] All of which more than strongly hints at an ancient source that by Nennius's day was rendered illegible in places by damage and time. (Folcwald does not appear in the Anglo-Saxon Chronicle. But it does appear in the Saxon epic poem *Widsith* [l. 27: 'Finn Folcwalding'], and in the poem *Beowulf* [l. 1089]).

Of equal significance is the unabashed way in which it is so early stated in Nennius's source that the Saxons worshipped Geat as a deified ancestor. It came across to the British annalist who originally recorded the information as a shocking fact, and it clearly horrified him. Indeed, as far as the Britons were concerned, it characterised the Saxons even more than their rapacity and violence, for it was one of the first facts about the Saxons of which the early Britons, who were certainly Christian long before the mid-5th century, became aware. Thus it is clear that such idolatrous practices are not the manufactured accusations of later Christian writers. It is equally clear that the Saxons themselves would have revered their ancestral lists just as much as the ancestors whose names were enshrined therein, making tampering and falsifying a most unlikely event, and certainly not one that would be knowingly tolerated by the Saxons.

Which brings us to the Icelandic list. There we encounter a much fuller pedigree that carries the lineage of Óthin (i.e. Odin or Woden) back to Seskef. The name Seskef is itself merely a variant of the Saxon Sceaf, who we noticed in the previous chapter as the biblical Japheth. But notice that the Icelandic list does not go back to Noah, an omission that places it right outside the pale of 'pious' forgeries. Iceland was first colonised by Norwegian Vikings in the 870s, and it cannot be pretended by any stretch of the imagination that either the Norwegian or Danish Vikings were Christian by this time. As in the case of the Saxon Sceaf, the Icelandic Seskef is a form of Japheth's name that would not have been used by any Christian forger who wished to falsify the records. For the Christian Icelanders, like the Christian Saxons, would have known Japheth under the Latin-cum-Hebrew form of his name, Iafeth, and not under the more ancient form that appears in the ancestral lists.

But the Icelandic list is practically identical to that of Norway and Denmark, and it is interesting to examine some of the characters who would have owned this list as their own ancestral tree. For example, just before the Norwegian settlement of Iceland in the 870s there lived one famous Viking who went by the name of Ragnar Lothbrok, known affectionately amongst his torture victims as 'Hairy Breeches'. His son, Ivor the Boneless (the Ingware of the Anglo-Saxon Chronicles) committed the pagan Rite of the Blood-eagle upon the living bodies of kings Aelle of Northumbria and Edmund of East Anglia.[6] This was a sacrificial rite to Odin, and it involved cutting out the lungs of a living man and laying them out on his shoulders, so that they resembled the outspread wings of an eagle. And it was such men as these who counted it an inestimable honour to be able to trace their descent from such patriarchs as Odin (Woden), Geat, Seskef and, in the case of the Norwegians and Danes, Noa. No friends of Christians these, and it is impossible to believe that they would have looked on as anyone, Christian or pagan, tampered with the sacred lists in which were enshrined the very ancestral gods of the nation, gods to whom even kings were sacrificed. The allegation is easy enough to make, but passing difficult to realise from a purely historical perspective.

It is simply impossible to imagine that any form of tampering with the royal lists would have been permitted in such an age and amongst such a people as these. And when we consider the purity and strictness with which these records were kept amongst such diverse languages and cultures, and the almost non-existent corruption of the names over the centuries, then such imaginings seem even more detached from reality. Indeed, it must stand as a lasting tribute to the scholars who were entrusted with the keeping of the ancient lists that those lists remained so pure and uncorrupted. They employed certain ingenious methods, of course, for preventing interference and damage to the lists, and one of these methods is demonstrated in Appendix 8, which deals with the descent of the East Saxon kings. But we shall see in the following chapter how the records of another race altogether were cherished and protected from age and interference, and how those same records added their own pagan but independent testimony to the historical reliability of the book of Genesis.

Notes

1. The earliest instance in the Anglo-Saxon Chronicle of Woden's lineage (back to Geat) appears under the year 547 (Parker Chronicle). An older instance by about a century occurs in Nennius. See below. The Parker list and Nennius list differ in several points of detail, so it cannot be pretended that the later Parker list is merely a copy of Nennius.
2. Morris. p. 4.
3. The list could hardly have been the ad lib invention of Hengist and his men as they landed. It was clearly a long-established and important part of their historical tradition that they brought with them from the continent, making it already ancient by the mid-fifth century.
4. Morris. p. 26.
5. Henry of Huntingdon. p. 39. See Bibliography. We see an interestingly similar corruption in William of Malmesbury (p. 97. See Bibliography), where he renders the name Sceaf as Strephius.
6. Campbell, J. *The Anglo-Saxons*. Penguin Books. 1982. p. 148.

Chapter 8

The Descent of the Irish Celtic Kings

> 'The Scots (originally Irish, but by now Scotch) were at this time inhabiting Ireland, having driven the Irish (Picts) out of Scotland; while the Picts (originally Scots) were now Irish ... and vice versa. It is essential to keep these distinctions clearly in mind... (!)' [1]

When Sellar and Yeatman penned these satirical words on the history of the Irish (and Scots), they were not entirely joking. The early history of Ireland, any single clear fact of which is virtually untaught in England's schools and colleges (and in Ireland's too, I suspect), has lain under a cloak of almost inextricable confusion since Victorian times. And on those rare occasions when the subject is broached at all, it is invariably broached at that point in history that gave rise to the hilarious misunderstanding quoted above, the so-called Dark Ages. The student will be taught nothing concerning the chronicles and genealogies that have survived from the very earliest times. Irish history before the Saxon period, is given only in terms with which we are already familiar from the history of the early Britons and the Saxons, where we hear of this culture or that method of farming, this particular stone age or that particular glacial period, but where no attempt is made to give an account of the individuals of early Ireland whose names and deeds appear in such great abundance in the early Irish chronicles. Nor is any account given of the surprisingly

EARLY IRISH GENEALOGY

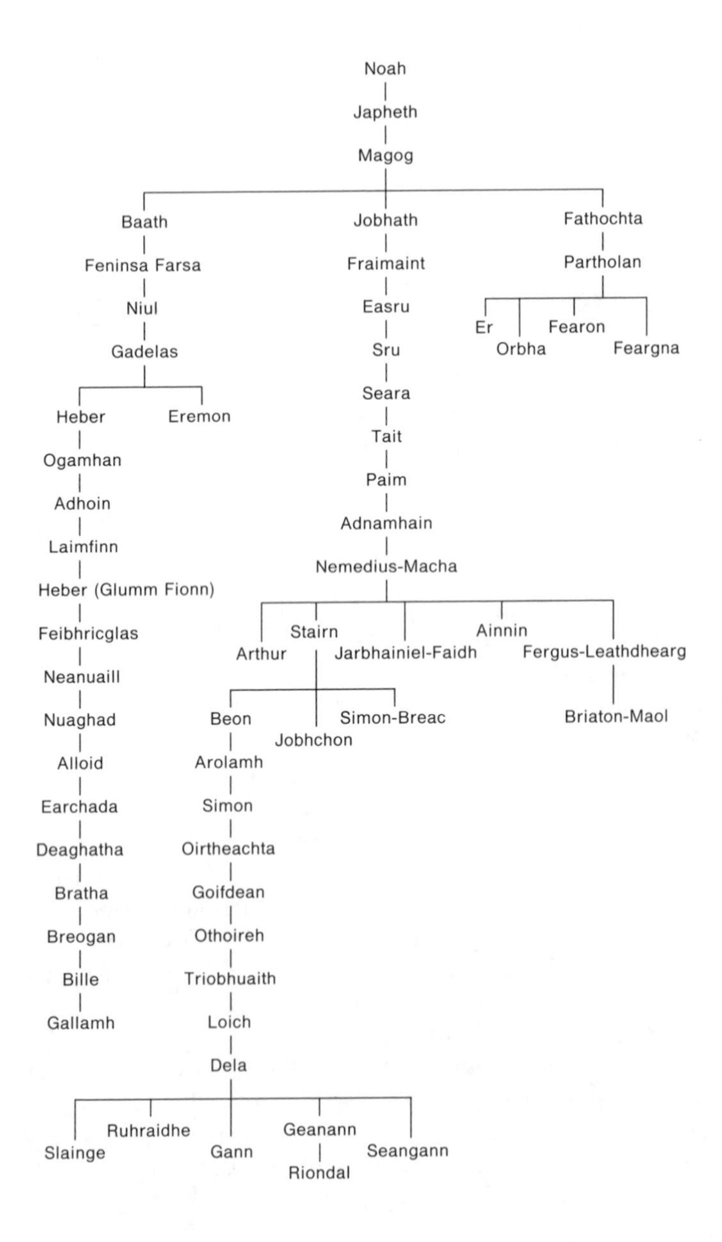

detailed chronology that the pagan scholars of Ireland were careful to weave into their histories. By this stage in our enquiry, it is perhaps superfluous to ask why this should be. So we shall concentrate our attention on what exactly it is that the early Irish records reveal.

The records in which early Irish history has been preserved, have been masterfully summarised by the scholar nun Cusack, [2] and for her history she drew upon an extensive number of manuscripts, many of which were known to her under such evocative names as *The Book of Leinster* (written ca AD 1130, and copied from the much older *Saltair* [Psalter] of Cashel); the *Book of Ballymote* (AD 1390); and the Annals of the Four Masters. But there are two others that received special mention, and they are the *Chronicum Scotorum*, and the even more important (because much earlier) *Cin of Drom Snechta*.

The *Cin of Drom Snechta*, otherwise known as The Book of Invasions, is now lost by all accounts, [3] but its contents were preserved by Keating, the Irish historian who wrote his own History from this and many other early manuscripts in about AD 1630. [4] The importance of the *Cin of Drom Snechta*, however, lies in the very early date of its compilation, concerning which a note in the 12th century Book of Leinster tells us:

> 'Ernín, son of Duach, that is son of the King of Connacht ... it was he that collected the Genealogies and Histories of the men of Erinn in one book, that is, the Cin of Drom Snechta.' [5]

The importance of this passage lies in the fact that Duach is known to have died in the year AD 365, [6] which places Ernín's gathering of the material well before the coming to Ireland of St Patrick (whose mission to Ireland took place in ca AD 432) and the later Christian monks whose sole business, some would have us believe, was to forge fake histories for the early nations of western Europe. Cusack provides further information from the *Book of Leinster* on another of these early chronicles inasmuch as the contents of the *Cuilmenn* (see Note 3 at the end of the chapter) were almost forgotten by as early as AD 580, showing that by that year it was already of great antiquity.[7]

Regarding the material of these early chronicles, however, whose contents were already of great age by the time Ernín copied them down, Keating writes:

> 'We will set down here the branching off of the races of Magog, according to the Book of Invasions (of Ireland), which was called the Cin of Drom Snechta . . .'[8]

There later follows a succession of strange and ancient names, of which the table of descent that opens this chapter is a somewhat simplified extract. The important thing for us to notice in this table of descent, though, is the unequivocal statement that the decidedly pagan Irish traced their origins back to the biblical patriarch, Magog, the son of Japheth. This is in direct contrast to the claims of the Britons and other European nations, whose genealogies were traced back to Javan, another son of Japheth. Now, Magog, as we shall see in Appendix 3, was considered, with Ashchenaz, the father of the Scythian peoples, and the early Irish chroniclers were most emphatic in their insistence that the Irish were of Scythian stock. And there is good etymological evidence for this. The Irish were long referred to as Scots even before some of them migrated to the country that today bears their name, and as Brewer tells us:

> 'Scot (is) the same as Scythian in etymology; the root of both is **Sct**. The Greeks had no **c**, and would change **t** into **th** making the root **skth**, and by adding a phonetic vowel we get **Skuthai** (Scythians), and **Skothai** (Skoths). The Welsh disliked **s** at the beginning of a word, and would change it to **ys**; they would also change **c** or **k** to **g**, and **th** to **d**; whence the Welsh root would be **Ysgd**, and Skuth or Skoth would become **ysgod**. Once more, the Saxons would cut off the Welsh **y**, and change the **g**

back again to **c**, and the **d** to **t**, converting the **Ysgod** to **Scot**.'[9]

It would be no strange thing to find Scythian peoples as far west as Ireland. After all, the land in Asia Minor known of old as Galatia, was populated by a migrating colony of Gallic Celts from whom the country got its name. St Paul wrote his famous epistle to their descendants. Many other examples from history are known of nations seemingly popping up in places where one would normally not expect to find them, so it requires no great stretch of the imagination to accept what the early Irish chroniclers so often insisted upon, namely their descent from the Scythian races.

But it is at this stage that we must notice those four particular patriarchs whose names we have already noted in the Table of European Nations passed down to us by Nennius. There we encountered the names of **Baath**, **Iobaath**, **Izrau** and **Esra**. And we see precisely the same names (allowing for linguistic variation) emerging from the early Irish genealogy, where they are rendered **Baath**, **Jobhath**, **Easru** and **Sru**. Now, it is known amongst archaeologists and ethnologists that the early Britons and many of the ancient peoples of Europe were Celts (Gk. *Κελτοί*), as were the early Irish. (The Saxons were not Celts. Hence the absence of these patriarchal names from the Saxon pedigree.) And this is known purely from archaeological evidence, without any reference whatever to these genealogies. Indeed, most modern scholars within these disciplines would scorn such a reference. So how do we account for the presence of these names in such diverse genealogies as the early British and the Irish?

There is one discrepancy. Nennius's Table of European Nations traces the descent of these four patriarchs from Javan, whereas the Irish genealogy traces them from Magog. Which is right? They both are. The discrepancy is explained by the fact that there was certainly a mixing of the various patriarchal lines before Babel. It was only after Babel that the nations were separated. From this moment in time, the pedigrees branched away from each other in a markedly emphatic way. But previously the families of mankind were uniting into a single people, which was their expressed intent of course,[10] and the dispersal of the nations as recorded in the Genesis account happened for the precise purpose of preventing this process of unification. Interestingly, the dispersal is depicted in Genesis as having occurred in the fifth generation after the Flood, and we note in these ancient genealogies that after the fifth generation the Irish and continental pedigrees diverge in a most pointed way in exact accordance with the Genesis account. The four patriarchs noted, then, were clearly the pre-Babel founders of both the British and the Irish Celts, which should give us some idea of the extreme antiquity of some of the material that is to be found in the early pagan Irish chronicles and Nennius's Table of European Nations.

The appearance of these names, however, may also go some way towards explaining another historical mystery, namely the origins of royalty, and the concept of hereditary royal families. The fact that all the royal families of Europe were, and indeed still are, interrelated is something that is accepted and well known. But what was the origin of these families (or rather this original family) who have always insisted that they were set above the common herd and entitled to rule their fellow man by a sort of divine right, a claim that cost Charles I of England, and the royal families of France and Russia, their very lives. Clearly, it was not a concept that was just thought up one day. Indeed, the aforementioned royal families took it so seriously that they pursued their right to the death. Rather, it has its roots right back in the very dawn of history, and was such an anciently established concept that the early Israelites felt somehow excluded from the rest of humanity because they did not have a royal family of their own.[11] So, were Baath, Iobaath, Izrau and Ezra the original stock from which the later royal families of Europe are descended? It would certainly seem to point in that direction. And what of Iobaath? Did his name become enshrined elsewhere in early European thought as Father Jove? It is all very intriguing.

The very notion of kingship was itself a decidedly pagan concept, where in Assyria, for example, the king was deemed to rule as a representative of the national god, the biblical Asshur, Assyria's founder, and in Egypt where the king was deemed to actually be a god himself,[12] as later were the Roman Caesars. This is what marked the Israelites' cry for a king to rule over them as a cry of apostasy. So it would seem that the concept of royalty and of a privileged and divinely appointed royal family whose rule was to embrace many nations originated initially amongst the pre-Babel patriarchs such as those noted above in the Irish and British genealogies, and was nurtured and developed as a unifying principle within and amongst the dispersed pagan societies. This would, of course, have been an act of open defiance towards God, and an attempt to repair or perhaps exploit the damage that was inflicted against a unifying of mankind at Babel.

Of further interest to us, however, is the pagan memory revealed in the early Irish chronicles, of the Creation and the Flood. These were remembered by the Irish as relatively recent and definitely historical events. Moreover, they reckoned the dates of other subequent and successive historical events by counting the years since the Creation, and this is examined more closely in the following chapter. But for the moment, we need note only that, according to this chronology, the first colonisation of Ireland seems to have taken place ca 1484 BC (the 2520th year after the Creation).[13]

It was the colony led by one Partholan, which landed in the estuary of the river Kenmare. Partholan himself was to die thirty years later in about 1454 BC or Anno Mundi [the year of the world] 2550. Some three hundred years later, it is recorded that the colony was wiped out by a plague, 9000 men, women and children dying in one week alone. The name of the area in which they had settled was later called Tallaght, denoting a place where plague victims lie buried, and it is interesting to note that it is still littered with ancient burial mounds today.[14]

Of added interest are certain details that have been handed down to us by Geoffrey of Monmouth.[15] We are told by him how Partholan's colony consisted of thirty ships. Interestingly, Nennius makes no mention of the number of ships, but does tell us that the colony consisted of 1000 souls, which indicates that he and Geoffrey were working from different sources.[16] However, Geoffrey also tells us that the colony had recently been expelled from the Spanish mainland, and moreover that they were called *'Basclenses'*, or Basques. Now, we know that the present-day Basques of northern Spain are of an entirely mysterious origin, and we also know that they speak a language that is quite unrelated to any known Indo-European tongue. In which context, it is interesting to note what Professor Mackie has written concerning the language of the early Picts who had more than a passing influence on both the early and later history of the Irish:

> 'The Picts certainly used a form of P-Celtic (the mother of Welsh, Cornish and Breton), with traces of Gaulish forms. However, it is clear, from the few scraps of evidence which survive, that the Picts also used another language, probably unrelated to any "Indo-European" tongue and therefore so different from modern European languages as to be incomprehensible to us.'[17]

Presumably, this information would not have been available to that allegedly incorrigible forger, Geoffrey of Monmouth, but it is instructive to compare Mackie's remarks with a comment by Cusack, when she says:

> '... those who have maintained the theory of a Gaulish colonisation of Ireland, have been obliged to make Spain the point of embarkation.'[18]

The next recorded invasion (or settlement) of Ireland took place, according to the chronicles, in Anno Mundi 2859, or ca 1145 BC in our terms. This colony was led by Nemedius (see genealogy), or Nemedh, and it is recorded that the people of Nemedh were credited with having built certain types of fort as well as clearing the land for a particular method of cultivation. A later outbreak of plague took its toll on the population, the remainder of whom are recorded as having fought off an invasion of Ireland by the Formorians, who, according to the Annals of Clonmacnois:

> '... were a sept descended from Cham (i.e. Ham), the son of Noeh, ... (who) ... lived by pyracie and spoile of other nations, and were in those days very troublesome to the whole world.'[19]

This is of particular interest to us, as we know from the chronicles of the early Britons that the British mainland was at this time being settled by Brutus and his people in ca 1104 BC according to the British chronology. Now, although Brutus is said to have been the first coloniser of Britain, the chronicles do emphatically state that he had to displace an indigenous race of 'giants'.[20] Whether physical giantism is here intended cannot be certainly resolved, as the early British word 'gawr' (like the Hebrew *gibbor*) could mean simply a great warrior as well as a giant man. But we do know from the biblical record that giantism was a particular physical trait amongst certain of Ham's descendants, Goliath of Gath being the best known example,[21] which lends both the British and Irish accounts a degree of hitherto unsuspected corroboration. The Formorians, it seems, were the displaced natives of Britain who were trying to seek a foothold on the Irish mainland only to be repelled by the Nemedians, thereafter having to live, like many other displaced peoples, by scavenging and piracy.

After the repulsion of the Formorians, the few Nemedian survivors settled further inland, presumably for safety while they consolidated their numbers. They are then recorded as subsequently dividing themselves into three 'bands', each with their respective leaders. One of these groups migrated to northern Europe, where they founded a nation known later to the Irish as the Tuatha de Danann. A second group settled, intriguingly, in the northernmost parts of Britain, apparently the first Pictish settlement of what is now Scotland. This settlement of Picts from 'Scythia' (so states the British record – note etymological derivation given above of Scot from Scythian) into Albany, is recalled in the early British chronicles as having taken place under the Pictish king Soderic. The British chronology seems to have slipped somewhat at this point, but the event is real enough and accurately portrayed.[22]

The third group are named as the Firbolgs, who migrated to Greece and then returned to Ireland which they subsequently divided up into five provinces. However, in Anno Mundi 3303, or ca 701 BC in our terms, the Firbolgs were subdued in their turn by the returning colony of Tuatha de Danann.

The last colonisation of Ireland is then recorded under Anno Mundi 3500 (i.e. ca 504 BC):

> 'The fleet of the sons of Milidh came to Ireland at the end of this year, to take it from the Tuatha de Danann, and they fought the battle of Sliabh Mis with them on the third day after landing.'[23]

The children of Milidh, known to us as the Milesians, had landed unobserved in the mouth of the river Slaney in what is today the county of Wexford, from where they marched to Tara, the central seat of government. The word Milesian is still used (though with increasing rarity) to denote the Irish people themselves, or things pertaining to Ireland. And of further interest to our enquiry is the fact that the Milesians were newly arrived (via the Spanish peninsula) from the city of Miletus, whose ruins still stand on the Turkish mainland, and which was finally destroyed by the Persian army in the year 494 BC. Given that the Irish records state ca 504 BC for the landing of the Milesian colony in Ireland, this is a spontaneous and unexpected chronological correlation that is close enough to give us serious pause for thought. For there's many an Egyptologist who wishes that he could get that close with Egyptian chronology!

The lives of the people of Miletus had been made precarious for decades prior to the fall of their city due to the increasingly threatening ambitions of the Persian army, and nothing would have been more natural than that a colony of Milesians should decide to flee in search of a safe haven. They would seek a land that was sufficiently far away to be safe, was fertile, and which was well known to the Phoenician mariners of the eastern Mediterranean, as was Ireland. And that the city of Miletus should also be known to us as an Ionian outpost whose population consisted of, amongst other races, Scythians and Phoenicians, tells us that we should take the claims of the early Irish chroniclers very seriously indeed.

Moreover, with regard to the equally often stated Phoenician element of Irish descent, we should also note that the ancient Greeks once held that Phoenicia was founded by one Phoenix, whose brother Cadmus had invented the alphabet. Likewise, the early Irish recalled the time when they lived under a king named '... Phenius, who devoted himself especially to the study of languages, and composed an alphabet and the elements of grammar.'[24] So it is clear that, at the very least, the early Irish chroniclers were passing on an account, albeit garbled in places, of authentic historical events and personages, and of the equally historic descent of their own race from Phoenician and Scythian stock. And on the subject of that descent, Cusack adds yet again to our store of knowledge:

> 'As the Milesians were the last of the ancient colonists ... only their genealogies, with a few exceptions, have been preserved. The genealogical tree begins, therefore, with the brothers Eber and Eremon, the two surviving leaders of the expedition, whose ancestors are traced back to Magog, the son of Japhet. The great southern chieftains, such as the MacCarthys and O'Briens, claim descent from Eber; the northern families of O'Connor, O'Donnell, and O'Neill, claim Eremon as their head. There are also other families claiming descent from Emer, the son of Ir, brother to Eber and Eremon; as also from their cousin Lugaidh, the son of Ith. From these four sources the principle Celtic families of Ireland have sprung ...'[25]

As we see in the genealogy, Eber and Eremon were able to trace their own descent from Gadelas, the father of the Gaels and the Gaelic languages, but just how seriously did the early Irish take the question of pedigree? Were they serious enough to take the trouble to keep accurate records over long periods of time? Once more, Cusack answers the question for us:

> 'The Books of Genealogies and Pedigrees form a most important element in Irish pagan history. For social and political reasons, the Irish Celt preserved his genealogical tree with scrupulous precision. The rights of property and the governing power were transmitted with patriarchal exactitude on strict claims of primogeniture, which claims could only be refused under certain conditions defined by law ... and in obedience to an ancient law, **established long before the introduction of Christianity**, all the provincial records, as well as those of the various chieftains, were required to be furnished every third year to the convocation at Tara, where they were compared and corrected.'[26] (Emphasis mine)

As in the case of the Norwegian and Danish Vikings (see previous chapter), it is easy to state, as many modernist articles do on the subject, that these patriarchal genealogies were faked. But it is impossible to imagine this happening when we consider the natural temperament of these various peoples and the gravity with which they viewed the importance of the records that contained the detailed accounts of their own patriarchal descent. It is impossible to see how anyone could have deliberately or even accidentally contrived even a minor alteration to their pedigree without everyone else becoming immediately aware of the fact, and to imagine an alteration on the scale of that required to give substance to the modernist scenario of things, would bring us firmly into the realms of fantasy. Historically, the modernist view on this simply cannot be justified. Such an attempt at fraud or forgery would have brought the full force of the law, or rather the more immediate remedy of someone's sword, crashing down upon the culprit's head. These records may be relied upon, therefore, to be as accurate as any record can be.

Notes

1. Sellar and Yeatman. *1066 And All That*. Penguin. 1962. p. 13.
2. Cusack, M.F. *The Illustrated History of Ireland*. 1868. Published in facsimile by Bracken Books. London. 1987.
3. Cusack tells us which Irish MSS were lost by her own day, and those which had survived. Those lost are: *The Cuilmenn*; the *Saltair of Tara*; *The Book of the Uachongbhail*; the *Cin of Drom Snechta*; and the *Saltair of Cashel*. Those surviving include: *The Annals of Tighernach*; *The Annals of Ulster*; *The Annals of Inis Mac Nerinn*; *The Annals of Innisfallen*; *The Annals of Boyle*; the *Chronicum Scotorum*; the *Annals of the Four Masters*; *The Book of Laws* (the Brehon laws), and 'many books of genealogies and pedigrees' (pp. 39–40).
4. Keating, G. (1634). *The History of Ireland*. Dublin. 1902–14. The Guildhall Library of London holds a copy of this intriguing work.
5. cit. Cusack. p. 43.
6. Cusack. p. 43n.
7. *The Book of Leinster* is kept in the library of Trinity College, Dublin, shelfmark H.2.18.
8. Keating. p. 109 and cit. Cusack. p. 43.
9. Brewer E.C. enl. ed. 1894. *Dictionary of Phrase and Fable*. p. 1112.
10. Genesis 11:6. '... *Behold the people is one, and they have all one language, and this they begin to do: and now nothing will be restrained from them, which they have imagined to do.*'
11. 1 Samuel 8:7: '*And the Lord said unto Samuel, Hearken unto the voice of the people in all that they say unto thee: for they have ... rejected Me, that I should not reign over them.*'
12. See, for example, the article 'King, Kingship'. *The New Bible Dictionary*. Inter-Varsity Press. London. 1972. pp. 692–3.
13. This is according to the *Annals of the Four Masters*. See Cusack. p. 58.
14. Cusack. p. 59.
15. Thorpe. pp. 100–1.
16. Nennius §13.
17. Mackie, J.D. *A History of Scotland*. Penguin Books. p. 16.
18. Cusack. p. 71.
19. (tr. Conell MacGeoghegan). cit. Cusack. p. 20.

20. See Geoffrey of Monmouth. pp. 72–3. Geoffrey's *Gogmagog* appears to be a corruption of the name Gawr Madoc, meaning the giant or great warrior Madog. Of these 'giants', we read, '...though their stature is exaggerated, yet it will be remembered that the stature of the ancient Britons was thought gigantic by the Romans.' Pope. p. 164.
21. 1 Samuel 17:4. See also *New Bible Dict.* pp. 466 & 481.
22. Geoffrey of Monmouth. p. 123.
23. *The Annals of the Four Masters.* cit. Cusack. p. 75.
24. Cusack. p. 69.
25. Cusack. p. 85.
26. Cusack. p. 82.

Chapter 9

Ancient Chronologies and the Age of the Earth

That the earth might be millions or even billions of years old is a fairly recent idea which did not really begin to be formed until the turn of the 18th and the 19th centuries, after the works of Hutton and Lyle were first published. They introduced an idea known as the uniformitarian theory, stating in effect that the processes of nature had always been the same slow processes that they are today, and that hence the earth's features formed gradually over aeons of time. It was a notion in which there was no room given to either a recent six-day Creation or the Flood of Noah. The notion of uniformitarianism, as well as laying the foundations for the theory of evolution which was to follow, was deemed sufficient in its own right to disprove the Genesis record, and the somewhat dubious philosophical attractions of this idea have led to the near universal acceptance of the theory. Indeed, the rejection of the Genesis account seems to have been the one objective behind the formulation of the theory in the first place. [1] There have been many learned and complex criticisms published of late against the uniformitarian theory by creationists and others, and I will not repeat here what they have said. All that concerns us in this present study is what our ancient forebears thought of the age of the earth, and exactly how old they reckoned it to be.

Particular interest was shown amongst the Anglo-Saxons and the early Britons in establishing a firm chronology for their histories, and although there may be good reasons today for questioning **some** of the dates provided by their systems of reckoning, we are nevertheless left with unequivocal evidence that shows them to have believed in a young earth (a recent Creation) and the Flood. For example, the version of the Anglo-Saxon Chronicle known as the *Parker Chronicle*,[2] states that from the beginning of the world until the year AD 6 were 5200 years. The *Laud Chronicle*[3] differs slightly from this, stating that the same period elapsed from the Creation to the year AD 11, indicating either a simple scribal error or a derivation from two distinct sources. However, both chronicles agree that from the Creation to the year AD 33, the year of the Crucifixion, was a period of 5226 years. In other words, as far as the Saxons were concerned, the world was created about 5200 BC.

Further to this, is the statement found elsewhere amongst the Anglo-Saxon records that:

> *Fram Adame* ... (to the) ... *flod* ... (were) ... *twa hund wintra & twa thusenda & twa & fiowertig*. (From Adam to the Flood were 2242 winters.')[4] (My translation)

It would be interesting to discover whence the Saxons got this figure of 2242 years for the antediluvian period, for it does not appear in the Latin Vulgate which gives 1656 years for this period, thus agreeing with the Hebrew; and they were not familiar with the Septuagint version which gives in any case a period of 2256 years for the antediluvian era. However, their figure does agree exactly with that of the Britons, as passed down to us by Nennius:[5]

> 'From the beginning of the world until the Flood (are) 2242 years.
> From the Flood until Abraham (are) 942 years.
> From Abraham to Moses (are) 640 years.
> From Moses to David (are) 500 years.

From David to Nebuchadnezzar are 569 years.
From Adam until the migration to Babylonia (i.e. the Captivity of the Jews) are 4879 years.
From the migration to Babylonia until Christ are 566 years.
From Adam therefore until the Passion of Christ are 5228 years.
From the Passion of Christ have been completed 796 years.
And from His Incarnation 831 years.'

(Nennius, chapters 1–4; my translation)

We would say today that there are certain points on which this early British chronology is patently wrong. For example, there were not 942 years between the Flood and Abraham, but only ca 427 until Abraham's entry into Canaan.[6] Again, adding the years given in lines 1–7, we have a period of 5459 years between Adam and Christ, whereas the chronology states towards the end that from Adam until Christ's Passion was only 5228 years, an error of 231 years! Assuming that Nennius was himself quite capable of doing simple arithmetic, we have to conclude that he passed down to us, characteristically unedited and uncorrected, a faulty (and therefore much older?) source. However, the early Britons and the Saxons are seen by their records to have looked back to a Creation of about 5200 BC.

The Irish chronology, on the other hand, seems to have favoured a date for the Creation of about 4000 BC. Now, there are admittedly certain complex difficulties concerning Irish chronology, but these have to do with events recorded for the period between the Flood and the Milesian colony of ca 500 BC. For example, Partholan, if we accept the Irish chronology, landed in Ireland in the 15th century BC, whereas the British chronicle dates him to the reign of Gurguit (who, it is said, gave Ireland to him) in the 4th century BC. These difficulties can be resolved however. It seems that it is the British chronology that is in error here, but how did this error of over a thousand years come about?

There are various possibilities. Firstly, it could be that Gurguit was mistaken for a much earlier British king. But when we consider that Partholan began his reign some 380 years before the British royal line was even founded (by Brutus in ca 1104 BC), then this possibility is immediately discounted. Could Partholan have been confused with a much later Irish king of similar name and whose reign was contemporary with that of Gurguit? That is just possible, although the Irish records are silent concerning such a king. Finally, we can consider the possibility that there was some kind of political agreement between the Irish and British monarchies during the 4th century BC (i.e. during the reign of Gurguit), and that Partholan's name, as the original founder of Irish kingship and in whose name the present kingship of Ireland was held, simply became embroiled with that of the king under whom the agreement was made. This way, the discrepancy becomes one of name only rather than one of chronology.

However, the Creation date of ca 4000 BC favoured by the early Irish chroniclers brings to mind the most famous of all proposed for the Creation, that of Ussher, who, in his 17th century work, *Annales Veteris et Novi Testamenti*, calculated a date of 4004 BC. Ussher was himself an Irishman, of course, who was doubtless steeped in the lore of his countrymen. But whether Ussher was influenced by this or not, we note that the favoured dates for the Creation between the Britons, Saxons and Irish were somewhere between ca 4000 BC on the one hand, and ca 5200 BC on the other. Which brings us to the following observation concerning the work of the 16th century chronologist, Scaliger.

Joseph Scaliger (1540–1609) was a scholar of immense ability who broke much new ground in the study of classical literature. Yet his chief claim to fame (if the comparative obscurity so far afforded him can be described as fame), lies in his work, *De Emendatione Temporum*, which he published in 1583 and which paved the way for the modern science of chronology. (This was followed by the publication in 1606 of his *Thesaurus Temporum*, in which he reconstructed Eusebius's *Chronicon*.)

Scaliger turned his interest from classical literature and languages to chronology primarily because chronology was a science that had degenerated into some disarray by his own day. Indeed, it was so beset with difficulties that it was nigh unworkable, and Scaliger set himself the task of either improving it or replacing it altogether. In his *De Emendatione Temporum*, Scaliger rightly recognised that the calendar as it now stands, i.e. the Gregorian Calendar which was introduced in Europe in 1582, and which he heavily criticised, was a somewhat cumbersome apparatus with which to reconstruct the chronology of past events. Its very complexity lent itself to mistakes, whilst its inherent inaccuracies lent themselves to yet further inaccuracies. So he decided to solve the problem, and his solution was as ingenious as it was simple. Instead of an event being said to have occurred at such a date in such a year BC or AD, it would henceforth be said to have occurred on a certain numbered day.

Now, although a daycount was the answer, it raised a further question. From which point in time should this daycount begin? The answer was obvious. It should begin from Day 1 of the Creation. But when did Day 1 occur? Well, Scaliger (partially) solved the problem by turning his attention to the three basic units upon which virtually all workable calendars are based, namely, the Solar Cycle, the Metonic Cycle and the Roman Indiction.

In simple terms, the Solar Cycle is completed every 28 years, the Metonic Cycle every 19 years, and the Roman Indiction every 15 years. Scaliger realised that there must obviously be points in time when all three cycles begin and end together, so, noting carefully the age of each cycle at the moment when he began his calculations, he counted the years backwards until he came to that year when all three cycles began together. And that was the year 4713 BC.

Simple arithmetic then told him that the three cycles would only meet together in time every 7980 years (this figure being the product of $28 \times 19 \times 15$), and given that they had begun together in 4713 BC, the period, which he named the Julian

Period in honour of his father Julius, would not end until the close of the year AD 3267 [7].

This was an excellent and broad base upon which to build his system of chronology, and for convenience's sake Scaliger counted 1st January 4713 BC as Day 1, building up his chronology from there. However, the fact that the three cycles (Solar, Metonic and Roman Indiction) began in the year 4713 BC will hold a certain significance for creationists, for Genesis is quite clear on the matter when it tells us that, apart from their light-giving properties, the solar system and its backdrop of stars were created so that we could measure by them times and seasons, days and years. In other words, God had created a gigantic clock, and what more natural than that the Creator should start that clock ticking, as it were, at a setting that would measure the age of the universe as well as the more mundane passing of the seasons here on earth?

But, before we recklessly assume that Scaliger had all unwittingly stumbled across the true date for the Creation, we must remember that Scaliger based his calculations on the present values of the Solar and Metonic Cycles, or at least the values of these cycles as they stood in the year 1582/3. Creationists should be painfully aware by now that values today may not necessarily be the values of the past. This is constantly argued by creationists in refutation of the uniformitarian hypothesis. Much damage, disruption and mayhem has occurred which will undoubtedly have altered those values to an extent we can only guess at. On a local (planet earth) level, we have had the global Flood of Noah and other geological disasters to alter the rotation of the earth and hence the lengths of the day and year. The moon has suffered local catastrophes of its own affecting no doubt the length of the lunar month, and the universe in general has degenerated noticeably in its values during the past six thousand years or so simply through the inexorable workings of the Second Law of Thermodynamics.

There is, moreover, much documentary evidence to suggest that calendar calculations underwent several revisions both during the more immediate centuries of the post-Flood era and later. Why were these revisions necessary? The deteriorations in the motions of the earth, moon and stars, and hence the calendar, seem to have occurred not gradually over an immense period of time, as implied by most modernist writers on the subject, but at certain points in history when one day the current calendar was workable and the next when it was not. Studying the revisions that had to be made and of which we have any record, intercalations were suddenly brought in to correct for suddenly observed discrepancies.

Now, if the deteriorations in the calendar, especially the lunar calendar, were indeed gradual, as some would have us believe, then why were the reforms that corrected for this deterioration not brought in in equally gradual stages? It is simply not good enough to assume, as most modern writers on the subject assume, that the early calendar makers were merely poor observers who possessed no theoretical astronomy and who could thus only make poor calendars that had to be corrected from time to time. If the people of the time had truly devised a calendar that was unworkably in error, then they would surely have discovered this within only a year or two of its inauguration, and would not have waited centuries to allegedly evolve sufficient acumen to notice that the seasons were wildly at variance with their own calculated harvest time. With ignorance and stupidity of that order, it is difficult to see how they would have coped with some of life's more challenging problems.

One such people who are said not to have possessed any mathematics of a particularly high order, nor any theoretical astronomy, are the Maya of South America. Now, the Maya instituted a daycount exactly like that which Scaliger devised in order to solve certain chronological and genealogical problems that they had come across whilst reconstructing their own ancient history. The unnerving aspect of this from the modernist point of view, however, is the fact that the Maya perfected their daycount some six hundred years or more before Scaliger was even thought of. Scaliger, we are rightly told, was a genius. The Maya, we are wrongly told, were not.

But why are we told that the Maya were not geniuses? Why

do modernist authors insist on telling us that the Maya had no theoretical astronomy and no system of theoretical mathematics in spite of much concrete evidence to the contrary? At Chichen Itza in Mexico stand the ruins of a gigantic observatory that the Maya built, whose passageways are aligned with the sun, moon and stars. With this, and in conjunction with other aligned observatories, the Maya were able to predict lunar and solar eclipses with great accuracy as well as measuring the synodic cycle of Venus with a precision that has only been matched and realised in modern times.[8] But perhaps there is method in the modernist madness.

If we correlate the Mayan daycount with that of Scaliger, we find that the Mayan Day 1 began on Julian Day 584283,[9] which equals in our terms 10th August 3113 BC (I make that a Thursday) for the start of the Mayan daycount. Now, the significance of this lies in the fact that although the Mayan concept of time was cyclic, they nevertheless knew that the world-destroying catastrophe that had closed the previous age was brought about by water, and that their own age had begun after that catastrophe. In other words, they looked back to the Flood as the close of the old age and the beginning of the new. And it is here that their daycount takes on an immense significance. Scaliger's daycount, we remember, took him back to the year 4713 BC, and it is more than probable that this corresponds **roughly** to the year of the Creation. The Mayans, however, did not begin their daycount from the Creation, but from the Flood, and this event was set in **their** chronology, not Scaliger's, in the year 3113 BC, and subtracting 3113 from 4713 leaves us with a 1600 year period between the two dates for the Creation and the Flood, a period of time which corresponds remarkably closely to the 1656 year period set out so precisely in the Genesis record. Little wonder that this information is precluded these days by a cursory dismissal of Mayan mathematics and astronomy. If I were a modernist, I'd dismiss it too!

But to briefly take stock of the situation, we may see by all the evidence noted above that not only did our ancient forebears look back, in pre-Christian times, to their descent from patriarchs that are named in the Table of Nations, but they also held that the earth was of recent creation and that it had once suffered a Flood. And they knew all this without any recourse to the book of Genesis, of which they were entirely unaware. In all, their records constitute a rather formidable body of evidence. But there is another subject that has a bearing on our enquiry, and again it was something that our forebears accepted without any problem at all. Indeed, they recorded its occurrence regularly in their annals and chronicles, blissfully unaware of the fact that today it would be a most controversial and sensitive subject. It is one that we deal with in the following chapter.

Notes

1. See Bowden's *Rise of the Evolution Fraud.*
2. Corpus Christi College Cambridge MS. 173. For an English translation see Garmonsway. pp. 6–7.
3. Bodleian MS. Laud 636. See also Garmonsway. pp. 6–7.
4. MS. Cotton. Vespasian. D. IV. fol. 69v.
5. *A principio mundi usque ad diluvium anni II CC XL II.*
   A diluvio usque ad Abraham anni D CCCC XL II.
   Ab Abraham usque ad Moysen anni D C XL.
   A Moyse usque ad David anni D.
   A David usque Nabuchodonosor anni sunt D LX VIIII.
   Ab Adam usque transmigrationem Babyloniae anni sunt IIII DCCC LXX VIIII.
   A transmigratione Babyloniae usque ad Christum D LX VI.
   Ab Adam vero usque ad passionem Christi anni sunt V CC XX VIII.
   A passione autem Christi peracti sunt anni D CC LXXXX VI.
   Ab incarnatione autem eius anni sunt D CCC XXX I.
   (Nennius 1–4; see also Morris. p. 59)
6. Osgood, John. *The Times of Abraham.* CEN Tech. J. Vol. 2. 1986. p. 79.
7. *Encyclopaedia Britannica.* 1985 ed. Vol. 15. p. 463.
8. The Mayans calculated a 584 day cycle, against the modern value of 583.92 days. See Ronan, C. *The Cambridge Illustrated History of the World's Science.* Newnes. Cambridge. 1983. p. 55.
9. *Encyclopaedia Britannica.* 1985 ed. Vol. 15. p. 474.

Chapter 10

Dinosaurs from Anglo-Saxon and other Records

I have spoken on the subject of the Table of Nations and the early post-Flood history of Europe, in Germany, Belgium and at many places now in England, and what surprised me at first was how, during question time, the subject turns so quickly to that of dinosaurs. Do they appear in the early chronicles? Do descriptions of them exist? And so on. So here I have set out as many examples of the mention of dinosaurs in the early records as I could immediately find, although there are doubtless many other instances to be noticed. Some of the examples mentioned here come from the very records that we have just been considering concerning the descent of the nations.

The progression is only logical, for if the earth is as young as our forebears thought and as the creation model of origins predicts, then evidence will be found which tells us that, in the recent past, dinosaurs and man have co-existed. There is, in fact, good evidence to suggest that they still co-exist, and this is directly contrary to the evolutionary model which teaches that dinosaurs lived millions of years before man came along, and that no man therefore can ever have seen a living dinosaur. And to test that assertion, we will now examine the issue by considering the written evidence that has survived from the records of various ancient peoples that describe, sometimes in the most graphic detail, human encounters with living giant reptiles that we would call dinosaurs. And as we shall see, some of those records are not so ancient.

There are, of course, the famous descriptions of two such monsters from the Old Testament, **Behemoth** and **Leviathan** (Job 40:15–41:34), Behemoth being a giant vegetarian that lived on the fens, and Leviathan a somewhat more terrifying armour-plated amphibian whom only children and the most foolhardy would want as a pet. The Egyptians knew Behemoth by the name **p'ih.mw**,[1] which is the same name, of course. Leviathan was similarly known as **Lotan** to the men of Ugarit.[2] Babylonian and Sumerian literature has preserved details of similar creatures, as has the written and unwritten folklore of peoples around the world. But perhaps the most remarkable descriptions of living dinosaurs are those that the Saxon and Celtic peoples of Europe have passed down to us.

The early Britons, from whom the modern Welsh are descended, provide us with our earliest surviving European accounts of reptilian monsters, one of whom killed and devoured king Morvidus (Morydd) in ca 336 BC. We are told in the account translated for us by Geoffrey of Monmouth, that the monster 'gulped down the body of Morvidus as a big fish swallows a little one.' Geoffrey described the animal as a **Belua**.[3]

Peredur, not the ancient king of that name (306–296 BC), but a much later son of Earl Efrawg, had better luck than Morvidus, actually managing to slay his monster, an **addanc** (pr. athanc: var. afanc), at a place called Llyn Llion in Wales.[4] At other Welsh locations the addanc is further spoken of along with another reptilian species known as the **carrog**. The addanc survived until comparatively recent times at such places as Bedd-yr-Afanc near Brynberian, at Llyn-yr-Afanc above Bettws-y-Coed on the River Conwy (the killing of this monster was described in the year 1693), and Llyn Barfog. A carrog is commemorated at Carrog near Corwen, and at Dol-y-Carrog in the Vale of Conwy.[5]

Moreover, 'dinosaurs', in the form of flying reptiles, were a feature of Welsh life until surprisingly recent times. As late as the beginning of the present century, elderly folk at Penllin in

Glamorgan used to tell of a colony of winged serpents that lived in the woods around Penllin Castle. As Marie Trevelyan tells us:

> 'The woods around Penllin Castle, Glamorgan, had the reputation of being frequented by winged serpents, and these were the terror of old and young alike. An aged inhabitant of Penllyne, who died a few years ago, said that in his boyhood the winged serpents were described as very beautiful. They were coiled when in repose, and "looked as if they were covered with jewels of all sorts. Some of them had crests sparkling with all the colours of the rainbow". When disturbed they glided swiftly, 'sparkling all over', to their hiding places. When angry, they "flew over people's heads, with outspread wings bright, and sometimes with eyes too, like the feathers in a peacock's tail". He said it was "no old story invented to frighten children", but a real fact. His father and uncle had killed some of them, for they were as bad as foxes for poultry. The old man attributed the extinction of the winged serpents to the fact that they were "terrors in the farmyards and coverts".'[6]

This account is intriguing in many respects, not the least being the fact that it is not a typical account of dragons. The creatures concerned were not solitary and monstrous beasts, but small creatures that lived in colonies. Not at all like the larger species of winged reptile that used to nest upon an ancient burial-mound, or tumulus, at Trellech-a'r-Betws in the county of Dyfed, for example. But whilst we are in Wales, it is worth noting that at Llanbardan-y-Garrag (is Garrag a corruption of carrog?), the church contains a carving of a local giant reptile whose features include large paddle-like flippers, a long neck and a small head. Glaslyn, in Snowdon, is a lake where an afanc was sighted as recently as the 1930s. On this occasion two climbers on the side of a mountain looked down onto the surface of Glaslyn and they saw the creature, which they described as having a long grey body, rise from the depths of the lake to the surface, raise its head and then submerge again.[7]

One could multiply such reports by the hundred. In England and Scotland, again until comparatively recent times, other reptilian monsters were sighted and spoken of in many places. The table at the end of this chapter lists eighty-one locations in the British Isles alone in which dinosaur activity has been reported (there are, in fact, nearly 200 such places in Britain), but perhaps the most relevant aspect of this as far as our present study is concerned is the fact that some of these sightings and subsequent encounters with living dinosaurs can be dated to the comparatively recent past. The giant reptile at Bures in Suffolk, for example, is known to us from a chronicle of 1405:

> 'Close to the town of Bures, near Sudbury, there has lately appeared, to the great hurt of the countryside, a dragon, vast in body, with a crested head, teeth like a saw, and a tail extending to an enormous length. Having slaughtered the shepherd of a flock, it devoured many sheep.'

After an unsuccessful attempt by local archers to kill the beast, due to its impenetrable hide:

> '...in order to destroy him, all the country people around were summoned. But when the dragon saw that he was again to be assailed with arrows, he fled into a marsh or mere and there hid himself among the long reeds, and was no more seen.'[8]

Later in the 15th century, according to a contemporary chronicle that still survives in Canterbury Cathedral's library, the following incident was reported. On the afternoon of Friday, 26th September, 1449, two giant reptiles were seen fighting on the banks of the River Stour (near the village of Little Cornard) which marked the English county borders of Suffolk and Essex. One was black, and the other 'reddish and spotted'. After an hour-long struggle that took place 'to the admiration of many [of the locals] beholding them', the black monster yielded and returned to its lair, the scene of the conflict being known ever since as Sharpfight Meadow.[9]

As late as August, 1614, the following sober account was given of a strange reptile that was encountered in St Leonard's Forest in Sussex. The sighting was near a village that was known as Dragon's Green long before this report was published:

> 'This serpent (or dragon as some call it) is reputed to be nine feete, or rather more, in length, and shaped almost in the form of an axletree of a cart: a quantitie of thickness in the middest, and somewhat smaller at both endes. The former part, which he shootes forth as a necke, is supposed to be an elle [3ft 9ins or 114cms] long; with a white ring, as it were, of scales about it. The scales along his back seem to be blackish, and so much as is discovered under his bellie, appeareth to be red . . . it is likewise discovered to have large feete, but the eye may there be deceived, for some suppose that serpents have no feete . . . [The dragon] rids away (as we call it) as fast as a man can run. His food [rabbits] is thought to be, for the most part, in a conie-warren, which he much frequents . . . There are likewise upon either side of him discovered two great bunches so big as a large foote-ball, and (as some thinke) will in time grow to wings, but God, I hope, will (to defend the poor people in the neighbourhood) that he shall be destroyed before he grows to fledge.'[10]

This dragon was seen in various places within a circuit of three or four miles, and the pamphlet named some of the still-living witnesses who had seen him. These included John Steele, Christopher Holder and a certain 'widow woman dwelling neare Faygate'. Another witness was 'the carrier of Horsham, who lieth at the White Horse [inn] in Southwark'. One of the locals set his two mastiffs onto the monster, and apart from losing his dogs he was fortunate to escape alive from the encounter, for the dragon was already credited with the deaths of a man and woman at whom it had spat and who consequently had been killed by its venom. When approached unwittingly, our pamphleteer tells us, the monster was...

> '...of countenance very proud and at the sight or hearing of men or cattel will raise his neck upright and seem to listen and looke about, with great arrogancy.'

...an eyewitness account of typically reptilian behaviour.

Again, as late as 27th and 28th May 1669, a large reptilian animal was sighted many times, as was reported in the pamphlet: *A True Relation of a Monstrous Serpent seen at Henham (Essex) on the Mount in Saffron Waldon.*[11]

In 1867 was seen, for the last time, the monster that lived in the woods around Fittleworth in Sussex. It would run up to people hissing and spitting if they happened to stumble across it unawares, although it never harmed anyone. Several such cases could be cited, but suffice it to say that too many incidents like these are reported down through the centuries and from all sorts of locations for us to say that they are all fairy-tales. For example, Scotland's famous Loch Ness Monster is too often thought to be a recent product of the local Tourist Board's efforts to bring in some trade, yet Loch Ness is by no means the only Scottish loch where monsters have been reported. Loch Lomond, Loch Awe, Loch Rannoch and the privately owned Loch Morar (over 1000ft deep) also have records of monster activity in recent years. Indeed, there have been over forty sightings at Loch Morar alone since the end of the last war, and over a thousand from Loch Ness in the same period. However, as far as Loch Ness itself is concerned, few realise that monstrous reptiles, no doubt the same species, have been sighted in and around the loch since the so-called Dark Ages, the most notable instance being that which is described in Adamnan's famous 6th century *Life of St Columba.*

There we read that in the year AD 565, Columba, on yet another of his missionary journeys in the north, needed to cross the River Ness. As he was about to do so, he saw a burial party. On enquiry he was informed that they were burying a man who had just been killed by a savage bite from a monster who had snatched him while swimming. On hearing this, and with never a thought for his own safety, the brave saint immediately ordered one of his followers to jump into the freezing water to see if the monster was still in the vicinity. Adamnan relates how the thrashing about of the alarmed and unhappy swimmer, Lugne Mocumin by name, attracted the monster's attention. Suddenly, on breaking the surface, the monster was seen to speed towards the luckless chap with its mouth wide open and screaming like a banshee. Columba, however, refused to panic, and from the safety of the dry land rebuked the beast. Whether the swimmer added any rebukes of his own is not recorded, but the monster was seen to turn away, having approached the swimmer so closely that not the length of a punt-pole lay between them.

Columba, naturally, claimed the credit for the swimmer's survival, although the reluctance of the monster to actually harm the man is the most notable thing in this incident. The first swimmer had been savaged and killed, though not eaten, and the second swimmer was likewise treated to a display of the creature's wrath, though not fatally. Most likely, the two men had unwittingly entered the water close to where the creature kept her young, and she was reacting in a way that is typical of most species. Gorillas, bull elephants, ostriches, indeed all sorts of creature will charge at a man, hissing, screaming and trumpeting alarmingly, yet will rarely kill him or harm him so long as the man takes the hint and goes away. We can rely on it that Columba's follower, utterly lacking his saintly master's fortitude, had begun the process of taking the hint in plenty of time for the monster to realise that killing him would not be necessary.

Yet not even Lugne Mocumin's experience is that uncommon. As recently as the 18th century, in a lake called Llyn-y-Gader in Snowdon, Wales, a certain man went swimming. He reached the middle of the lake and was returning to the shore when his friends who were watching him noticed that he was being followed by:

> '...a long, trailing object winding slowly behind him. They were afraid to raise an alarm, but went forward to meet him as soon as he reached the shore where they stood. Just as he was approaching, the trailing object raised its head, and before anyone could render aid the man was enveloped in the coils of the monster...'[12]

It seems that the man's body was never recovered.

At about the turn of this present century, the following incident took place. It was related by a Lady Gregory of Ireland in 1920:

> '...old people told me that they were swimming there, [in an Irish lake called Lough Graney] and a man had gone out into the middle, and they saw something like a great big eel making for him...'[13]

Happily, on this occasion the man made it back to the shore, but the important thing for us to notice is that these are only a few of a great many reports concerning the sightings in recent times of lake-dwelling monsters which, if only their fossils had been found, would have been called dinosaurs.

But the British Isles are not the only place where one can find such reports. They occur, quite literally, all over the world.[14] William Caxton, for example, England's first printer, recorded for us in 1484 the following account of a reptilian monster in medieval Italy. I have modernised the spelling and punctuation:

> 'There was found within a great river [i.e. the Po in Italy] a monster marine, or of the sea, of the form or likeness which followeth. He had the form or making of a fish, the which part was in two halves, that is to wit double. He had a great beard and he had two wonderfully great

horns above his ears. Also he had great paps and a wonderfully great and horrible mouth. And at the both [of] his elbows he had wings right broad and great of fish's armour wherewith he swimmed and only he had but the head out of the water. It happed then that many women laundered and washed at the port or haven of the said river [where] that this horrible and fearful beast was, [who] for lack or default of meat came swimming toward the said women. Of the which he took one by the hand and supposed to have drawn her into the water. But she was strong and well advised and resisted against the said monster. And as she defended herself, she began to cry with an high voice, "Help, help!" To the which came running five women which by hurling and drawing of stones, killed and slew the said monster, for he was come too far within the sound, wherefore he might not return to the deep water. And after, when he rendered his spirit, he made a right little cry. He was of great corpulence more than any man's body. And yet, saith Poge [Pogius Bracciolini of Florence] in this manner, that he, being at Ferrara, he saw the said monster and saith yet that the young children were accustomed for to go bathe and wash them within the said river, but they came not all again. Wherefore the women [neither] washed nor laundered their clothes at the said port, for the folk presumed and supposed that the monster killed the young children which were drowned.'[15]

Caxton also provided the following account of a 'serpent' which left a cow badly bruised and frightened, although we should bear in mind that a serpent in Caxton's day was not the snake that we would imagine today, for the word serpent has changed its meaning slightly since the Middle Ages. There are one or two intriguing woodcut illustrations of these serpents in Caxton's book, and they are all bipedal, scaled reptiles with large mouths:

> '... about the marches of Italy, within a meadow, was sometime a serpent of wonderful and right marvellous greatness, right hideous and fearful. For first he had the head greater than the head of a calf. Secondly, he had a neck of the length of an ass, and his body made after the likeness of a dog. And his tail was wonderfully great, thick and long, without comparison to any other. A cow ... [seeing] ... so right horrible a beast, she was all fearful and lift herself up and supposed to have fled away. But the serpent, with his wonderfully long tail, enlaced her two hind legs. And the serpent then began to suck the cow. And indeed so much and so long he sucked that he found some milk. And when the cow might escape from him, she fled unto the other cows. And her paps and her hind legs, and all that the serpent touched, was all black a great space of time.'[16]

These accounts are clearly factual and witnessed reports rather than fairy-tales, and are as close to journalistic reporting as we shall ever see in works from the Middle Ages. But for a more modern example of such journalistic reporting, let us consider the following article that appeared recently in that most sober of British journals, *The Times*:

> 'Japanese fishermen caught a dead monster, weighing two tons and 30 feet in length, off the coast of New Zealand in April, it was reported today. Believed to be a survivor of a prehistoric species, the monster was caught at a depth of 1000 feet off the South Island coast, near Christchurch. Palaeontologists from the Natural Science Museum near Tokyo have concluded that the beast belonged to the pleisiosaurus family – huge, small-headed reptiles with a long neck and four fins ... After a member of the crew had photographed and measured it, the trawler's captain ordered the corpse to be thrown back into the sea for fear of contamination to his fish.'[17]

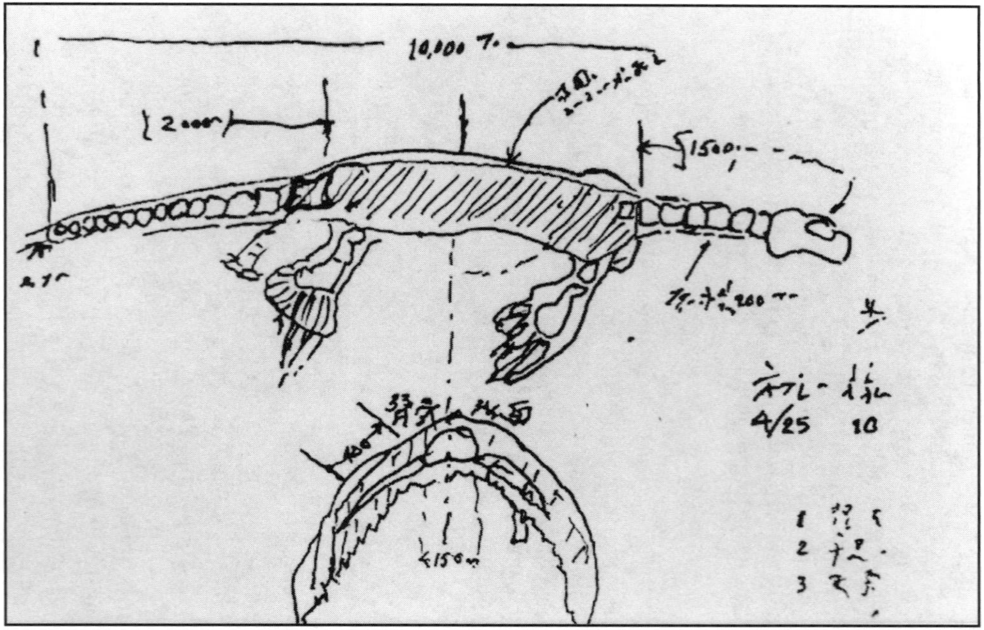

Figure 10.1 The drawing and measurements made by Michihiko Yano of the creature's skeleton that was dredged up off the New Zealand coast in 1977, and which the BBC and British Museum of Natural History would assure us was the body of a dead shark.

It is thought-provoking to consider that the Japanese have no problem with officially owning up to the present-day existence of dragons, sea-monsters or dinosaurs. Indeed, they even issued a postage-stamp with a picture of a pleisiosaurus to commemorate the above find. Only we in the West seem to have a problem with the present-day existence of these creatures, for only nine days after the appearance of the *Times* article, it was sombrely announced on the 30th July 1977 by the BBC that the monster only looked like a pleisiosaurus. It in fact was a shark that had decomposed in such a way as to convey the impression that it had a long neck, a small head and four large paddles. How they, or their informants at the Natural History Museum in Kensington, could tell this since the creature was no longer available for examination, we can only guess at, especially considering that the marine biologist on board the vessel, the *Zuiyo-maru*, had sketched the creatures skeletal structure and it is nothing like that of a shark (see Figure 10.1). Marine biologists are highly trained scientists whose ability to detect disease and mutations in fish and marine mammals is crucial to the health of the consumer let alone the profits of the fishing vessel concerned, so their knowledge of marine life is necessarily very great. Yet the BBC would have us believe that Michihiko Yano, the government-trained and highly qualified marine biologist who examined, photographed and measured the monster, wouldn't know a dead shark when he saw one!

But western officialdom has not always been as averse as this at acknowledging and even mentioning in official reports the existence of creatures which are supposed by today's establishment to have died out millions of years ago. The following, for example, was penned only two hundred years ago in 1793 and describes creatures that sound suspiciously like pterodactyls or similar. Remember, it is an official and very sober government report that we are reading:

> 'In the end of November and beginning of December last, many of the country people observed ... dragons ... appearing in the north and flying rapidly towards the

east; from which they concluded, and their conjectures were right, that ... boisterous weather would follow.'[18]

This report is intriguing for the fact that exactly one thousand years before an almost identical report made its appearance in the Anglo-Saxon Chronicle under the year 793. The two accounts are nothing more than country people being able to predict the weather by observing the behaviour of the animals, which is a skill that they have always possessed and used, and these accounts, combined with later records of the years 1170, 1177, 1221 and 1222, of 1233 and of 1532, suggest that these creatures could tell the approach of bad weather coming in off the Atlantic and simply migrated to calmer regions while the bad weather lasted. Considering the flimsiness and fragility of the wings of pterodactyls and similar creatures, the reports make eminent sense.

But now we come to the most notable records of all. They are written works that are remarkable for the graphic detail with which they portray the giant reptiles that the early Saxons, Danes and others encountered in Northern Europe and Scandinavia. In various Nordic sagas the slaying of dragons is depicted in some detail, and this helps us to reconstruct the physical appearance of some of these creatures. In the *Volsungassaga*,[19] for example, the slaying of the monster **Fafnir** was accomplished by Sigurd digging a pit and waiting, inside the pit, for the monster to crawl overhead on its way to the water. This allowed Sigurd to attack the animal's soft under-belly. Clearly, **Fafnir** walked on all fours with his belly close to the ground.

Likewise, the *Voluspa* tells us of a certain monster which the early Vikings called a **Nithhoggr**, its name (*'corpse-tearer'*) revealing the fact that it lived off carrion. Saxo Grammaticus, in his *Gesta Danorum*, tells us of the Danish king Frotho's fight with a giant reptile, and it is in the advice given by a local to the king, and recorded by Saxo, that the monster is described in great detail. It was, he says, a serpent:

> '... wreathed in coils, doubled in many a fold, and with a tail drawn out in winding whorls, shaking his manifold spirals and shedding venom ... his slaver [saliva] burns up what it bespatters ... yet [he tells the king in words that were doubtless meant to encourage rather than dismay] ... remember to keep the dauntless temper of thy mind; nor let the point of the jagged tooth trouble thee, nor the starkness of the beast, nor the venom ... there is a place under his lowest belly whither thou mayst plunge the blade ...'[20]

The description of this reptilian monster closely resembles that of the monster seen at Henham (see Note 11), and the two animals could well have belonged to the same or similar species. Notable, especially, is their defence mechanism of spitting corrosive venom at their victims.

But it is the epic Anglo-Saxon poem *Beowulf*[21] that provides us with truly invaluable descriptions of the huge reptilian animals which, only 1400 years ago, infested Denmark and other parts of Europe, and we shall turn our attention now to a close and very detailed examination of this most remarkable account.

Some Sites of 'Dinosaur' Activity Throughout Britain

Aller, Somerset; Anwick, Lincolnshire; Bamburgh, Northumberland; Beckhole, North Yorkshire; Bedd-yr-Afanc, Wales; Ben Vair, Scotland; Bignor Hill, West Sussex; Bishop Auckland, Durham; Bisterne, Hampshire; Brent Pelham, Hertfordshire; Brinsop, Hereford and Worcester; Bures, Suffolk; Cadbury Castle, Devon; Carhampton, Somerset; Castle Carlton, Lincolnshire; Castle Neroche, Somerset; Challacombe, Devon; Churchstanton, Somerset; Cnoc-na-Cnoimh, Scotland; Crowcombe, Somerset; Dalry, Scotland; Deerhurst, Gloucestershire; Dol-y-Carrog, Wales; Dragonhoard (nr Garsington), Oxfordshire; Drake Howe, North Yorkshire; Drakelow,

Derbyshire; Drakelowe, Worcestershire; Filey Brigg, North Yorkshire; Handale Priory, North Yorkshire; Henham, Essex; Hornden, Essex; Kellington, North Yorkshire; Kilve, Somerset; Kingston St Mary, Somerset; Lambton Castle,, Durham; Linton, Scotland; Little Cornard, Suffolk; Llandeilo Graban, Wales; Llanraeadr-ym-Mochnant, Wales; Llyn Barfog, Wales; Llyn Cynwch (nr Dolgellau), Wales; Llyn Llion, Wales; Llyn-y-Gader, Wales; Llyn-yr-Afanc, Wales; Loch Awe, Scotland; Loch Maree, Scotland; Loch Morar, Scotland; Loch Ness, Scotland; Loch Rannoch, Scotland; Longwitton, Northumberland; Ludham, Norfolk; Lyminster, West Sussex; Manaton, Devon; Money Hill, Northumberland; Moston, Cheshire; Newcastle Emlyn, Wales; Norton Fitzwarren, Hereford and Worcester; Nunnington, North Yorkshire; Old Field Barrows (nr Bromfield), Shropshire; Penllin Castle, Wales; Penmark, Wales; Penmynydd, Wales; St Albans, Hertfordshire; St Leonard's Forest, West Sussex; St Osyth, Essex; Saffron Waldon, Essex; Sexhow, North Yorkshire; Shervage Wood, Hereford and Worcester; Slingsby, North Yorkshire; Sockburn, Durham; Stinchcombe, Gloucestershire; Strathmartin, Scotland; Walmsgate, Lincolnshire; Wantley, South Yorkshire; Well, North Yorkshire; Wherwell, Hampshire; Whitehorse Hill, Oxfordshire; Winkleigh, Devon; Wiston, Wales; Wormelow Tump, Hereford and Worcester; Wormingford, Essex.

Notes

1. See e.g. 'Behemoth'. *The New Bible Dictionary*. Inter-Varsity Press. London. 1972. p. 138.
2. *ibid*. pp. 729–30. See also Pfeiffer, C.F. 'Lotan and Leviathan'. *Evangelical Quarterly*. XXXII. 1960. pp. 208 ff.
3. Thorpe, Lewis tr. *The History of the Kings of Britain, Geoffrey of Monmouth*. Guild Publishing. London. 1982. pp. 101–2.
4. Jones, G. and Jones, T. [tr.]. *The Mabinogion*. Revis. ed. Everyman's Library. J.M.Dent & Sons Ltd. 1974. pp. 209–212 & 217.
5. See Westwood, J. *Albion*. Granada. London. 1985. pp. 270, 275, 289.

6. Trevelyan, M. 1909. *Folk-Lore and Folk Stories of Wales*. (cit. Simpson, J. *British Dragons*. B.T. Batsford Ltd. London. 1980).
7. Whitlock, R. 1983. *Here Be Dragons*. Allen & Unwin. Boston. pp. 133–4.
8. This chronicle was begun by John de Trokelow and finished by Henry de Blaneford. It was translated and reproduced in the Rolls Series. 1866. IV. ed. H.G. Riley. (cit. Simpson, J. *British Dragons*. B.T. Batsford Ltd. 1980. p. 60).
9. *ibid*. p. 118. See also 'The Fighting Dragons of Little Cornard'. *Folklore, Myths and Legends of Britain*. Reader's Digest. 1973. p. 241.
10. *True and Wonderful: A Discourse Relating a Strange and Monstrous Serpent (or Dragon.#lately discovered, and yet living, to the great Annoyance and divers Slaughters of both Men and Cattell, by his strong and violent Poison: in Sussex, two Miles from Horsham, in a Woode called St Leonard's Forrest, and thirtie Miles from London, this present month of August 1614. With the true Generation of Serpents*. cited in Harleian Miscellany. 1745. III. pp. 106–9. (also cit. Simpson. p. 118).
11. *ibid*. p. 35.
12. *ibid*. p. 21.
13. Gregory, Lady. *Visions and Beliefs in the West of Ireland*. 1920. (repr. 1976). (cit. Simpson. pp. 42–3).
14. See Steiger, B. *Worlds Before Our Own*. W. & J. Mackay Ltd. Chatham (England). 1980. pp. 41–66. (Steiger is by no means a creationist).
15. Caxton, Wm. 1484. *Aesop*. folio 138. The only surviving copy of this book lies in the Royal Library at Windsor Castle. This extract appears here by gracious permission of Her Majesty the Queen.
16. *ibid*. This extract appears here by gracious permission of Her Majesty the Queen.
17. *The Times*. 21st July 1977.
18. 'Flying Dragons at Aberdeen'. *A Statistical Account of Scotland*. 1793. Vol. VI. p. 467.
19. See Morris, W. *Volsungassaga*.
20. Elton's translation cited by Klaeber, p. 259.
21. The Anglo-Saxon text relied on in this study is that of Klaeber. See bibliography.

Chapter 11

Beowulf and the Creatures of Denmark

The *Beowulf* poem survives in a single manuscript copy that was made in ca AD 1000. Moreover, this manuscript[1] is often stated by modern critics to be a copy of a mid-8th century Anglo-Saxon (i.e. Old English) original, now lost. This original is in turn described as an essentially Christian poem. Yet, the continually repeated assertion of the supposedly Christian origins of the poem not only contributes toward a serious misunderstanding of the poem's nature and purpose, but notably fails to take into account the following facts.

Firstly, there are no allusions whatever in the poem to any event, person or teaching of the New Testament. This is in sharp contrast to other Anglo-Saxon poems (The Dream of the Rood, and so on) that certainly are Christian in sentiment. There are definite allusions to certain facts and personages contained in the Old Testament, namely to God, the Creation, to Abel and to Cain, but these are no more than those same historical allusions that are to be met with in the other pre-Christian Anglo-Saxon genealogies and records that we have already studied in chapter 7 of this book. Like those records, and whilst likewise showing a most interesting historical knowledge of certain events and personages that also appear in the Genesis record, the *Beowulf* poem clearly pre-dates any knowledge among the Anglo-Saxons of Christianity *per se*.

In view of this, it is hardly surprising to find that the sentiments of the poem are strongly pagan, extolling the highly questionable virtues of vengeance, the accumulation of plunder and the boasting of and reliance upon human strength and prowess. Allusions are also made to blatantly pagan oaths, sacrifices, sentiments and forms of burial. But there are certainly no exclusively Christian sentiments expressed anywhere in its 3182 lines of text.

Nowhere in the poem is any reference made to the British Isles or to any British (or English) king, personage or historical event. This is simply because this epic poem pre-dates the migration of the Saxons to these isles. And what are we to make of the following passage?:

> '...*fortham* ***Offa*** *waes geofum ond guthum garcene man wide geweorthod wisdome heold ethel sinne thonon* ***Eomer*** *woc haelethum to helpe*...'[2] (Emphases mine)

Which Alexander (see bibliography) translates thus:

> 'So it was that Offa [i.e. king of the continental Angles], brave with the spear, was spoken of abroad for his wars and his gifts; he governed with wisdom the land of his birth. To him was born Eomer, helper of the heroes...'[3]

The Offa who is mentioned here was the pre-migration ancestor of his 8th century namesake, King Offa of Mercia (AD 757–796), whom we have already met (along with this same ancestor), in the early Saxon genealogies. We have also met Eomer in the same genealogies, where his name is rendered Eomaer and where he is, strictly speaking, the grandson, and not the son, of Offa. These ancient genealogies were clearly fresh in the mind of the writer of *Beowulf*, which again tells us something of the times in which the poem was composed.[4]

There is, moreover, no sycophantic dedication of the poem to any Christian Anglo-Saxon English king, not even to that King Offa whose ancestor is immortalised in the poem and under whose auspices some modern scholars suggest the poem was written. Many other scholars would plump for an even later date for the poem, yet the characters in the poem can be historically dated to the late 5th and early 6th centuries, years that long preceded the adoption of Christianity by the Saxons. In other words, the poem belongs very firmly indeed to the pagan times which it describes.

A detailed study of the historical characters contained in the *Beowulf* epic and their relationships to each other, is set out in Appendix 9. But to briefly summarise here, Beowulf, the character in whose honour the poem was written, was no mythical figure. His place is firmly set in history. He was born the son of Ecgtheow in AD 495. At the age of seven, in AD 502, he was brought to the court of Hrethel, his maternal grandfather (AD 445–503) who was then king of the Geatingas, a tribe who inhabited what is today southern Sweden (and whose eponymous founder, Geat, also appears in the early genealogies – see chapter 7). After an unpromising and feckless youth, during which years were fought the Geatish/Swedish wars, in particular the Battle of Ravenswood [**Hrefnawudu**] in the year AD 510, Beowulf undertook his celebrated journey to Denmark, to visit Hrothgar, king of the Danes. This was in AD 515, Beowulf's twentieth year. (This was also the year of his slaying the monster Grendel which we shall examine shortly.) Six years later, in AD 521, Beowulf's uncle, King Hygelac, was slain.

Hygelac himself is known to have lived from AD 475–521, having come to the throne of the Geatingas in AD 503, the year of his father Hrethel's death. He is independently mentioned in Gregory of Tour's *Historiae* **Francorum**, where his name is rendered **Chlochilaichus**.[5]

There, and in other Latin Frankish sources,[6] he is described as a Danish king (**Chogilaicus Danorum rex**), not a Geat, but this is the same mistake that our own English chroniclers made when they included even the Norwegian Vikings under the generic name of Danes. The *Liber Monstrorum*, however, did correctly allude to him as **rex Getarum**, king of the Geats. Saxo also mentions him as the **Hugletus** who destroyed the Swedish chief **Homothus**.

Homothus, in turn, is the same as that Eanmund who is depicted in line 2612 of the *Beowulf* poem. [7]

On Hygelac's death, Beowulf declined the offer to succeed his uncle to the throne of the Geatingas, choosing instead to act as guardian to Hygelac's son, prince Heardred, during the years of Heardred's minority. (Heardred lived from AD 511–533. He was therefore in his tenth year when he became king.) Heardred, however, was killed by the Swedes in AD 533 (for giving shelter to the Swedish king's nephews – see Appendix 9), and it was in this year that Beowulf took over the reins of kingship. Beowulf went on to rule his people in peace for fifty years, dying at some 88 years of age in the year AD 583. The manner of his death, though, is particularly relevant to our study, as we shall see.

But first, we must dispel one particular and erroneous notion that has bedevilled studies in this field for years. Since the poem's rediscovery in the early 18th century (although it was brought to the more general attention of scholars in the year 1815 when it was first printed), scholars have insisted on depicting the creatures in their translations of the poem as **'trolls'**. [8] The monster Grendel, it is said, was a troll. And the older female who was assumed by the Danes to have been his mother, is likewise called by modern translators a troll-wife.

The word **'troll'** is of Nordic origin, and in the fairy-tales of Northern Europe it is supposed to have been a human-like, mischievous and hairy dwarf who swaps troll children for human children in the middle of the night. For good measure, trolls are sometimes depicted as equally mischievous and hairy giants, some of whom lived under bridges or in caves. Which would be all well and good but for the singular observation that the word **'troll'** is entirely absent from the original Anglo-Saxon text of Beowulf! The poem is full of expressions that we would call zoological terms, and these relate to all kinds of creatures, (see Appendix 10). But none of them have anything whatever to do with dwarves, giants, trolls or fairies, mischievous or otherwise. And whilst we are on the subject, the monster Grendel preyed on the Danes for twelve long years (AD 503–515). Are we seriously to believe then that these

Danish Vikings, whose berserker-warriors struck such fear into the hearts of their neighbours, were themselves for twelve long years rendered helpless with terror by a hairy dwarf, even a 'giant' one? For that is what certain of today's mistranslations of the poem would have us believe.

By the time of his slaying the monster Grendel in AD 515, Beowulf himself had already become something of a seasoned hunter of large reptilian monsters. He was renowned amongst the Danes at Hrothgar's court for having cleared the local sea lanes of monstrous animals whose predatory natures had been making life hazardous for the open boats of the Vikings. Fortunately, the Anglo-Saxon poem, written in pure celebration of his heroism, has preserved for us not just the physical descriptions of some of the monsters that Beowulf encountered, but even the names under which certain species of these animals were known to the Saxons and Danes.

However, in order to understand exactly what it is that we are reading when we examine these names, we must appreciate the nature of the Anglo-Saxon language. The Anglo-Saxons (like the modern Germans and Dutch) had a very simple method of word construction, and their names for everyday objects can sometimes sound amusing to our modern English ears when translated literally. A body, for example, was simply a bone-house (**banhus**), and a joint a bone-lock (**banloca**). When Beowulf speaks to his Danish interrogator, he is said quite literally to have unlocked his word-hoard (**wordhord onleoc**). Beowulf's own name means bear, and it is constructed in the following way. The **Beo**-element is the Saxon word for bee, and his name means literally a bee-wolf. The bear has a dog-like face and was seen by those who wisely kept their distance to apparently be eating bees when it raided their hives for honey. So they simply called the bear a bee-wolf. Likewise, the sun was called **woruldcandel**, lit. the world-candle. It was thus an intensely literal but at the same time highly poetic language, possessing great and unambiguous powers of description.

The slaying of Grendel is the most famous of Beowulf's encounters with monsters, of course, and we shall come to look closely at this animal's physical description as it is given in the Beowulf epic. But in Grendel's lair, a large swampy lake, there lived other reptilian species that were collectively known by the Saxons as **wyrmcynnes** (lit. wormkind, a race of monsters and serpents – the word serpent in those days meant something rather more than a snake). Beowulf and his men came across them as they were tracking the female of Grendel's species back to her lair after she had killed and eaten King Hrothgar's minister, Asshere, whose half-eaten head was found on the cliff-top overlooking the lake.

Amongst them were creatures that were known to the Saxons and Danes as giant **saedracan** (sea-drakes or sea-dragons), and these were seen from the cliff-top suddenly swerving through the deep waters of the lake. Perhaps they were aware of the arrival of humans. Other creatures were lying in the sun when Beowulf's men first saw them, but at the sound of the battle-horn they scurried back to the water and slithered beneath the waves.

These other creatures included one species known to the Saxons as a **nicor** (pl. **niceras**), and the word has important connotations for our present study inasmuch as it later developed into **knucker**, a Middle English word for a water-dwelling monster or dragon. The monster at Lyminster in Sussex (see table of previous chapter) was a knucker as were several of the other reported sightings of such creatures in this country. The pool where the Lyminster dragon lived is known to this day as the Knucker's Hole. The Orkney Isles, whose inhabitants, significantly, are Viking, not Scots, likewise have their **Nuckelavee**, as do also the Shetland Islanders. And on the Isle of Man, they have a **Nykir**.

However, amongst the more generally named **wyrmas** (serpents) and **wildeor** (wild beasts) that were present at the lake on this occasion, there was one species in particular that was called an **ythgewinnes**,[9] evidently a surface-swimming monster if its name is anything to go by, rather than a creature that swam at depth like the **saedracan**. Intrigued by it, Beowulf shot an arrow into the creature, and the animal was then harpooned by Beowulf's men using **eoferspreotum**, modified boar-spears. Once the monster was dead, Beowulf and his men then dragged the **ythgewinnes** out of the water and laid its body out for examination. They had, after all, a somewhat professional interest in the animals that they were up against. Moreover, of the monstrous reptiles that they had encountered at the lake, it was said that they were such creatures as would sally out at midmorning time to create havoc amongst the ships in the sealanes, and one particular success of Beowulf's, as we have already seen, was clearing the narrow sea lanes between Denmark and Sweden of certain monsters which he called **merefixa** and **niceras**. Following that operation, the carcases of nine such creatures (**niceras nigene** – Alexander mistakenly translates **nigene** as seven) were laid out on the beaches for display and further inspection.

The last monster to be destroyed by Beowulf (and from which encounter Beowulf also died in the year AD 583) was a flying reptile which lived on a promontory overlooking the sea at Hronesness on the southern coast of Sweden. Now, the Saxons (and presumably the Danes) knew flying reptiles in general as **lyftfloga** (air-fliers), but this particular species of flying reptile, the specimen from Hronesness, was known to them as a **widfloga**, lit. a wide (or far-ranging) flyer, and the description that they have left us fits that of a giant **Pteranodon**. Interestingly, the Saxons also described this creature as a **ligdraca**, or fire-dragon, and he is described as fifty feet in length (or perhaps wing-span?) and about 300 years of age. (Great age is a common feature even among today's non-giant reptiles.) Moreover, and of particular interest to us, the name **widfloga** would have distinguished this particular species of flying reptile from another similar species which was capable of making only short flights. Such a creature is portrayed in Figure 11.1, a shield-boss from the Sutton Hoo burial which shows a flying dragon with its wings folded along its sides. Its long tooth-filled jaws are readily seen, and the shield-boss can be seen to this day in its showcase at the British Museum. Modern palaeontologists, working from fossilised remains, have named such a creature **Pterodactyl**.

But our attention must now be drawn towards another

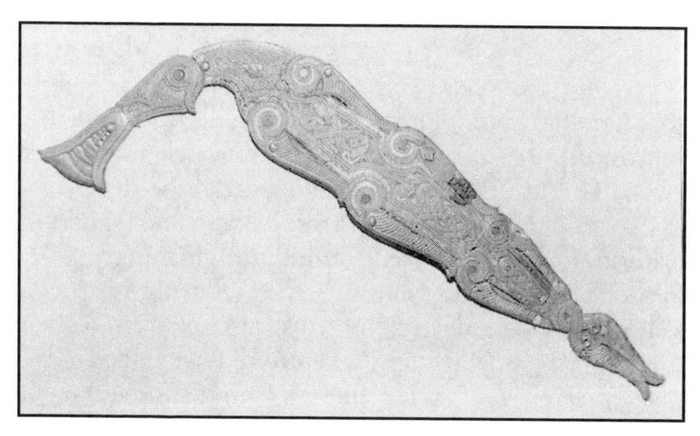

Figure 11.1 The portrayal from a Saxon shield of a flying reptile at rest. Note the wings folded along its sides, as well as the long tooth-filled jaws. Comparison of this with a modern reconstruction of a Pterodactyl or similar creature is most instructive.

reptilian monster which was surely the most fiercesome of all the animals encountered by Beowulf, the monster called Grendel.

It is too often and mistakenly thought that the name Grendel was merely a personal name by which the Danes knew this particular animal. In much the same way as a horse is nicknamed Dobbin, or a dog Fido, this monster, it is assumed, was called Grendel. But, in fact, Grendel was the name that our forebears gave to a particular species of animal. This is evidenced by the fact that in the year AD 931, King Athelstan of Wessex issued a charter in which a certain lake in Wiltshire (England) is called (as in Denmark) a **grendles mere.**[10] The Grendel in *Beowulf*, we note with interest, also lived in a mere. Other place-names mentioned in old charters, **Grindles bec** and **Grendeles pyt**, for example, were likewise places that were (or had been) the habitats of this particular species of animal. Grindelwald, lit. Grendelwood, in Switzerland is another such place. But where does the name Grendel itself come from?

There are several Anglo-Saxon words that share the same root as Grendel. The Old English word **grindan**, for example, and from which we derive our word **grind**, used to denote a destroyer. But the most likely origin of the name is simply the fact that Grendel is an onomatopoeic term derived from the Old Norse **grindill**, meaning a storm or **grenja**, meaning to bellow. The word Grendel is strongly reminiscent of the deep-throated growl that would be emitted by a very large animal and it came into Middle English usage as **grindel**, meaning angry.

To the hapless Danes who were the victims of his predatory raids, however, Grendel was not just an animal. To them he was demon-like, one who was **synnum beswenced** (afflicted with sins). He was **godes ansaca** (God's adversary), the **synscatha** (evil-doer) who was **wonsaeli** (damned), a very **feond on helle** (devil in hell)! He was one of the **grund-wyrgen**, accursed and murderous monsters who were said by the Danes to be descended from Cain himself. And it is descriptions such as these of Grendel's nature that convey something of the horror with which the men of those times anticipated his raids on their homesteads.

But as for Grendel's far more interesting physical description, his habits and the geography of his haunts, they are as follows:

At one point in the poem, Hrothgar, king of the Danes, relates to Beowulf the following information when describing Grendel and one of the monster's companions:

> *'Ic thaet londbuend leode mine seleraedende secgan hyrde thaet hie gesawon swylce twegen micle mearcstapan moras healdan ellorgaestas. Thaera other waes thaes the hie gewislicost gewitan meahton* ***idese onlicnes****, other earm-sceapen on* ***weres waestmum*** *sraeclastas traed naefne he waes mara thonne aenig man other thone on geardagum Grendel nemdon foldbuende...'*[11] (Emphases mine)

...the best translation of which is Alexander's:

> 'I have heard it said by subjects of mine who live in the country, counsellors in this hall, that they have seen such a pair of huge wayfarers haunting the moors,

> otherworldly ones; and one of them, so far as they might make it out, was in woman's shape; but the shape of a man, though twisted, trod also the tracks of exile – save that he was more huge than any human being. The country people have called him from of old by the name of Grendel . . .'[12]

The key words from this passage, and from which we gain important information concerning the physical appearance of Grendel, are **idese onlicnes** when referring to the female monster, and **weres waestmum** when referring to the male. Those Danes who had seen the monsters thought that the female was the older of the two and supposed that she was Grendel's mother. She may have been. But what exactly do the descriptive terms tell us that is of such importance? Simply this: that the female was in the shape of a woman (**idese onlicnes**) and the male was in the shape of a man (**weres waestmum**), 'though twisted'. In other words, they were both **bipedal**, but larger than any human.

Further important detail is added elsewhere in the poem concerning Grendel's appearance, especially when the monster attacked the Danes for what was to prove the last time. In lines 815–8, we are told, in the most graphic detail, how Beowulf inflicted a fatal injury on the monster by holding the creature in an armlock, which he then twisted – **'wrythan'**. line 964). The poem then goes on to tell us that:

> *'Licsar gebad atol aeglaeca him on eaxle wearth syndolh sweotol seonowe onsprungon burston banlocan.'*

Which may be translated thus:

> 'Searing pain seized the terrifying ugly one as a gaping wound appeared in his shoulder. The sinews snapped and the (arm-)joint burst asunder.' (My translation)

For twelve years the Danes had themselves attempted to kill Grendel with conventional weapons, knives, swords, arrows and the like. Yet his impenetrable hide had defied them all, and Grendel was able to attack the Danes with impunity. Beowulf considered all this and decided that the only way to tackle the monster was to get to grips with him at close quarters. The monster's forelimbs, which the Saxons called **eorms** (arms) and which some translate as claws, were small and comparatively puny. They were the monster's one weak spot, and Beowulf went straight for them. He was already renowned for his prodigious strength of grip, and he used this to literally tear off one of Grendel's weak, small arms.

Grendel, however, is also described, in line 2079 of the poem, as a **muthbona**, i.e. one who slays with his mouth or jaws, and the speed with which he was able to devour his human prey tells us something of the size of his jaws and teeth (he swallowed the body of one of his victims in large 'gobbets'). Yet, it is the very size of Grendel's jaws which paradoxically would have aided Beowulf in his carefully thought out strategy of going for the forelimbs, because pushing himself hard into the animals chest between those forelimbs would have placed Beowulf tightly underneath those jaws and would thus have sheltered him from Grendel's terrible teeth.

We are told that as soon as Beowulf gripped the monsters claws (and we must remember that Grendel was only a youngster, and not by all accounts a fully mature adult male of his species), the startled animal tried to pull away instead of attacking Beowulf. The animal instinctively knew the danger he was now in and he wanted to escape the clutches of the man who now posed such an unexpected threat and who was inflicting such alarming pain. However, it was this action of trying to pull away that left Grendel wide open to Beowulf's strategy. Thus, Beowulf was able in the ensuing struggle eventually to wrench off one of the animal's arms as so graphically described in the poem. As a result of this appalling injury, the young Grendel returned to his lair and simply bled to death.

But is Beowulf's method of slaying Grendel unknown elsewhere in the historical record? Are there no depictions to

Figure 11.2 Was Beowulf's method of mortally wounding Grendel entirely novel, or was he merely employing a tried and tested strategy? This illustration is from an early Babylonian cylinder seal, and it portrays a man seizing and about to amputate the forelimb of a Grendel-like bipedal monster.

be found of similar creatures being killed in a similar way? It would seem that there are, the illustration below being one example (see Figure 11.2). It is taken from an impression of an early Babylonian cylinder seal now in the British Museum, and clearly shows a man about to amputate the forelimb of a bipedal monster whose appearance, though stylistic, fits the descriptions of Grendel very closely. I know of no scholar who would venture to suggest that the Old English author of *Beowulf* filched his idea from his knowledge of Babylonian cylinder seals. So we may, I think, safely assume that Beowulf's method of slaying this particular kind of animal was not entirely unknown in the ancient world. Nor, indeed, was the Grendel itself entirely unknown in the ancient world, as is evident from the following item depicted in Figure 11.3.

Here we are presented with a truly remarkable scene. The stone in which these strange animals are carved, is preserved in the church of SS. Mary and Hardulph at Breedon-on-the-Hill in Leicestershire. This church used to belong to the Saxon kingdom of Mercia. The stone itself is part of a larger frieze in which are depicted various birds and humans, all of them readily recognisable. But what are these strange creatures represented here? They are like nothing that survives today

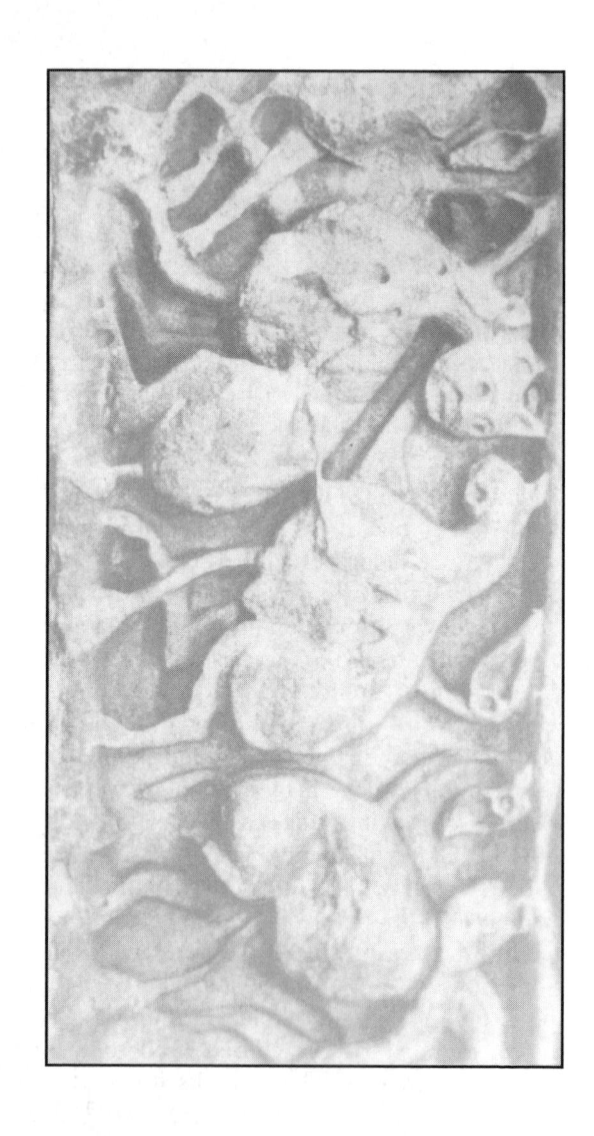

Figure 11.3 A most graphic portrayal from Saxon times of an attack on a herd of long-necked quadrupeds by a bipedal predator. Note the predator's two large legs and puny forelimbs. This portrayal conforms very closely indeed to the description of Grendel, and is a clear indication that such creatures were to be seen on the British mainland as well as the Continent, as is also shown by Athelstan's and other charters. The stone can be seen inside the church of SS. Mary and Hardulph at Breedon-on-the-Hill in Leicestershire.

in England, yet they are depicted as vividly as the other creatures. There are long-necked quadrupeds, one of whom on the right seems to be biting (or 'necking' with) another. And in the middle of the scene appears a bipedal animal who is clearly attacking one of the quadrupeds. He stands on two great hindlegs and has two smaller forelimbs, and carries what appears to be armour plating on his back. His victim seems to be turning to defend himself, but with his hindlegs buckled in fear.

Now it cannot be pretended that these are merely caricatures of ordinary animals that are indigenous (these days) to the British Isles, for none of our present native species have long necks or are bipedal. So how are we to satisfactorily account for them? Is there a predatory animal from the fossil record known to us, who had two massive hindlegs and two comparatively puny forelimbs? There is indeed. In fact there are several such species, but how was our Saxon artist to know about such creatures if he'd never seen one? Are we looking here at a depiction in stone of the creature known to the Saxons and Danes as Grendel? Considering the close physical descriptions that we find in *Beowulf*, it would seem that we are.

The *Beowulf* epic tells us that as for his haunts and habits, Grendel hunted alone, being known by the understandably frightened locals who sometimes saw his moonlit shape coming down from the mist-laden fens as the **atol angengea**, the terrifying solitary one. He was a **mearcstapa** (lit. a marsh-stepper), one who stalked the marshes or outlying regions, ('haunting the moors', as Alexander so powerfully renders it). He hunted by night, approaching human settlements and waiting silently in the darkness for his prey to fall asleep before he descended on them as a **sceadugenga** (lit. a shadow-goer, a nightwalker). Gliding silently along the **fenhlith** (the waste and desolate tract of the marshes), he would emerge from the dense black of night as the **deathscua** (death's shadow). The Danes employed an **eotanweard** (lit. a giant-ward, a watcher for monsters), to warn of Grendel's approach, but often in vain. For so silent was Grendel's approach when he was hunting in the darkness of the night that sometimes the **eotanweard** himself was surprised and eaten. On one particular and long-remembered night, no less than thirty Danish warriors were killed by Grendel. Little wonder then that Beowulf was rewarded so richly and was so famed for having slain him.

In all, a comprehensive and somewhat horrifying picture of Grendel emerges from the pages of Beowulf, and I doubt that the reader needs to be guided by me as to which particular species of predatory dinosaur the details of his physical description fit best. Modern commentators who have been brought up on evolutionary ideas are compelled to suggest that monsters like Grendel are primitive personifications of death or disease, and other such nonsense. (It had even once been suggested that he was a personification of the North Sea!) But really, the evidence will not support such claims. One modern and refreshingly honest publication on the poem makes a far more telling comment:

> 'In spite of allusions to the devil and abstract concepts of evil, the monsters are very tangible creatures in *Beowulf*. They have no supernatural tricks, other than exceptional strength, and they are vulnerable and mortal. The early medieval audience would have accepted these monsters as monsters, not as symbols of plague or war, for such creatures were a definite reality.'[13]

Notes

1. Brit. Mus. Cotton. Vitellius. A. XV.
2. lines 1957–61 (Klaeber).
3. Alexander, M. *Beowulf*. Penguin Classics. Harmondsworth. pp.112–3.
4. Which incidentally verifies the pre-Christian origins of the Mercian, and therefore other pedigrees, proving that the early Saxon genealogies were in existence before the Saxons migrated to England.

5. *Historiae Francorum*. Book III. chap. 3. See Thorpe, Lewis tr. *Gregory of Tours: The History of the Franks*. Penguin Classics. Harmondsworth. 1974. p. 163.
6. cit. Klaeber. p. xli.
7. *ibid.*
8. This is the one flaw that mars Michael Alexander's otherwise excellent translation of *Beowulf*. Surprisingly, Klaeber also makes the same error, having actually edited the original text of the poem.
9. **Ythgewinnes**. lit. a wave-thrasher. Its surface-swimming nature would explain the ease with which the creature was harpooned from the shore of the mere. It is also probably the **ythgewinnes** whose likeness was portrayed so often on the prow of Viking ships. Rather than being merely a superstitious emblem, perhaps that likeness had the very practical purpose of deterring other wave-thrashers from attacking the vessel.
10. *Cartularium Saxonicum*. (W. de Gray Birch ed.). ii. 363 ff. (cit. also by Klaeber. p. xxiv).
11. *Beowulf*. lines 1345–1355 (Klaeber).
12. Alexander. p. 93.
13. Longman Literature Guides. (York Notes Series). *Beowulf*. p. 65.

Chapter 12

Conclusion

It is astonishing how much information comes to the surface once a document has been released from the veil of obscurity that modernism has thrown over it. Who would believe, when reading a modernist commentary on the book of Genesis, that so much evidence was available to prove, not its falsity, but its authenticity? Not its mythical nature, but its truth and astonishing historical accuracy? Who would believe, when reading a modern evolutionary book on dinosaurs, that so many records were available to demonstrate that these creatures did not die out millions of years before man came along, as the evolutionary scheme of things would have it, but have lived alongside man who recorded their activities and physical appearance in records both ancient and modern? And who would have believed, when reading a modern history book on the ancient world, that so many peoples from such diverse cultures actually recorded their own descent from the patriarchs of Genesis long before they could have heard of the Bible or have been taught any of its contents? And who would have believed that the creation/evolution controversy was such an ancient debate? It is a sobering matter, and one which presents us with a picture of our past that is quite unlike that which we are used to seeing.

It must certainly give us pause, and in the light of it all, we should surely now consider adopting a more reasonable and constructive approach to the study of the early history of mankind, and of the Genesis record in particular. Some, no doubt, will be quick to decry such an acceptance of the truth of the biblical record as an act of blind faith. But where does blind faith come into it when that record is so fully endorsed by the writings of so many disinterested, not to say antagonistic, witnesses, many of whose voices we have listened to both in the preceding chapters and the appendices which follow? When we read a book about king Henry VIII of England, we are not learning about him by way of blind faith, for we know that there are many independent sources to which we can go in order to verify what we have read. Rather, we believe the historical accounts of Henry VIII by way of informed reason, not faith. And exactly the same thing applies when we read the history that is contained in the book of Genesis and other parts of the Bible. We accept that history as well because, in the face of so many disinterested witnesses and corroborative statements, that is simply the reasonable thing to do. To discard such a vast weight of independent testimony would be most unreasonable, and would itself be a most irrational act of faith in the approach and highly questionable tenets of modernistic philosophy.

Thus it is by our accepting the overwhelming testimony of so many witnesses that we come to accept the Genesis record as a truly factual and historical account, surely a most reasonable approach. And if this leads us on to a saving faith in the God of Whom Genesis so eloquently testifies, then that faith too is seen to be a reasonable and informed faith, whatever our critics might think.

The student who has read thus far and would like to pursue some or all of the matters raised in this book, will find in the following appendices a great deal of information and source-material that should point him or her in the right direction. The casual reader also will find much of interest there which will expand his or her thought with profit. And on that note, I shall now leave the reader to either browse or burrow, hopeful that this book has shed a little light at least on a vast and complex subject, the early history of mankind. Most of all, though, I hope that when the Christian reader turns once more to the pages of Genesis, then he or she will do so with the added confidence that its contents are factual and accurate and that they have every sound reason for believing it, whatever modern biblical commentators might tell them to the contrary.

Those who have been stimulated by what they have read in this book, and who would like to join the Creation Science Movement in its work of restoring to beleaguered Christians the world over a confidence in the Bible's historical and scientific accuracy, may like to read carefully the following chapter which will tell them all about our work and aims. We are the oldest creationist organisation in the world and our workload is increasing all the time. But we cannot work alone.

The CSM needs *you*.

Chapter 13

What the CSM is all about

The **Creation Science Movement** started in 1932 protesting about the influence of Darwin's theory of evolution; in fact it was called the Evolution Protest Movement in those days.

The prime movers were Mr Douglas Dewar, barrister and Auditor General of the Indian Civil Service, and Captain Bernard Acworth, DSO who developed the asdic sonar device (Who's Who). They called the first Creationist meeting (EPM) at 21 Essex Gardens, The Strand, London, in 1932. The first public meeting was reported in *The Times* on February 12, 1935. Sir Ambrose Fleming presided and what he said then still stands for what the Creation Science Movement believes in today. He declared that

> 'of late years the Darwinian anthropology had been forced on public attention by numerous books ... in such a fashion as to create a belief that it was a certainly settled scientific truth. The fact that many eminent naturalists did not agree that Darwin's theory of species production had been sufficiently established as a truth was generally repressed. If there had been no creation, there was no need to assume any Creator; the chief basis for all religion was taken away and morality reduced to mere human expediency. It had seemed to a large number of thoughtful persons that it was of national importance to ... counteract the effects of reckless and

> indiscriminate popularisation of the theory of the wholly animal origin of mankind, especially among the young, by the diffusion of a truly scientific ... cause for all those altruistic, aesthetic, intellectual, spiritual and religious faculties ... in man, of which not the very slightest trace was seen in the animal species ... they desired to oppose a one-sided materialistic presentation of human origin which rejected altogether any suggestion of creation ... They said that the arguments of the Darwinian anthropologists were defective in logic and did not give the proof they assumed.'

This was reported over half a century ago! Today society witnesses to the effect of atheistic humanism which belief in the theory of evolution has brought – fragmented family units, abortion, child abuse etc. In fact in all these intervening years the evidence has mounted up arguing that of course a Creator must have made this planet Earth and the heavens. There is a wealth of further scientific evidence supporting Creation which these eminent men in the early 1930s did not then know. Advances in our knowledge of genetics, biochemistry and information theory are just some areas where progress in the last sixty years has made belief in evolution even less logical.

The sense of high purpose expressed in *The Times* account is still what motivates CSM today. We are concerned that people today are rarely confronted with a straight-forward reading of the Bible starting at Genesis chapter one. In fact most people have been told that they cannot trust the beginning of God's Word. They rehearse Satan's own words, 'Hath God said?'. CSM declares that the doctrine of original sin is not based on myth or fable but rather on the solid foundation of the 'lively oracles' of the Lord God. A blurring of this truth affects the wonder of the Atonement by the peerless Son of God which in turn can lead to a shallow commitment to Him. CSM ringingly declares that the beginning of God's Word may be trusted as well as all that follows.

What else does CSM do? A pamphlet on different subjects giving evidence of Creation is published every other month together with the *Creation Journal* which carries up-to-the-minute news and comment. These pamphlets form an information resource on the Creation/evolution issue. One of our pamphlets shows how Creation is the foundation of the Gospel (249) while others trace Creation in Genesis (260) and Isaiah (243). Others are critical of aspects of evolution theory such as alleged vestigial organs (258) and supposed intermediate forms such as Archaeopteryx (76) and ape-men (151, 234). Many pamphlets consider particular creatures and show how they could not possibly have evolved. These include whales (114) where the design of the mouth of the young whale fitting into the mother enables it to be suckled while at sea. The Bombardier Beetle (233) had to have a perfectly functioning explosive defence or it would have blown itself up! The Palisade moth (248), birds' feathers (255), bats' sonar systems (247), the bee's informative dance (264), and butterflies' metamorphoses (257) could not have evolved. Other pamphlets consider the so-called chemical evolution of life (267). Evidence is cited that the universe is only thousands of years old (265). Measurements of salinity of the oceans (221) show they are young. The eruption of Mount St. Helens (252) in 1980 produced sediments which evolutionary geologists would normally interpret as taking very long periods of time to form. Three distinct lines of experimental evidence from scientists of repute in Australia, America and Russia strongly suggest that the speed at which light travels has diminished with time (262, 256). This affects the radiometric dating of rocks (207) and the time taken for light to reach us from distant galaxies. It indicates that the universe is less than 10,000 years old. Scientific observations support the genealogies (219) in the Bible, a book of amazingly accurate science (254), that life was created and did not evolve and that Adam was created in the beginning.

CSM provides able speakers on Creation who major on the scientific evidence which is increasingly weighty. Today many eminent scientists who do not even argue from the Christian standpoint, find this evidence against the theory of evolution sufficient to convince them that there is no evolution at all.

This evidence is ignored in school textbooks and TV nature programmes. CSM lecturers regularly address universities, colleges, sixth forms and Church groups throughout the UK. In the 1960s our Creationist speakers toured the Far East, Australia, New Zealand and North America, while in the 1990s we are beginning to meet the need in Eastern Europe.

CSM has charitable status (Charity no: 801745). We are members of the Evangelical Alliance. May we admit that we need you as a member? The hard-nosed humanism of evolutionism has become entrenched in the British educational system and in society at large. We need your dedicated support to topple it! Your subscription will help; and if you could arrange a meeting as well, even better!

At heart CSM wishes to give glory to the Lord Jesus Christ who created man in the image of the Tri-une God and then stooped to redeem us.

The address of the CSM is:

Creation Science Movement
50 Brecon Avenue
Cosham, Portsmouth
PO6 2AW
England

APPENDICES

Note on Appendices 1, 2 and 3

It would be pointless giving references to the following historical notices that are either obscure or difficult to get hold of (and there are plenty of them). Therefore I have given sources that are within the easy reach of anyone whose interest in the subject will prompt them to investigate further any or all of the names given here. Four main sources are given, namely:

1. *The Interpreter's Dictionary of the Bible*. Four volumes with Supplementary. Abingdon Press. New York. 1962.
2. *The New Bible Dictionary*. Inter-varsity Press. London. 1972.
3. Josephus. *The Antiquities of the Jews*. Translated by William Whiston.
4. Poole, Matthew. *Commentary on the Holy Bible*. Three vols. (1685). Facsimile published by Banner of Truth Trust. London. 1962.

Reference 1 is abbreviated and followed by volume number and page thus: IDB 3:247.

Reference 2 is simply abbreviated NBD followed by page number.

Reference 3, due to the many varied editions of Josephus's *Antiquities*, is abbreviated followed by book number, chapter number and paragraph number thus: JA 1.vi.2.

Reference 4 is abbreviated and followed by volume and page number thus: P 1:26.

All, with the exception of Josephus, provide valuable reference material of their own for their sources. Josephus is valuable because he has preserved many of the names and spellings by which the names contained in the Table of Nations were known to the classical world.

Appendix 1

The Nations of Shem

1. ***Shem:*** The father of all the Semitic nations.
(Refs: IDB 4:321. NBD 1175. JA 1.vi.4. P 1:28)

2. ***Elam:*** The founder of the Elamites, who were known to the Babylonians as the **Elamtu**, to the Greeks as **Elymais**, and whom the Romans knew as the **Elymaei**. The Elamites recorded their own name as the **Haltamti**. Subsequently, in the Old Persian inscriptions their name is rendered **(h)uju**, and **huz** in the Middle Persian, which is the archaic form of the modern Persian name of **Khuzistan**, which now covers what used to be the land of Elam (see Map 2).
(Refs: IDB 2:70. NBD 355–6. JA 1.vi.3. P 1:28)

3. ***Asshur:*** The founder of the nation to whom he gave his name, Assyria. It may be possible to identify Asshur in the early king-lists of Assyria as Puzur Asshur I. According to these lists, Puzur Asshur I would have lived and reigned ca 1960 BC, which accords rather well with the biblical chronology. Asshur was one of the earliest men to be deified and worshipped by his descendants. Indeed, as long as Assyria lasted, that is until 612 BC, accounts of battles, diplomatic affairs and foreign bulletins were daily read out to his image; and every Assyrian king held that he wore the crown only with the express permission of Asshur's deified ghost (see Map 2).
(Refs: IDB 1:261. NBD 'Assyria' 100–7. JA 1.vi.3. P 1:27)

Appendix 1

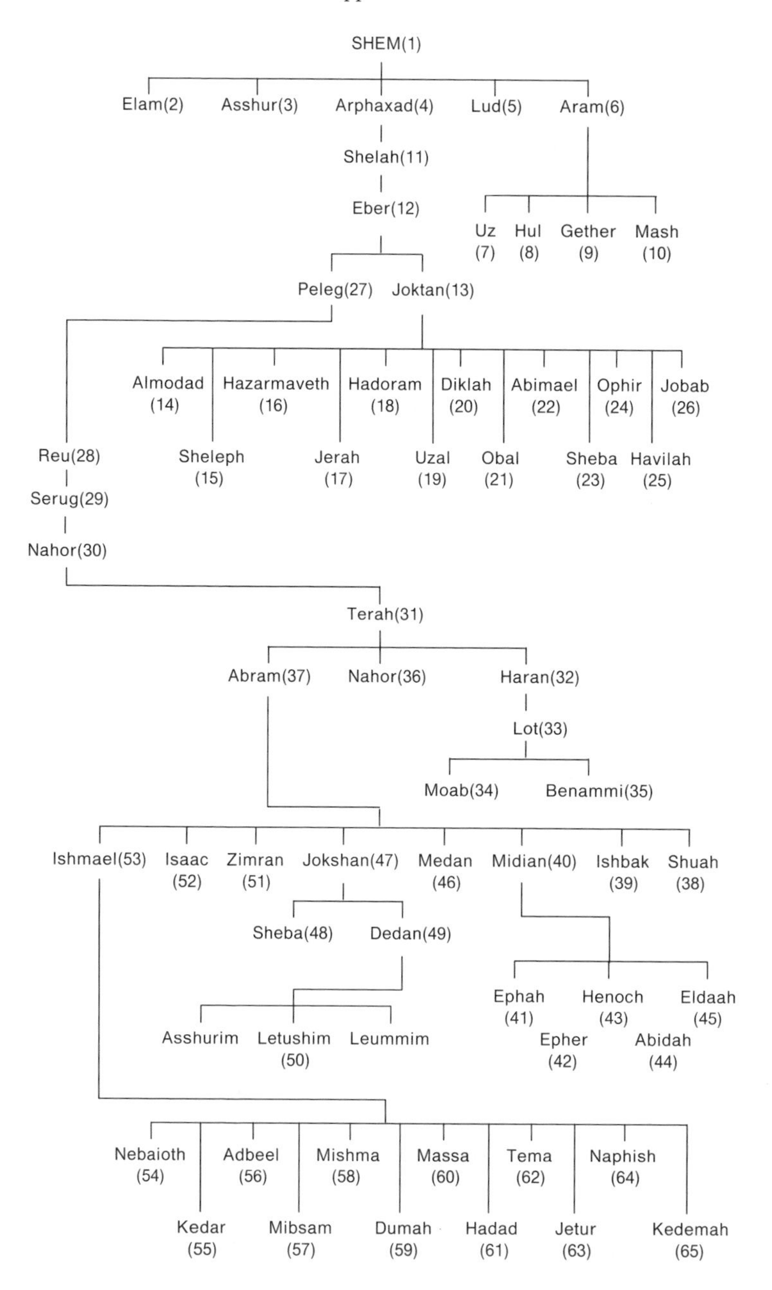

SHEM(1)
Elam(2)
Asshur(3)
Arphaxad(4)
Lud(5)
Aram(6)
Shelah(11)
Eber(12)
Uz (7)
Hul (8)
Gether (9)
Mash (10)
Peleg(27)
Joktan(13)
Almodad (14)
Hazarmaveth (16)
Hadoram (18)
Diklah (20)
Abimael (22)
Ophir (24)
Jobab (26)
Reu(28)
Sheleph (15)
Jerah (17)
Uzal (19)
Obal (21)
Sheba (23)
Havilah (25)
Serug(29)
Nahor(30)
Terah(31)
Abram(37)
Nahor(36)
Haran(32)
Lot(33)
Moab(34)
Benammi(35)
Ishmael(53)
Isaac (52)
Zimran (51)
Jokshan(47)
Medan (46)
Midian(40)
Ishbak (39)
Shuah (38)
Sheba(48)
Dedan(49)
Ephah (41)
Henoch (43)
Eldaah (45)
Epher (42)
Abidah (44)
Asshurim
Letushim (50)
Leummim
Nebaioth (54)
Adbeel (56)
Mishma (58)
Massa (60)
Tema (62)
Naphish (64)
Kedar (55)
Mibsam (57)
Dumah (59)
Hadad (61)
Jetur (63)
Kedemah (65)

4. ***Arphaxad:*** He was the progenitor of the Chaldeans, his name, apparently, corresponding to that of **arp-keshed**, the border marches of Chaldea. That he was indeed the forebear of the Chaldeans is confirmed by the Hurrian (Nuzi) tablets, which render the name as **Arip-hurra** – the founder of Chaldea. The name was also known to the Akkadians as **Arraphu**. Some scholars have endeavoured to treat his name as a derivative of the Assyrian phrase **arba-kishshatu**, meaning the four corners of the world. The Assyrians knew his descendants as the **Kaldu**, who were adept astrologers, magicians and mathematicians. Ptolemy recorded the name of their land as **Arrapichitis**, whilst it was known to others as **Arphaxitis**. Their very earliest settlement, however, would appear to be what is today a 2½ acre ruin that still bears the name **Arpachiya**. It lies some four miles to the east of ancient Nineveh, and is the remains of a very early farming community (see Map 2). (Refs: IDB 1:231. NBD 86. JA 1.vi.3. P1:28)

5. ***Lud:*** The early descendants of Lud, the **Ludim**, were known to both the Assyrians and Babylonians as the **Ludu**. Josephus tells us that their land was later known as **Lydia** (a direct Greek derivation of the name Lud) which lay in western Asia Minor. (Josephus rendered the name **Laud**.) The Lydians were famed in the old world for the skill of their archers. They spoke an Indo-European (Japhetic) language, examples of which are to be found on certain Egyptian monuments. The land of Lydia was finally conquered by Cyrus, king of Persia, in the year 546 BC (see Map 4).
(Refs: IDB 3:178–9. NBD 755. JA 1.vi.3. P1:28)

6. ***Aram:*** He was the founder of the Aramaeans, known to the Akkadians as the **Aramu**, but who were later known to the Greeks as the **Syrians** (from Serug? see 29). In an Assyrian inscription of Tiglath-pileser I, from ca 1100 BC, the Aramaeans are depicted as living to the east of the river Tigris. By the time of Tiglath-pileser III, however, some 400 years later, they were living all over Mesopotamia. After this they settled to the west, occupying roughly the same area that makes up modern Syria. A clay tablet from Ur bears the name

of **Aramu**, and it is of interest to note that Aramaic is still spoken today (see Map 2).
(Refs: IDB 1:185. NBD 55–9. JA 1.vi.3. P 1:28)

7. ***Uz:*** There is still considerable disagreement as to the precise area in which the descendants of Uz settled, and given the somewhat nomadic nature of the Aramaeans (Aram was the father of Uz), this is hardly surprising. Northern Arabia, between Babylon and Edom, seems the most likely area of settlement (see Map 2). (Josephus, probably correctly, identifies it as the classical **Trachonitis.**)
(Refs: IDB 4:741. NBD 1306–7. JA 1.vi.4. P1:28)

8. ***Hul:*** His descendants settled to the north of the sea of Galilee, where they gave their name to the lake and vale of **Huleh** (the biblical **Waters of Merom**, which were known to Josephus as **Ul**). The place was notorious amongst Victorian explorers of Palestine for its tribes of Bedhouin robbers, and its far from healthy marshes and swamps which today have been drained, the reclaimed land being farmed and settled. The modern Israelis have also set up a nature reserve there, and know the place under its ancient name of the vale of **Hula.** The lake of Hula is formed by the accumulation of water from the two sources of the Jordan before beginning their descent to Galilee (see Map 4). (Refs: IDB 2:658. JA 1.vi.3. P 1:28)

9. ***Gether:*** His descendants (known to Josephus as **Gather**) settled to the south of Damascus. Josephus identifies them as the latter-day **Bactrians**, famous amongst other things for a breed of camel. Whether this identification is correct or not cannot now be determined. It should, however, be noted that Bactria was populated by Aryan, or Japhetic, tribes in late Assyrian times, whereas the children of Gether were, of course, Semites (see Map 4). (Refs: IDB 2:387. JA 1.vi.3. P 1:28)

10. ***Mash:*** The Akkadians rendered the name **Mashu**, which in turn was known to the Egyptians as **Msh'r.** It was also rendered **Mishal**, all of which names referred to a people that dwelt in Lebanon (see Map 4). However, in 1 Chronicles 1:17, the name is rendered **Meshech**, and this should not be

confused with the Japhetic Meshech. Such confusion arises in Josephus and later in the 9th century historian Nennius (see chapter 4). (Refs: IDB 3:294. P 1:28)

11. ***Shelah:*** I have not yet been able to find his name in secular sources, although Josephus renders the name **Sala.**
(Refs: IDB 4:319. NBD 1175. JA 1.vi.4)

12. ***Eber:*** Known to Josephus as **Heber**, he gave his name to the Hebrew race. Some have tried to identify him with **Ebru**, erstwhile king of Ebla, but this is unlikely on both chronological and ethnic grounds. The attempt to identify the children of Eber with the **Habiru** of the Egyptian chronicles may also be somewhat forced, although it is fair to add that, although we tend today to think only of the Jewish nation as Hebrews, in fact all of Eber's descendants, technically speaking, would have been Hebrew also, the Joktanite Arabs included.
(Refs: IDB 2:5. NBD 331. JA 1.vi.3 and 5. P 1:28)

13. ***Joktan:*** The progenitor of no less than thirteen southern Arabian tribes, he is remembered amongst modern Arabs as **Yaqtan**. Only the purest Arabs, it is still maintained, are those Semitic Arabs descended from Joktan; whilst Hamitic Arabs are referred to somewhat disdainfully as Musta 'rabs, pretended Arabs. Joktan's name is preserved in that of the ancient town of **Jectan** near present-day Mecca (see Map 2). Josephus knew him as **Joctan.**
(Refs: IDB 2:963–4. NBD 652. JA 1.vi.3. P 1:28)

14. ***Almodad:*** Young gives Almodad's name as meaning 'The Agitator', which, if correct, hides what is no doubt a most interesting background. The name is certainly Arabic, his descendants being known to early Arab historians as the **al-Morad** tribe, who are seemingly to be identified with the **Gebonites** (the name is rendered **Elmodad** in Josephus). Their precise area of settlement cannot now be determined (see Map 2). (Refs: IDB 1:86. JA 1.vi.3. P 1:28)

15. ***Sheleph:*** Rendered **Saleph** in Josephus, the name is that of a southern Arabian tribe who were known to the pre-Islamic

Arabs as the **Salif**. They were a Yemeni tribe whose capital, **Sulaf**, lay some sixty miles due north of present-day San'a (see 19 and Map 2). (Refs: IDB 4:320. JA 1.vi.4. P 1:28)

16. ***Hazarmaveth:*** Known as **Asermoth** in Josephus, his descendants populated the 200 mile long valley that runs parallel to the southern coast of Arabia. It is known to this day as the **Hadramaut**, a direct transposition into Arabic of the name Hazarmaveth. In pre-Islamic inscriptions, the name is variously rendered **hdrmt** and **hdrmwt**. Strabo tells us that the tribe of Hazarmaveth was one of the four main tribes of Arabs in his day. The name seems to mean *'town of death'* – Hadramaut means the same in Arabic – although we can now only ponder the possible tragedy that lies behind it (see Map 2). (Refs: IDB 2:539. NBD 507. JA 1.vi.3. P 1:28)

17. ***Jerah:*** There lies, on the shores of Galilee, a ruined mound that is named **Beth-Yerah**, the house of Jerah, although this may not refer to the subject here. It is more likely that his descendants migrated into the southern regions of Arabia. Indeed, the Arab city that bore Jerah's name, and which was rendered by Ptolemy as **Jerakon Kome**, lay on the Mara coast close to the Hadramaut (see 16 and Map 2). The name appears as **Jera** in Josephus and as **Yarki** in the inscriptions of Ashurbanipal.
(Refs: IDB 2:821–2. NBD 605–6. JA 1.vi.3. P 1:28)

18. ***Hadoram:*** Rendered **Adoram** in Josephus, it is that of a southern Arabian tribe, the name of whose town appears as **Hurarina (Haroram)** in the inscriptions of Ashurbanipal. It lay close to Yarki (see 17).
(Refs: IDB 2:508. NBD 500. JA 1.vi.3. P 1:27)

19. ***Uzal:*** Arab historians render the name of Uzal as **Azal** (Josephus gives **Aizel**), and it is the ancient, pre-Islamic name for the city of **San'a**, the modern capital of the Yemen (see 15). Uzal's descendants are still doubtless thriving in the area. The Assyrians knew the tribe of Uzal as the **Azalla** (see Map 2).
(Refs: IDB 4:741. NBD 1307. JA 1.vi.4. P 1:28)

20. ***Diklah:*** The name Diklah appears in Akkadian records as **Diklat**, the Aramaeans knew it as **Diklath**, and the Assyrians gave it as **Idiklat**, all of which transpose into Greek as **Tigris**, the name of the valley and river that cuts through Mesopotamia. (Josephus renders it **Decla**). This would give a clear indication as their place of settlement, either north of the Persian Gulf or at least in the north-east extremity of the Arabian peninsula (see Map 2). Procopius gives it as **Phoinikon**, which lay at the southern end of the Wadi Sirhan.
(Refs: IDB 1:843. JA 1.vi.4. P 1:29)

21. ***Obal:*** A southern Arabian tribe whose name was rendered by Arab historians as **Ebal**. (Josephus has the same rendering). Ancient inscriptions from the Yemen give it as **Abil**, which elsewhere appears as **Ubal**. According to these sources the location of this tribe's place of settlement lies between the ancient Yemeni cities of Hadeida and San'a (see 19 and Map 2).
(Refs: IDB 3:579. NBD 'Ebal' 330. JA 1.vi.4. P 1:29)

22. ***Abimael:*** His descendants settled in southern Arabia, where their existence is known from ancient Sabean inscriptions (see Map 2). (Refs: IDB 1:9. JA 1.vi.4. P 1:29)

23. ***Sheba:*** There are no less than three Shebas in the Table of Nations (see 48 and Ham 7)! Due to the presence in Arabia of both the Cushite and Jokshanite tribes of Sheba, it is impossible to determine where this particular patriarch's descendants settled. Josephus may give a clue in rendering the name as **Sabeus**.
(Refs: IDB 4:311–2. NBD 1171. JA 1.vi.4. P 1:27)

24. ***Ophir:*** Its existence being duly noted in the pre-Islamic Arabian inscriptions, this tribe's area of settlement is given by them as lying between Saba in the Yemen and Hawlan (or Havilah, see 25). The name has been preserved in that of the coastal town of **Ma'afir** in south-west Arabia (see Map 2).
(Refs: IDB 3:605–6. NBD 911. JA 1.vi.4. P 1:29)

25. ***Havilah:*** There were two Arabian tribes known under the name of Havilah. The first was of Hamitic descent (see Ham 4), which settled in the eastern regions of the Arabian peninsula. Their land was known to Arabian cosmographers as **Hawlan**. Kautsch identifies them as the **Huwailah**, a people who settled on the Arabian shore of the Persian Gulf. The Semitic tribe, however, with whom we are dealing here, remained distinct, and occupied areas on the opposite side of the peninsula. In Strabo's day, they were still occupying areas of northern Arabia, their name being recorded by him as the **Khaulotaei**. Josephus knew them as the **Euilat**. The Arabian cosmographer, Yakut, informs us that their dialect, **Hawil**, was spoken by *'the descendants of Midian, the son of Abraham'*. This Semitic tribe of Havilah also occupied the southernmost tip of the Arabian peninsula, crossing from there the Bab-el-Mandeb to the African coast. Here, both Ptolemy and Pliny refer to their city of **Aualis** on the Red Sea coast of Africa, which lay next to the modern state of Djibouti. This city (Aualis) is known today as **Zeila** (see Map 2).

(Refs: IDB 2:537. NBD 506. JA 1.vi.4. P 1:29)

26. ***Jobab:*** Jobab's descendants were known to the Akkadians as the **Iabibi**. They settled in the town that has long borne their founder's name, **Juhaibab**, which, according to Sabean inscriptions, lay close to modern Mecca (see Map 2).

(Refs: IDB 2:925. NBD 637. JA 1.vi.4. P 1:29)

27. ***Peleg:*** Genesis tells us that in his day the earth was divided. The meaning of his name, as rendered in Hebrew, corresponds exactly with the Akkadian noun **pulukku**, which means a dividing up of territory by means of boundaries and borders (the Akkadian verb for 'to divide' is **palaku**). Likewise, the Assyrian word, **palgu**, referes to the dividing up of land by canals and irrigation systems. It is in this sense that the Hebrew word **peleg** is used in Job 29:6 and 38:5. The man named Peleg, (whose name appears as **Phaleg** in Josephus), was so named, however, after the division and scattering of the nations from Babel. In fact, one of the ancient names of Babylon (Babel) is nowadays translated as *'the place of canals'*,

though surely a better translation would be *'the place of division'*, or even the place of Peleg. There is an ancient city that bore the name of Peleg, however, the Akkadian town of **Phalgu**, whose ruins lie at the junction of the Euphrates and Chaboras rivers (Chebar. see Ezekiel 1:1). Of further interest to us is the fact that the division of the nations is recorded in Genesis as occurring in the fifth generation after the Flood. We will encounter striking confirmation of this when we study the descent of certain European kings later.

(Refs: IDB 3:709. NBD 957. JA 1.vi.4. P 1:28)

28. ***Reu:*** This name appears as a personal name in Akkadian records where it is rendered **Ra'u**. The early Greeks knew it as **Ragau**, as did Josephus. Reu was to give his name to an island in the Euphrates that lies just below the city of Anat, and which the Akkadians knew as **Ra'ilu**. It was known to the Greeks as **Ragu** (see Map 2).

(Refs: IDB 4:53. JA 1.vi.5. P 1:30)

29. ***Serug:*** He gave his name to the city and district that was known to the Akkadians as **Sarugi**. This lay to the west of Haran (see 32). It is normally assumed that the name of the land of Syria came about because the Greeks confused it with Assyria. But surely it is more likely that Syria is merely a transposition into Greek of the patriarchal name of Serug who, after all, settled in that part of the world (see Map 2).

(Refs: IDB 4:291. JA 1.vi.5. P 1:30)

30. ***Nahor:*** There seems to be no secular record that mentions him as an individual (but see 36).

(Refs: IDB 3:497. NBD 860. JA 1.vi.5. P 1:30)

31. ***Terah:*** The father of Abraham, he later settled in Haran (see 32), where he died. The name Terah is associated in Jewish literature with the moon-god, and there seems to be a direct etymological link between his name and the **teraphim**, small idolatrous images that were kept in most households. In this context, it is interesting to note that Joshua 24:2 describes Terah as an idolater. However, near to the city of Haran, there was a place that bore Terah's name, known to the

Assyrians as **Turahi** and to the Akkadians as **Turahu**, the ruins of which city were later known to them as **Til-Sa-Turahi** (see Map 2).

(Refs: IDB 4:574. NBD 1252–3. JA 1.vi.5. P 1:30)

32. ***Haran:*** Haran was the youngest of his father's sons. He was born at Ur and died there at a young age. To his father, Terah, is attributed the building of the city of Haran, Terah naming the place in his son's memory and honour. The city lay on the main highway to Nineveh from Carchemish, and it is interesting to note in this context that the Assyrian noun for main road is **harranu**. From its earliest days, Haran was one of the chief centres of moon-worship, and we frequently read of its temple being restored and embellished by successive kings of Assyria. Its temple was, indeed, every bit as famous and well-subscribed as that at Ur (where the family originated, of course). Nimrod also was worshipped here (see Ham 10), he being referred to in the inscriptions concerning him as the *'prince of the men of Haran'* (see Map 2).

(Refs: IDB 2:524. NBD 504. JA 1.vi.5. P 1:30)

33. ***Lot:*** I have not yet noticed any secular reference to him, save that the Dead Sea has always been known to the Arabs as the Sea of Lot (see Map 2).

(Refs: IDB 3:162–3. NBD 752)

34. ***Moab:*** He was the founder of the Moabite nation. This nation was known as **Mu'abu** to the Akkadians, and as **M-'-b** in the Egyptian inscriptions (see Map 4).

(Refs: IDB 3:409. NBD 834–5)

35. ***Benammi:*** He founded the Ammonite nation, and his name is still perpetuated in the modern city of **Amman** that lies some 25 miles to the north-east of the Dead Sea. Present-day Amman, in fact, was once the capital city of the Ammonite nation, and was known in the old world as **Rabbath-ammon**. We know from the first book of the Maccabees that Judas Maccabaeus confronted the Ammonites, and hence that the Ammonites had survived as a distinct nation until at least the 2nd century BC. However, in the 1st century BC, their lands

were occupied by the Nabataeans (see Nebaioth 54) and it is here that the Ammonites disappear from the historical scene. The personal name of Benammi is known from certain clan-lists of Ugarit. There also survives from Nimrud in Assyria an inscription bearing the name of **banu Ammanaia**. The Assyrians generally knew the Ammonites nation as **bit-Amma-na-aia**, or the House of Ammon (see Map 4).

(Refs: IDB 1:381. NBD 140 and 'Ammonite' 30)

36. ***Nahor:*** The name Nahor is known from Babylonian inscriptions, and from the clay tablets of Mari, which render the name **Nahur**. Nahor settled in Haran (see 32) which was later to become known as the Town of Nahor. This appears in inscriptions from the reign of Ashurbanipal, as **Nahuru**, the city's later ruins being known to the Assyrians as til-**Nahiri**, the mound or hill of Nahor (see Map 2).

(Refs: IDB 3:497. NBD 860. JA 1.vi.5. P 1:30)

37. ***Abraham:*** The well-known founder of the Jewish people. There exists from Babylonia an early clay tablet that bears the name of a man called **Abi-ramu**, which is rendered **Abarama** in the Eblaite tablets. Another bears the name of Sarai. Josephus quotes the Babylonian historian, Berosus, as saying, *'In the tenth generation after the Flood, there was a man among the Chaldeans who was righteous and great... '* Josephus, rightly in my opinion, regarded this remark as a direct reference to Abraham, even though Berosus didn't name him. Josephus tells us also that Hecataeus and Nicolaus of Damascus both mention Abraham in their own histories.

(Refs: IDB 1:14–22. NBD 5–7. JA 1.vi.5. P 1:30)

38. ***Shuah:*** The founder of the biblical **Shuites**, one of whose descendants (Bildad) counselled Job. The Assyrians knew Shuah's posterity as the **Suhu**, and describe their land as lying adjacent to the Euphrates, south of Carchemish, between the Balikh and Khabur rivers (the Khabur river was recorded as the Chaboras by Ptolemy, and as the Chebar by Ezekiel. See Map 2). (Refs: IDB 4:341. NBD 1183)

39. ***Ishbak:*** He was the progenitor of a tribe who seem to have settled to the east of Canaan. Otherwise, secular records seem to be silent concerning them (see Map 2).
(Ref: IDB 2:747)

40. ***Midian:*** The founder of the Midianite tribe of Arabs. The Arabian historian, Yakut, tells us that they spoke the Hawil dialect of Arabic (see 25). He also confirms the fact that Midian was the son of Abraham. The tribes of Midian are also known from Egyptian and other sources, Ptolemy, for example, recording the name as **Modiana**, whilst the ancient pre-Islamic Arab city of **Madyan** is today known as **Magha'ir Shu'aib** (see Map 2). (Refs: IDB 3:375–6. NBD 821)

41. ***Ephah:*** Ephah's descendants settled in what is now **Ghuwafa**, to the south-west of Tebuk in the north-west Arabian peninsula. They are known to us in the annals of Tiglath-pileser III, who refers to them as the **Hayapa**. They are last heard of in an inscription of Sargon II that dates to the year 715 BC (see Map 2). (Ref: IDB 2:107)

42. ***Epher:*** Known to Arab cosmographers as **'ofr**, Ashurbanipal of Assyria recorded the name of Epher's descendants as the **Apparu**. The city in which they settled still bears the name of their founder, **Ghifar**. It lies close to Medina (see Map 2). (Ref: IDB 2:107)

43. ***Henoch:*** He founded the famous Kenite tribe of Midianite Arabs. They were coppersmiths who settled to the south-west of the Gulf of Aqaba (see Map 2).
(Ref: IDB 2:523)

44. ***Abidah:*** Minean inscriptions from the Yemen record the name of Abidah's posterity as the **Abiyadi'**. Their precise area of settlement is unknown, although it must have been in the south-west regions of the Arabian peninsula (see Map 2).
(Ref: IDB 1:7)

45. ***Eldaah:*** The descendants of Eldaah are known to us from ancient Sabean inscriptions, which refer to them as the

Yada'il. We do not know their precise area of settlement, although it was certainly within the Yemen (see Map 2).
(Ref: IDB 2:72)

46. ***Medan:*** He founded various northern Arabian tribes, and his name is still preserved in the modern family name of **Abd-al-Madan**. His posterity settled in the town of **Madan**, which is mentioned in the inscriptions of Tiglath-pileser III that date to the year 732 BC. He renders the name as **Badan**, but the letters 'm' and 'b' are interchangeable in Arabic. The town lay to the west of Tema (see 62 and Map 2).
(Refs: IDB 3:318. NBD 801)

47. ***Jokshan:*** Seemingly unknown outside the biblical records, he appears to have settled with his descendants in northern Arabia (see Map 2). (Refs: IDB 2:963. NBD 652)

48. ***Sheba:*** In the often unrecorded and sometimes complex turmoil of these times, this people seemingly made up the Semitic Arabs who were to supercede the earlier Hamitic tribe, the original Sheba.
(Refs: IDB 4:311-2. NBD 1171. JA 1.vi.4. P 1:27 and 29)

49. ***Dedan:*** Like Sheba, this Semitic tribe of Dedan seemingly superseded the Hamitic tribe of the same name, and we notice here the derivation of the Hebrew word **'rab** (Arab) from **ereb**, which means a mixed multitude. The city of Dedan (modern **Daidan**) is mentioned in the inscriptions of Nabonidus, king of Babylon, who spent his years of exile at Tema. There are some ruins west of Tema called **Daidan**, that lies in an area known in modern times as Medain Salih. (see 62 and Map 2). (Refs: IDB 1:812. NBD 305. P 1:27)

50. ***The Sons of Dedan:*** These founded the three tribes of Dedanite Arabs, of whom nothing further is learned from extra-biblical sources save for the fact that in later Jewish literature the Asshurim (not to be confused with the Assyrians) were described as travelling merchants; the Letushim were those who sharpened weapons and cutlery; and the Leummim were somewhat enigmatically described as the *'chief of those*

who inhabit the isles', the significance of which phrase is now lost to us. From this information, it would appear that the Asshurim and Letushim would travel the country selling and repairing various items, rather like the numerous tribes of gypsies and tinkers who were once a common feature of the English and European scenes.

(Ref: For Asshurim, IDB 1:261)
(Ref: For Letushim, IDB 3:115)
(Ref: For Leummim, IDB 3:115)

51. ***Zimran:*** The chieftain and founder of an Arab tribe whose chief city lay to the west of Mecca. Ptolemy recorded its name as **Zabram**, the letters 'm' and 'b' being interchangeable in Arabic (see Map 2). (Refs: IDB 4:958. NBD 1360)

52. ***Isaac:*** I have so far found no mention of him in extra-biblical sources. (Refs: IDB 2:728. NBD 568–9)

53. ***Ishmael:*** Among the Babylonian documents that have come down to us from the days of Hammurabi, there is a list of witnesses to certain documents. One of these witnesses is registered as *'Abuha, son of Ishmael'*.

(Refs: IDB 2:747–8. NBD 577–8)

54. ***Nebaioth:*** He settled with his descendants to the south of the Dead Sea, where they were known to the Chaldeans as the **Nabat**, and to the Assyrians as the **Nabaiate**. Their own inscriptions render the name as **'nbtw'**. The Greek historian, Diodorus, mentions them, and Ptolemy knew them as the **Nabatei**. The Nabataeans' final demise was brought about by Augustus Caesar, who cut off the trade routes of Arabia. By the time of Tiberius Caesar, all the land east of Judea was known as **Nabataea**. (Refs: IDB 3:528. NBD 872)

55. ***Kedar:*** Known to the Hebrews as the **Qedar**, and the Assyrians as the **Qidri**, his descendants became the great tribe of Arabs who settled in the north-west Arabian peninsula, and whose black tents were to become proverbial in the ancient world. We are informed in Babylonian sources that the armies of Nebuchadnezzar confronted the tribe of Kedar in a major

skirmish of the year 599 BC, an incident that was foretold by Jeremiah (49:28 and 29). The tribe of Kedar is also mentioned in the annals of Ashurbanipal, with whom they clashed, and in various other Assyrian documents. In these, the men of Kedar are mentioned in close association with the men of Nebaioth (see 54). The founder of Islam, Mohammed, was to trace his own direct descent from Kedar (see Map 2).

(Refs: IDB 3:3–4. NBD 688)

56. ***Adbeel:*** He was the founder of a tribe who were known to the Akkadians as the **Idibilu**. This same people were subsequently mentioned in the annals of Tiglath-pileser III, who tells us how he conquered the **Idiba'leans** and employed them to guard the approaches to Egypt's borders. Their area of settlement was in north-west Arabia, close to the lands of Kedar (see 55) and Nebaioth (see 54 and Map 2).

(Ref: IDB 1:45)

57. ***Mibsam:*** An otherwise unknown Bedhouin chieftain.

(Ref: IDB 3:369)

58. ***Mishma:*** He settled with his descendants in what is known today as **Jebel Mishma** in the vicinity of Tema (see 62 and Map 2).

(Ref: IDB 3:404)

59. ***Dumah:*** The Assyrians and Babylonians knew Dumah's descendants as the **Adammatu**. Nabonidus later tells us how he conquered the **Adummu**. Ptolemy referred to them as the **Domatha**; and Porphyry recorded their name as the **Dumathii**. We know them today as the **Idumaeans**. The name of Dumah is still preserved in the modern Arab city of **Dumat-al-Jandal**, the erstwhile capital of his tribe (see Map 2).

(Refs: IDB 1:873–4. NBD 328)

60. ***Massa:*** The descendants of Massa were known to the Assyrians as the **Mas'a**, who with the tribe of Tema (see 62) were forced to pay tribute to Tiglath-pileser III. He tells us how he conquered them along with the peoples of Haiappa (see 41), the Idiba'leans (see 56) and others. Ptolemy knew the tribe as the **Masanoi**, who lived to the north-east of Dumah

(see 59). Josephus records their name as the **Mesanaeans**, and that in his day their lands were known to the Romans as **Charax Spasini** (see Map 2).

(Refs: IDB 3:299. NBD 793. JA 1.vi.3)

61. ***Hadad:*** The name is rendered as **Haddu** in Akkadian inscriptions as the name of a pagan god. Hadad himself, however, seems to be unknown in extra-biblical sources.

(Refs: IDB 2:507. NBD 497)

62. ***Tema:*** Still known by today's Arabs as **Taima'**, the city of Tema's descendants lies some 70 miles north-east of Dedan (see 49). Nabonidus, king of Babylon, (556–539 BC), passed his years of exile in this city, which he also knew as **Tema**. The city of Tema, with those of Dedan and Dumah (see 59) formed stages in the caravan route from Babylon to Sheba (see 48 and Map 2). (Refs: IDB 4:533. NBD 1241)

63. ***Jetur:*** He was the progenitor of the **Ituraeans**, who were known to the Greeks as the **Itouraia**. The Ituraeans are mentioned in the works of Dio Cassius, Josephus, Pliny, Strabo and others; and were known to the Roman authorities as a tribe of robbers. The descendants of Jetur perpetrated a massacre of Lebanese Christians in AD 1860 (see Map 4).

(Ref: IDB 2:897)

64. ***Naphish:*** He and his lineage are variously known in the biblical records as **Nephish**, the children of the **Nephusim**, and the **Nephishesim**. They are seemingly unknown from extra-biblical sources. (Refs: IDB 3:508. NBD 864)

65. ***Kedemah:*** He and his descendants settled in what was later known as the Wilderness of Kedemoth. The tribe dwelt in the city that is known today as **es-Za'feran** (see Map 4).

(Refs: IDB 3: 4 and 557. NBD 688)

Appendix 2

The Nations of Ham

1. ***Ham:*** *'Yt is observed that Cham, and his famely, were the only far Travellers, and Straglers into diverse unknowne countries, searching, exploring and sitting downe in the same; as also yt is said of his famely that what country soever the Children of Cham happened to possesse, there beganne both the Ignoraunce of true godliness ... and that no inhabited countryes cast forth greater multytudes, to raunge and stray into diverse remote Regions.'* Thus far the comments of one William Strachey, who added to these words in 1612 the following damning indictment, accusing Ham's posterity of instigating: '*... the Ignoraunce of the true worship of God ... the inventions of Heathenisme, and [the] adoration of falce godes and the Devill ...*' cit. Hogden, p. 262. See Bibliography.

(Refs: IDB 2:515. NBD 500. JA 1.vi.2. P 1:27)

2. ***Cush:*** Josephus writes: *'Time has not at all hurt the name of Cush; for the Ethiopians, over whom he reigned, are even at this day, both by themselves and by all men in Asia, called Cushites.'* The name of Cush (originally rendered **Chus** in Josephus) is preserved in Egypt's heiroglyphic inscriptions as **Kush**, these records referring to the country that lay between the second and third cataracts of the Nile. This same land was later known as **Nubia**. Additional information on this location is gleaned from the records of Esarhaddon, king of Assyria, (681–668 BC), who tells us that he made himself king of

Appendix 2

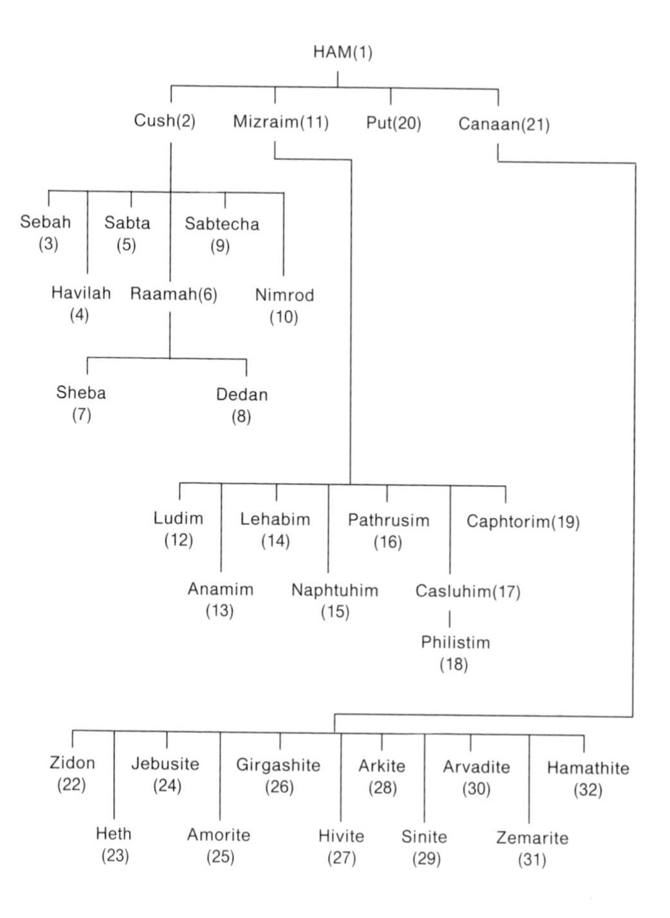

HAM(1)
Cush(2)
Mizraim(11)
Put(20)
Canaan(21)
Sebah (3)
Sabta (5)
Sabtecha (9)
Havilah (4)
Raamah(6)
Nimrod (10)
Sheba (7)
Dedan (8)
Ludim (12)
Lehabim (14)
Pathrusim (16)
Caphtorim(19)
Anamim (13)
Naphtuhim (15)
Casluhim(17)
Philistim (18)
Zidon (22)
Jebusite (24)
Girgashite (26)
Arkite (28)
Arvadite (30)
Hamathite (32)
Heth (23)
Amorite (25)
Hivite (27)
Sinite (29)
Zemarite (31)

Musur (see 11), of **Paturisi** (see 16), and **Cush**. Some have claimed also that the name of Cush was likewise perpetuated in that of the Babylonian city of **Kish**, one of the earliest cities to be built after the Flood.

(Refs: IDB 1:751. NBD 284. JA 1.vi.2. P 1:27)

3. ***Sebah:*** He founded the nation that was known to later history as the **Sabaeans**. Strabo writes of their city of **Sabai** along with its harbour of **Saba** (same spelling as in Josephus), which lay on the west coast of the Arabian peninsula (see Map 2). (Refs: IDB 4:260. JA 1.vi.2)

4. ***Havilah:*** The progenitor of the Hamitic tribe of Havilah. (There were two tribes of Havilah, one of them Semitic in origin, see Shem 25.) His descendants settled on the east coast of Arabia looking out onto the Persian Gulf. Their land was known to the pre-Islamic writers as **Hawlan**, and to Josephus as **Evilas**. Kautsch renders the name as **Huwailah**, and confirms their settlement on the east coast of Arabia (see Map 2). (Refs: IDB 2:537. NBD 506. JA 1.vi.2. P 1:29)

5. ***Sabta:*** Josephus records the name of his (Sabta's) descendants as the **Sabateni** or **Sabathes**. Ptolemy knew them as the **Saptha**, and Pliny called them the **Messabathi**. They settled on the eastern side of the Arabian peninsula. Sabta's name is also preserved in that of the ancient city of **Shabwat** (modern **Sabota**), the capital of the Hadramaut (Hazarmaveth. See Shem 16).

(Refs: IDB 4:146. NBD 1112. JA 1.vi.2. P 1:27)

6. ***Raamah:*** We know from the inscriptions of ancient Sheba (see 7) that Raamah's descendants settled near to the land of Havilah (see 4), and to the east of Ophir (see Shem 24). They are known from other sources to have traded with the children of Zidon (see 22) in the city of Tyre. Ptolemy agreed with the LXX in the name **Ragma**, which Josephus rendered **Ragmas**. There is still a place called **Raamah** near Ma'in in south-west Arabia (see Map 2).

(Refs: IDB 4:1. NBD 1072. JA 1.vi.2. P 1:27)

7. ***Sheba:*** Minaean inscriptions from the north Yemen, and which date to the 9th century BC, tell us that Sheba was that kingdom's southern neighbour. The land of Sheba is also known to us from Assyrian inscriptions of the 8th century BC. Sheba was famous as the Land of Spices (there were four 'spice kingdoms' - Minaea, Kataban, and Hadramaut. See Shem 16), and we know from the vast archaeological ruins, some of whose walls still stand some 60 feet above the desert sands, that the land was extremely fertile, being watered by ingenious irrigation systems controlled by a great dam that once spanned the river Adhanat. In the year 542 BC, the dam collapsed after more than a thousand years of service, an event that is recalled in the Koran and described there as a judgment of God upon the people.

(Refs: IDB 4:311-2. NBD 1171. JA 1.vi.4. P 1:27)

8. ***Dedan:*** His posterity are known to have traded with the Phoenicians. Identified from various cuneiform inscriptions, their main place of settlement was the city that is known today as **Al-ula**, and which lies some 70 miles south-west of modern Taima (see Shem 62 and Map 2).

(Refs: IDB 1:812. NBD 305)

9. ***Sabtecha:*** Identified by Josephus as the **Sabactens** or **Sabactas**, Sabtecha's descendants appear to have settled in southern Arabia, the modern Yemen (see Map 2).

(Refs: IDB 4:146. NBD 1112. JA 1.vi.2. P 1:27)

10. ***Nimrod:*** Writing in 1876, George Smith tells us that: *'Nearly thirteen hundred years before the Christian era, one of the Egyptian poems likens a hero to the Assyrian chief,* ***Kazartu****, a great hunter ... and it has already been suggested that the reference here is to the fame of Nimrod. A little later, in the period BC 1100 to 800, we have in Egypt many persons named after Nimrod, showing a knowledge of the mighty hunter there.'* (Chaldean Genesis. p. 313). Nimrod was undoubtedly the most notorious man in the ancient world who is credited with instigating the Great Rebellion at Babel, and of founding the very worst features of paganism, including the practice of

magical arts, astrology and even human sacrifice. Moreover, there is much evidence to suggest that he himself was worshipped from the very earliest times. His name, for example, was perpetuated in those of **Nimurda**, the Assyrian god of war; **Marduk**, the Babylonian king of the gods; and the Sumerian deity **Amar-utu**. His image was likewise incorporated very early on in the Chaldean zodiac as a child seated on his mother's lap, and both mother and child were worshipped, she as the Queen of Heaven, and he as her erstwhile sacrificial son, the precursor of today's worship of the Madonna and Child. Nimrod was also worshipped by the Romans under the name of **Bacchus**, this name being derived from the Semitic **bar-Cush**, meaning the son of Cush. A mountain not far from Ararat, has been called **Nimrud Dagh** (Mount Nimrod) from the earliest times since the Flood, and the ruins of **Birs Nimrud** bear the remains of what is commonly reputed to be the original Tower of Babel. The Caspian Sea was once called the **Mar de Bachu**, or Sea of Bacchus, as is witnessed by the map appearing in Sir Walter Raleigh's History of the World, published in 1634. One of the chief cities of Assyria was named **Nimrud**, and the Plain of Shinar, known to the Assyrians as Sen'ar and the site of the Great Rebellion, was itself known as the Land of Nimrod. Iraqi and Iranian Arabs still speak his name with awe, and such was the notoriety of the man that his historical reality is beyond dispute (see Map 2). (Refs: IDB 3:551. NBD 888. JA 1.vi.2. P 1:27)

11. ***Mizraim:*** A collective name, these people settled in Egypt. Modern Israelis still use the name for that country; it is preserved as **Msrm** in the Ugaritic inscriptions; as **Misri** in the Amarna tablets; and in the Assyrian and Babylonian records as **Musur** and **Musri** respectively. Modern Arabs still know it as **Misr**. Josephus (rendering the name **Mesraites**) relates a curious episode that he called the Ethiopic War, an incident that was apparently well-known throughout the ancient world. According to Josephus, some six or seven of the nations descended from the Mizraim were destroyed, clearly a major conflict that would have had profound and

far-reaching repercussions in the world of those times. Josephus lists those nations as the Ludim (see 12); the Anamim (see 13); the Lehabim (see 14); the Naphtuhim (see 15); the Pathrusim (see 16); the Casluhim (see 17); and the Caphtorim (see 19).

(Refs: IDB 3:409. NBD 833. JA 1.vi.2. P 1:27)

12. ***Ludim:*** Seemingly known in later records as the **Lubim** (which Josephus renderd **Ludieim**) this people settled on the north coast of Africa and gave their name to the land of **Lybia**. They are known to have provided Egypt on more than one occasion with mercenary troops. The records that tell us this give the Ludim's name as **Lebu**. Otherwise, Josephus records their destruction, or rather defeat, in the Ethiopic War (see Map 3).

(Refs: IDB 3:178–9. NBD 755. JA 1.vi.2. P 1:28)

13. ***Anamim:*** Few occurrences of this name can now be found in the surviving records. This may be due to the devastations of the Ethiopic War. However, the Assyrian king, Sargon II, does tell us in his inscriptions of the land of the **A-na-mi** which lay adjacent to that of Kaptara (see 19). Josephus rendered the name **Enemim**.

(Refs: IDB 1:124. JA 1.vi.2. P 1:28)

14. ***Lehabim:*** The Egyptians recorded this name as **'rbw'**, although it is uncertain where they settled. Some authorities (including Josephus who renders the name **Lybyos**) give Lybia as their country. This people were, however, destroyed in the Ethiopic War (see Map 3).

(Refs: IDB 3:110. NBD 728. JA 1.vi.2. P 1:28)

15. ***Naphtuhim:*** This people are known to have settled in the Nile delta and the western parts of Egypt, where early records refer to them as the **p't'mhw** – literally, they of the delta or marshland. Their name also appears as **Na-patoh-im** in the same records. Josephus records their destruction in the Ethiopic War (see Map 3).

(Refs: IDB 3:510. NBD 865. P 1:28)

16. ***Pathrusim:*** The people of this name migrated to Upper Egypt, where the Egyptians recorded their name as the **p't'rs** or **Ptores**. The district of **Pathros** thus bears their name. Esarhaddon, king of Assyria from 681–668 BC, records his conquest of the **Paturisi**, thus showing that this particular tribe at least were not totally destroyed in the Ethiopic War as asserted by Josephus, who renders the name **Phethrosim** (see Map 3). (Refs: IDB 3:676. NBD 938. JA 1.vi.2)

17. ***Casluhim:*** The precise whereabouts of their country is uncertain, although the book of Genesis does record that the Philistines came from this people. Some cite Crete as their possible place of settlement, which, if true, would make the Ethiopic War of Josephus a truly international conflict, as he records the destruction of the Casluhim in that war. This, however, only serves to make Crete a most unlikely place for their settlement, the northern areas of Egypt being a far more reasonable proposition (but see 18 and 19 and Map 3). Josephus gives their name as the **Chesloim**.
(Refs: IDB 1:541. NBD 201. JA 1.vi.3. P 1:28)

18. ***Philistim:*** Better known to us as the Philistines, they were known to the Assyrians as the **Palashtu** and the **Pilisti**, and to the Greeks as **he Palastine** – hence the later name of **Palestine**. After the Assyrian conquests of the 8th century BC, the Philistines effectively disappear as a coherent nation. It is currently but wrongly believed that the Philistines did not appear until the 13th century BC, and that they are to be identified as the 'Sea Peoples' of Egyptian literature. But this view is erroneous. The Genesis record states emphatically that the Philistim occupied parts of Canaan as early as the time of Abraham, and far from implying that their place of origin was Crete, as currently taught, it is much more likely to have been northern Egypt (but see 19 and Map 3).
(Refs: IDB 3:791–5. NBD 'Philistines' 988–991. JA 1.vi.2. P 1:28)

19. ***Caphtorim:*** Some confusion has reigned in recent years over the question of the geographical location of the

Caphtorim. This is mainly due to modernist efforts to identify Caphtor as Crete. This would allow the assertion that the Philistines (see 18) were the Sea Peoples of the 13th century BC, and that the Genesis record therefore errs when it speaks of the Philistines as the 19th century BC contemporaries of Abraham. In opposition to this view, however, the Genesis record gives the commonsense and verifiable place of the Caphtorim's settlement as Egypt, or Mizraim (see 11) where the name of the Caphtorim was rendered **Keftiu** in a record that is conventionally dated to ca 2200 BC. Genesis tells us that the Caphtorim were descended from the Mizraim, and, through the absence of any qualifying remarks, leaves us with the strong implication that the Caphtorim therefore dwelt on the mainland of Egypt or North Africa either amongst, or in close proximity to, their forebears the Mizraim. Only the descendants of Japheth are said to have occupied the isles of the sea, e.g. Cyprus or Crete *et al*, whereas this qualification is entirely absent with either the Semitic or Hamitic races. The early Cretans, we know, were not a Hamitic people, but rather were Indo-European in race, language and culture, which confirms their descent from Japheth (and not Ham) as provided in the Genesis account. Furthermore, Josephus relates the involvement and subsequent defeat of the Caphtorim (whom he names the **Cephtorim**) in the Ethiopic War, a conflagration that was confined to the borders of Egypt and Ethiopia, and which did not, as far as we know, involve the isles of the sea. Moreover, Jeremiah 47:4 describes the Philistines as the *'remnant of the country of Caphtor'*, thus implying that by his own day the Caphtorim were a depleted nation. There is also strong evidence of a direct etymological link between the **ai-Kaphtor** of the Old Testament and the **Aiguptos** of Greek literature, **Aiguptos** being merely the archaic form of the western name for **Egypt.** That Caphtor's descendants were mainland dwellers is also confirmed in the Assyrian inscriptions in which they are named as the **Kaptara**; and in the Ugaritic inscriptions as the **'kptr'**. Later, Egyptian records speak of the **'kftyw'** or **Kaphtur**, a term that was used in relation to **Phoenicia**, not Crete. Intriguingly, the

Septuagint translates the name as **Kaphtoriim** in Genesis 10:14; whereas in the book of Deuteronomy (2:23) the name is rendered **Kappadokes** or **Cappadocians**. Likewise, the Latin Vulgate gives the rendering **Caphtorim** in Genesis 10:14, thus following the original Hebrew; whereas in Deuteronomy 2:23 it follows the Greek Septuagint in the rendering **Cappadoces** and **Cappadocia** – Cappadocia, of course, referring to mainland Asia Minor. Thus, to identify the Caphtorim as early Cretans is clearly untenable.

(Refs: IDB 1:534. NBD 199. JA 1.vi.3. P 1:28)

20. ***Put:*** The country in which the descendants of Put settled is well known to us from Egyptian records, which render the name **Put** or **Punt**. (Josephus calls it **Phut**.) It is always spoken of as closely associated with Egypt, and its close geographical proximity to Egypt is confirmed by an inscription from the archives of Darius the Great, king of Persia from 522–486 BC. Here the land of **Puta** is shown as lying in the proximity of Cyrenaica, i.e. on the North African coast to the west of Egypt. This same land was known as **Puta** to the Babylonians, and as **Putiya** in the Old Persian inscriptions (see Map 3). (Refs: IDB 3:971. NBD 1066. JA 1.vi.2. P 1:27)

21. ***Canaan:*** The posterity of Canaan settled in the land that was later to be given to Israel. At the time of the Israelite conquest of Canaan, the population consisted of all the tribes descended from Canaan (see 22–32). Both Sanchuniathon and Phylo of Byblos confirm the fact that the Canaanites derived their name from their founder. The Greeks and Phoenicians rendered the name **Kna'an**; the Egyptians knew it as **Kn'nw** and **Kyn'n.w**; the Assyrians rendered the name **Kinnahu**; and the Hurrians described certain dyed cloths as **Kinahne** or Canaanite cloth. In spite of their Hamitic descent, however, the Canaanites spoke a Semitic language (see Map 4).

(Refs: IDB 1:494. NBD 183–6. JA 1.vi.2. P 1:27)

22. ***Zidon:*** He settled, with his descendants, on the Mediterranean coast of Canaan, where his name is still perpetuated in the modern-day city of **Sidon**. Originally known as

Zidonians, his posterity were later known as **Phoenicians**. They are known to us from many and various inscriptions of the old world, the Akkadians, for example, rendering the name **Sidunu**, and the Armana tablets as **Sa'idunu** (see Map 4). Josephus adopted this spelling when he rendered the name **Sidonius**. (Refs: IDB 4:343–5. NBD 'Sidon' 1184–5. JA 1.vi.2. P 1:28)

23. ***Heth:*** Heth was the progenitor of the Hittite nation, whose name was known to the Assyrians as the **Khatti**. The Hittites were apparently the first nation to smelt iron on any appreciable scale. The Armana tablets contain letters that were sent between the Hittite emperor Subbiluliuma and Amenhotep IV of Egypt. Rameses II tells us how he engaged the Hittites in what was the earliest recorded battle involving massed battle chariots. This was the famous battle of Kadesh, and it appears that the Hittites got the better of the Egyptian forces. Heth's name was perpetuated in the Hittite capital of **Hattushash**, modern Boghazkoy in Turkey (see Map 4).
(Refs: IDB 2:597. NBD 'Hittites' 528–9. P 1:28)

24. ***Jebusite:*** The posterity of Jebus (whom Josephus knew as **Jebuseus**) settled in the mountainous regions of Judea where, due to their strong and natural fortifications they were able to withstand the armies of Israel. The chief city of the Jebusites came later to be known as Jerusalem, the **Urusalimmu** of the Armana tablets.
(Refs: (IDB 2:807. NBD 601–2. JA 1.vi.2. P 1:28)

25. ***Amorite:*** Known to the Sumerians as the **Martu**, and to the Akkadians as the **Amurru**, this people settled in the land of Canaan. They appear to have initially adopted a nomadic way of life, although they were soon to organise themselves into a very powerful and aggressive nation. Indeed, the Amorites were later to conquer Babylonia, subsequently producing one of the most famous of Babylonian kings, Hammurabi, whose own name perpetuates the designation **Amurru**. Josephus knew the name as **Amorreus** (see Map 4).
(Refs: IDB 1:115. NBD 31–2. JA 1.vi.2. P 1:28)

26. ***Girgashite:*** The name of the Girgashites has been discovered in the Ugaritic inscriptions as **'grgs'** and **'bn-grgs'**, in other words Girgash and the sons of Girgash. They are also known to us in Hittite documents as the **Karkisa** or **Qaraqisha**; and in Egyptian records as the **Kirkash**. They settled to the east of the river Jordan, between Galilee and the Dead Sea, and their descendants are probably to be identified with the **Gadarenes** of the NT. Josephus rendered the name **Gergesus** (see Map 4).

(Refs: IDB 2:399. NBD 471. JA 1.vi.2. P 1:28)

27. ***Hivite:*** Known to the ancient Greeks as the **Heuaios**, and to Josephus as **Eueus**, this people moved from Canaan to the foothills of Lebanon during the Israelite conquest under Joshua. King Solomon was later to use Hivites as builders (see Map 4). (Refs: IDB 2:615. NBD 529. JA 1.vi.2. P 1:28)

28. ***Arkite:*** This people come to our notice in the inscriptions of Shalmaneser II and Tiglath-pileser III, both kings of Assyria, and both of whom describe the Arkites as *'rebellious'*. The Arkites were known also to the Egyptians and are mentioned in the Armana tablets as the **Irkata**. They were known for their worship of Astarte. Their city is known to this day as **Tell-Arqa**, a place known to Thutmose III of Egypt as **Arkantu**. Josephus calls it **Arucas**, and it was known to the Romans as **Caesari Libani** (see Map 4).

(Refs: IDB 1:226. NBD 82. JA 1.vi.2. P 1:28)

29. ***Sinite:*** The name of this people is still to be found in the modern-day towns of **Nahr as-Sinn** and **Sinn addarb**, which are both in close proximity to Arqa (see 28). The Phoenicians knew the Sinites as the **Usnu**; the Assyrians called them the **Usana** and **Siannu**; and the Ugaritic tablets refer to them as the **'sn'**. Strabo called their town **Sinna**, and Heironymous rendered it **civitas Sini** (which Josephus gave as **Sineus** (see Map 4).

(Refs: IDB 4:379. NBD 1194. JA 1.vi.3. P 1:28)

30. ***Arvadite:*** This people settled on the island that bore their founder's name, **Arvad**. Today it is called **Ruad** and lies

north of the bay of Tripoli about two miles out to sea. The Arvadites were famed in the old world for their skilful seamanship, drawing for this even the grudging admiration of the Assyrians. Later, the Arvadites were to play an important part in the conquests of Alexander the Great. The Arvadites were known in the Armana tablets as the **Arwada**, to the Akkadians as the **Aruda**, and the Armana tablets as **Aruadi**. Josephus renders the name **Arudeus** (see Map 4).

(Refs: IDB 1:242. NBD 93. JA 1.vi.2. P 1:28)

31. ***Zemarite:*** The posterity of Zemar were known to the Assyrians as the **Simirra**, and to the Egyptians as the **Sumur**. The name is still perpetuated in the modern city of **Sumra**, just north of Tripoli.

(Refs: IDB 4:950. NBD 1357-8. P 1:28)

32. ***Hamathite:*** The city where this people settled lay on the Orontes, and was named after their forebear, **Hamath**. Sargon II of Assyria tells us how he conquered the city, and it was at Hamath that Nebuchadnezzar defeated the Egyptian armies in 605 BC. The city was known to the Akkadians as **Amatu**, to the Egyptians as **Hmtu**, and to the Arabs as **Hamat**. The Greeks and Romans subsequently knew the city as **Epiphaneia**, although today it has reverted to its ancient name, **Hamah**. In 853 BC the men of Hamath were able to successfully defeat Assyrian advances in the west by mobilising an army of no less than 63,000 foot, 2,000 light horse, 4,000 battle chariots and 1,000 camels. This is the Assyrian estimate of their forces, not an exaggerated Hamathite boast! (see Map 4). (Refs: IDB 2:516. NBD 501. P 1:28)

Appendix 3

The Nations of Japheth

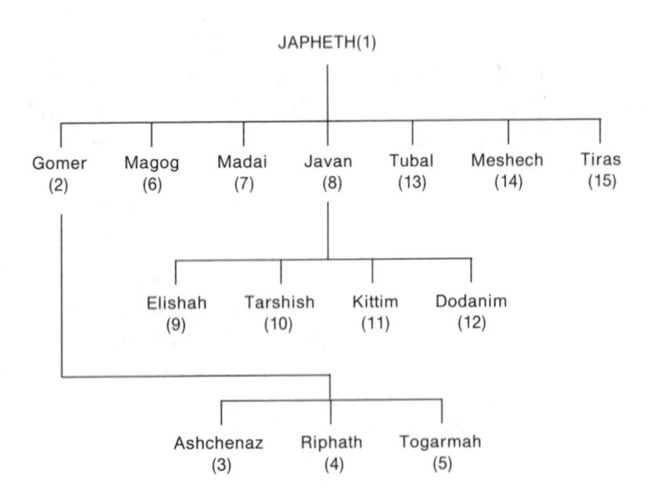

1. ***Japheth:*** The father of all the Indo-European peoples, it would be surprising indeed if his name had gone unremembered among them. As it is, we find that the early Greeks worshipped him as **Iapetos**, or **Iapetus**, whom they regarded as the son of heaven and earth, the father of many nations. Likewise, in the ancient Sanskrit vedas of India he is remembered as **Pra-Japati**, the sun and ostensible Lord of Creation. As time went by, his name was further corrupted, being assimilated into the Roman pantheon as **Iupater**, and eventually **Jupiter** (see Appendix 11). None of these names are of Greek, Indian or Latin origin, but are merely corruptions of the original name of Japheth. Both the early Irish Celts and the early Britons traced the descent of their royal houses from Japheth, as did also the early Saxons who corrupted his name to **Sceaf**, – pr. 'sheaf' or 'shaif' (see chapter 7).

(Refs: IDB 2:802. NBD 599. JA 1.vi.1. P 1:26)

2. ***Gomer:*** He was the founder of the **Cimmerians** who settled originally on the shores of the Caspian Sea. They were later driven away by the Elamites (see Shem 2). At the time of the Babylonian Exile, the Jews knew them as the tribes that dwelt in the **'uppermost parts of the north'** (Ezekiel 38:6). The Assyrians referred to them as the **Gimirraya**. Esarhaddon (681–668 BC) records his defeat of the **Gimirrai**; whilst King Ashurbanipal tells us in his records of the Cimmerian invasion of Lydia (see Shem 5) in the days of the Lydian king Gugu around the year 660 BC (see Map 1).

(Refs: IDB 2:440. NBD 481. JA 1.vi.1)

3. ***Ashchenaz:*** The descendants of Ashchenaz first settled in what is today Armenia, although in later Jewish writings he was associated (with his father Gomer) with the Germanic races. Hence, Germanic Jews are still known as **Ashkenazim**. More immediately, the Assyrians tell us in their inscriptions of the **Askuza**, a tribe who allied themselves with the Mannai in a revolt of the 7th century BC, an event that is also mentioned in the Old Testament (Jeremiah 51:27). Indeed, it is in this statement that Jeremiah incidentally confirms the identity of the Ashkenazim with the Askuza. This name, the Askuza of the

Assyrian records, later became the **Skythai** (Scythians) of Herodotus. Other early sources confirm their place of settlement to be the area later known as Pontus and Bythinia, where the peoples of Ashchenaz gave their name to the lake and harbour of **Ascanius**, and to the land of **Ascania**. Josephus tells us that they were subsequently known to the Greeks as the **Rheginians** (see Map 1).

(Refs: IDB 1:254. NBD 96. JA 1.vi.1. P 1:26)

4. ***Riphath:*** His descendants gave their name to the **Riphaean** mountains, which early cosmographers thought of as constituting the then northernmost boundary of the earth. Pliny, Melo and Solinus record the name of Riphath as that of the **Riphaei**, **Riphaces** and **Piphlataei** who were later known to history as the **Paphlagonians**, the descent and identification of which is confirmed by Josephus (see Map 1).

(Refs: IDB 4:100. JA 1.vi.1. P 1:26)

5. ***Togarmah:*** His earliest descendants settled in Armenia. We know from certain Hittite documents that in the 14th century BC, the then region of **Tegarama**, which lay between Carchemish and Haran, was sacked by the *'enemy from Isuwa'*, i.e. the enemy from beyond the Euphrates. The records of both Sargon II and Sennacherib mention the city of **Til-gari-manu**, the capital of **Kammanu** which lay on the border of Tabal (see 13). **Til-gari-manu** lay some thirty miles due east of present-day Malatya (it is known today as **Gürün**, anciently **Gauraena**), and was not finally destroyed until the year 695 BC. It was after the destruction of Til-gari-manu that the descendants of Togarmah became lost in obscurity. In line with the Assyrian policy of that time, the survivors were uprooted and transported to other lands within the Assyrian empire (see Map 1). The name was given as **Thrugramma** by Josephus.

(Refs: IDB 4:662. NBD 1285. JA 1.vi.1. P 1:26)

6. ***Magog:*** His immediate descendants were known as the **Magogites**, being later known to the Greeks as the Scythians, according to the testimony of Josephus. However, given the

subsequent history of the peoples of Ashchenaz (see *3*), who are far more certainly identified as the later Scythians (Gk. *Skythai*, and Assyr. *Askuza*), it is more likely that the early Magogites were assimilated into the peoples of Ashchenaz, thus making up merely a part of the Scythian hordes. The early Irish Celts traced their own lineage from Japheth through the line of Magog (see chapter 9 and Map 1).

(Refs: IDB 3:226. NBD 'Gog and Magog' 480–1. JA 1.vi.1. P 1:26)

7. ***Madai:*** His descendants were the **Madaeans**, who are better known to us as the **Medes**. The Assyrians recorded the name as **Amada**; the Greeks as the **Medai**; and the Old Persian inscriptions speak of them as the **Mada**. The earliest surviving reference to the Medes that is found in secular documents, appears in the inscriptions of Shalmaneser III, king of Assyria from ca 858–824 BC, in which he tells us that he invaded the land of the Medes to plunder them of their fine horses. Both Strabo and Herodotus confirm the fact that the Medes were of Indo-European (Japhetic) origin, and we know also that their language was of this group. After 631 BC, the Medes joined with the people of Askuza (or the Ashchenazim, see *3*) and those of Gomer (the Cimmerians, see *2*) in an attempt to throw off the Assyrian yoke (see Map 1).

(Refs: IDB 3:220. NBD 'Medes' 801–2. JA 1.vi.1. P 1:26)

8. ***Javan:*** The name of Javan's descendants appears in Assyrian documents as the **Iamanu**, where we are told that they engaged the Assyrians in a major sea battle during the reign of King Sargon II (721–705 BC). The Archaemenian inscriptions refer to them as the **Yauna**. Homer tells us in the Iliad that **Iawones** (Hebrew **Iawan**) was the progenitor of the **Ionians** (Gk. *Iones*), while the Hebrews knew the Greeks as the **Jevanim (Iewanim)**. Pre-Islamic Arab cosmographers gave the name as **Yuban** (see Map 1).

(Refs: IDB 2:805. NBD 600. JA 1.vi.1. P 1:26)

9. ***Elishah:*** He was the ancestor of the **Aeolians**, his name being frequently referred to in Greek history and mythology.

Two Greek cities were named after him, these being **Elis** and **Elissus**. Likewise, an entire area was named **Ellas** in his memory. His name lies behind the origin of the term **Hellenic**, and there is every reason to believe that his name is also perpetuated in the Greek paradise, the **Elysian Fields**. The Armana tablets referred to his descendants as the **Alashia**, the Hittites knew them as the **Alasiya**, and the Egyptians as **A-ra-sa**. Josephus rendered the name as **Elisa**. The name also appears in the Ugaritic inscriptions (see Map 1).

(Refs: IDB 2:92. NBD 366, JA 1.vi.1. P 1:26)

10. ***Tarshish:*** The father of the peoples of Tarshish, or **Tartesis**, who are thought by most to have settled in Spain. The Mediterranean Sea was once known as the Sea of Tarshish, and it is known that the Phoenicians built a class of vessel called a ship of Tarshish. (It was in one of these that Jonah tried to flee from Joppa in the 8th century BC.) Phoenician inscriptions found on Sardinia, and dating to the 9th century BC, mention Tarshish without, unfortunately, providing us with a positive identification of its geographical location. Josephus records the name as **Tharsus**, and tells that it used to be the name under which Cilicia was known, the chief and noblest city of which was **Tarsus**. However, for various reasons the identification is unlikely, and the matter remains unresolved.

(Refs: IDB 4:517. NBD 1239–40. JA 1.vi.1. P 1:26)

11. ***Kittim:*** This is a collective name of a people who are spoken of in the Old Phoenician inscriptions as the **kt** or **kty**, and who settled on the island of Cyprus. They were to give their name to the ancient Cypriot city of **Kition** (modern-day Larnaka). The Romans preserved the name when they named the city **Citium**, and Josephus gave the name as **Cethimus**.

(Refs: IDB 3:40–1. JA 1.vi.1. P 1:26)

12. ***Dodanim:*** This also is a collective name of a people descended from Dodan, who were known to the Greeks as the **Dardani**, the **Dardanians** of Asia Minor. They settled initially around the area of Troy whose coastal regions are known to

this day as the **Dardanelles**. The founder of this people was deified by his descendants and worshipped under the name of Jupiter **Dodonaeus**. (Here we have a mingling of the names of Japheth and Dodan.) The propagators of this cult built the city of **Dodona** as the chief seat of his worship. Egyptian records refer to the **drdny** who were allied to the Hittites (see Ham 23) at the battle of Kadesh. The early Britons were to trace their descent from **Dardanus** (Appendix 7).

(Refs: IDB 1:861. NBD 321. P 1:26)

13. ***Tubal:*** The descendants of Tubal first come to our notice in the inscriptions of Tiglath-pileser I, king of Assyria in about 1100 BC. He refers to them as the **Tabali** whose original area of settlement (i.e. **Tabal**) was adjacent to that of Tegarama (see 5). Subsequently, Josephus recorded the name of Tubal's descendants as the **Thobelites**, who were later known as the **Iberes**. Their land, in Josephus' day, was called by the Romans Iberia, and covered what is now the (former Soviet) state of Georgia whose capital to this day bears the name Tubal as **Tbilisi**. From here, having crossed the Caucasus mountains, this people migrated due north-east, giving their tribal name to the river **Tobol**, and hence to the famous city of Tobolsk.

(Refs: IDB 4:717. NBD 'Meshech' 811. JA 1.vi.1)

14. ***Meshech:*** The descendants of Meshech are often spoken of in close association with those of Tubal (see 34), the Assyrians for example mentioning **Tabal** and **Musku**, whilst Herodotus writes of the **Tiberanoi** and **Moschoi**. A very much earlier reference to the peoples of Meshech, is an inscription of ca 1200 BC which tells us how they overran the Hittite kingdom; and an inscription of Tiglath-pileser I of Assyria from ca 1100 BC, who tells us that, in his own day, the **Mus-ka-a-ia** were able to put into the field an army of 20,000 men. The activities of this same people are also subsequently reported by Tukulti-ninurta II, Ashurnasipal II, Sargon and Shalmaneser III, the last of whom refers to them as the **Mushki**. Josephus knew them as the **Mosocheni** (LXX **Mosoch**), whom, he says, were known in his own day as the

Cappadocians. Some later writers have pointed out that the name of Meshech is preserved in the old tribal name of the **Muscovites** of Russia, after whom **Moscow** is named. Such an identification, it must be said, is not at all unlikely, especially when we consider the subsequent history of their historically close associates the people of Tubal, and the fact that the city is still known today in the Russian tongue as **Moskva**, an exceedingly close, not to say identical relationship to the Assyrian form, **Musku**.

(Refs: IDB 3:357. NBD 811. JA 1.vi.1. P 1:26)

15. ***Tiras:*** Merenptah of Egypt, who reigned during the 13th century BC, provides us with what is so far our earliest reference to the people of Tiras, recording their name as the **Tursha** (or **Turusha**), and referring to them as invaders from the north. The Greeks later knew them as the **Tyrsenoi**, a nation of marauding pirates. Josephus identifies them as the tribe who were known to the Romans as the **Thirasians**, and who we now know as the **Thracians**. They were a *'ruddy and blue-eyed people'*, who spent most of their time in state of *'tipsy excess'*, as one authority put it! Tiras himself was worshipped by his descendants as **Thuras** (i.e. **Thor**), the god of war. The river **Athyras** was named after him, and it is not at all unlikely that the **Etruscans**, a nation of hitherto mysterious provenance, owe to him both their name and descent. The ancient city of **Troas** (Troy) appears to perpetuate his name, as does also the **Taurus** mountain range.

(Refs: IDB 4:652. NBD 1283. JA 1.vi.1. P 1:26)

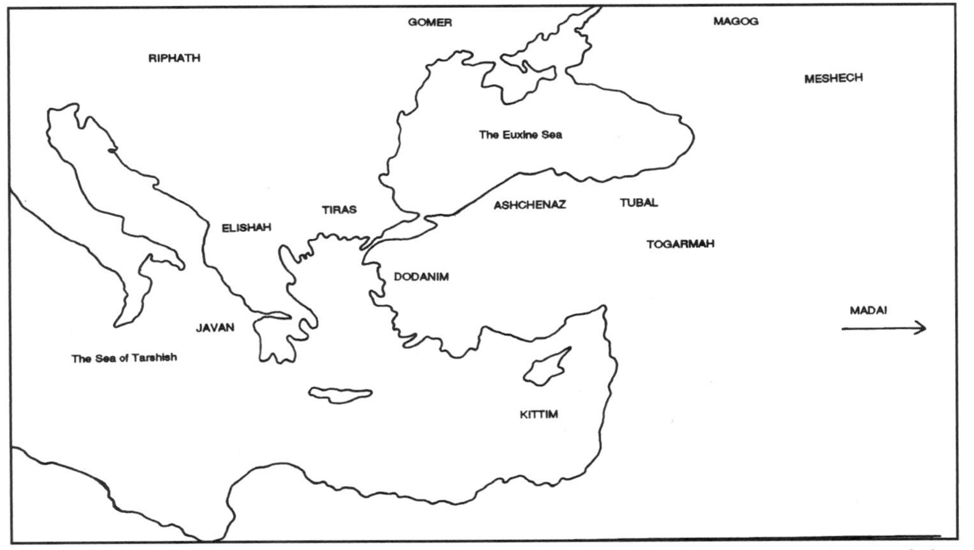

Map 1 The geographical distribution of Japheth's immediate descendants. It should, however, be noted that these given areas of settlement are not necessarily contemporaneous with one another. For example, the area shown for the people of Ashchenaz has been deduced from Assyrian documents from the 7th century BC; whereas that of Meshech has been deduced from inscriptions of the 13th century BC. Naturally, a great deal of 'adjustment' would have taken place concerning the borders of each respective nation in that 600 year period, and this must be borne in mind if certain descrepancies are to be successfully resolved.

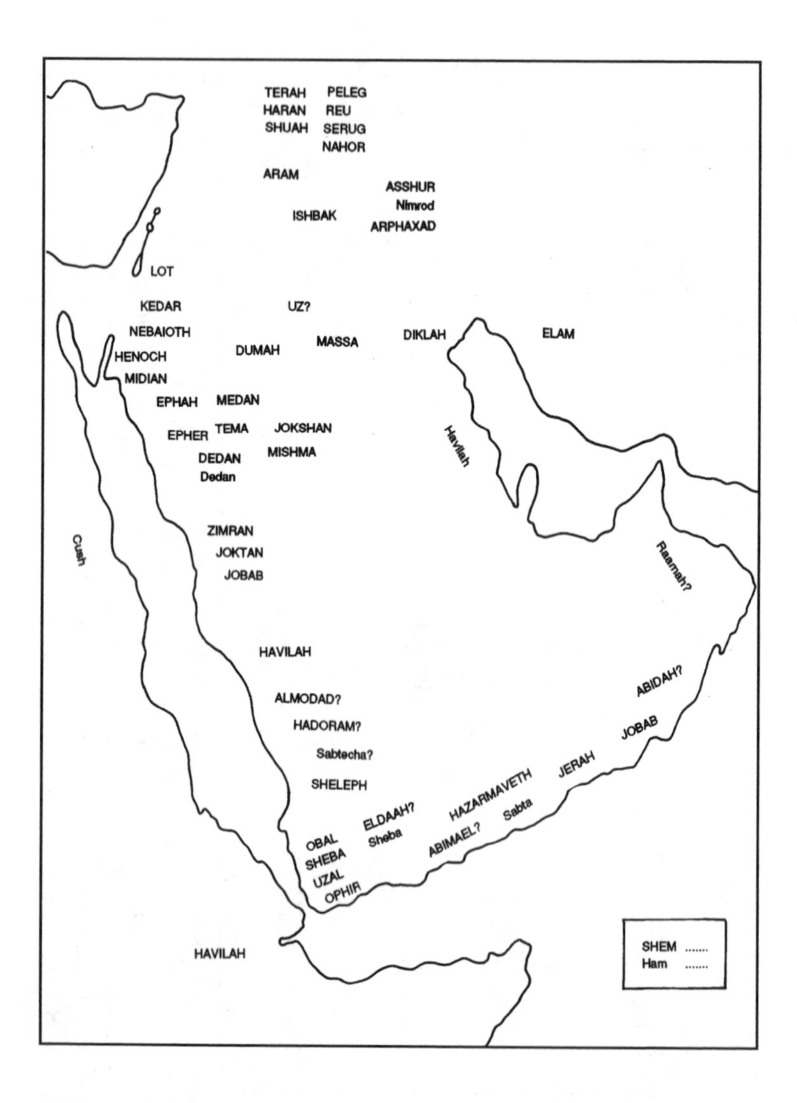

Map 2 The distribution of Semitic peoples throughout the Arabian Peninsula, and certain areas of Asia Minor. Among them are shown eight Hamitic peoples, who clearly make up only a minority of the Arab nations. Again, these areas of settlement are not necessarily contemporaneous with one another.

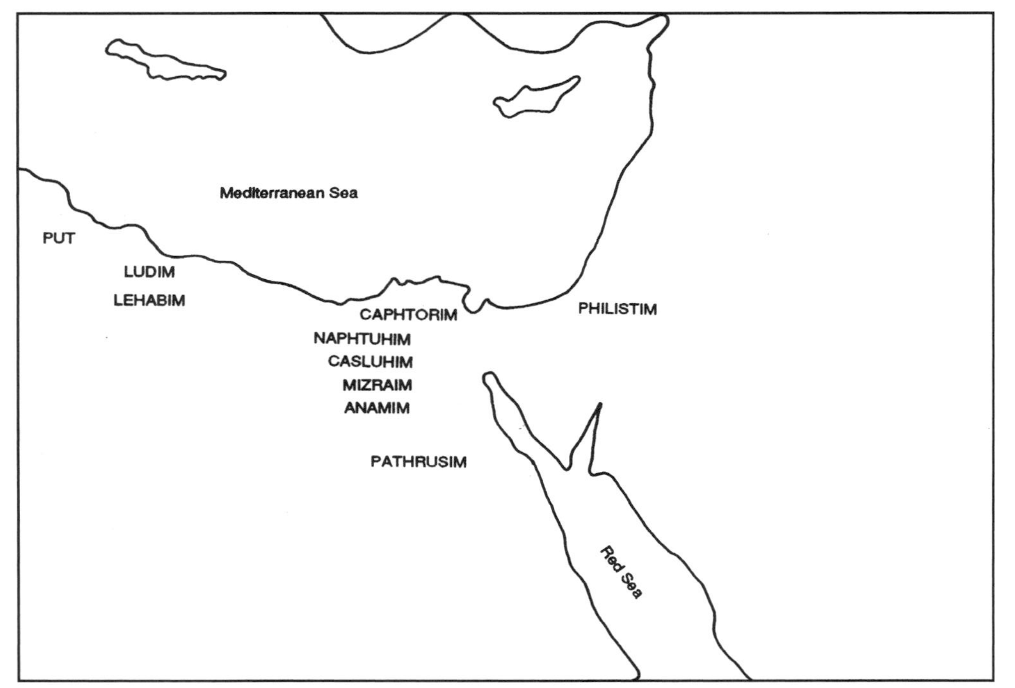

Map 3 The approximate areas of settlement of the descendants of Mizraim throughout Egypt and Libya.

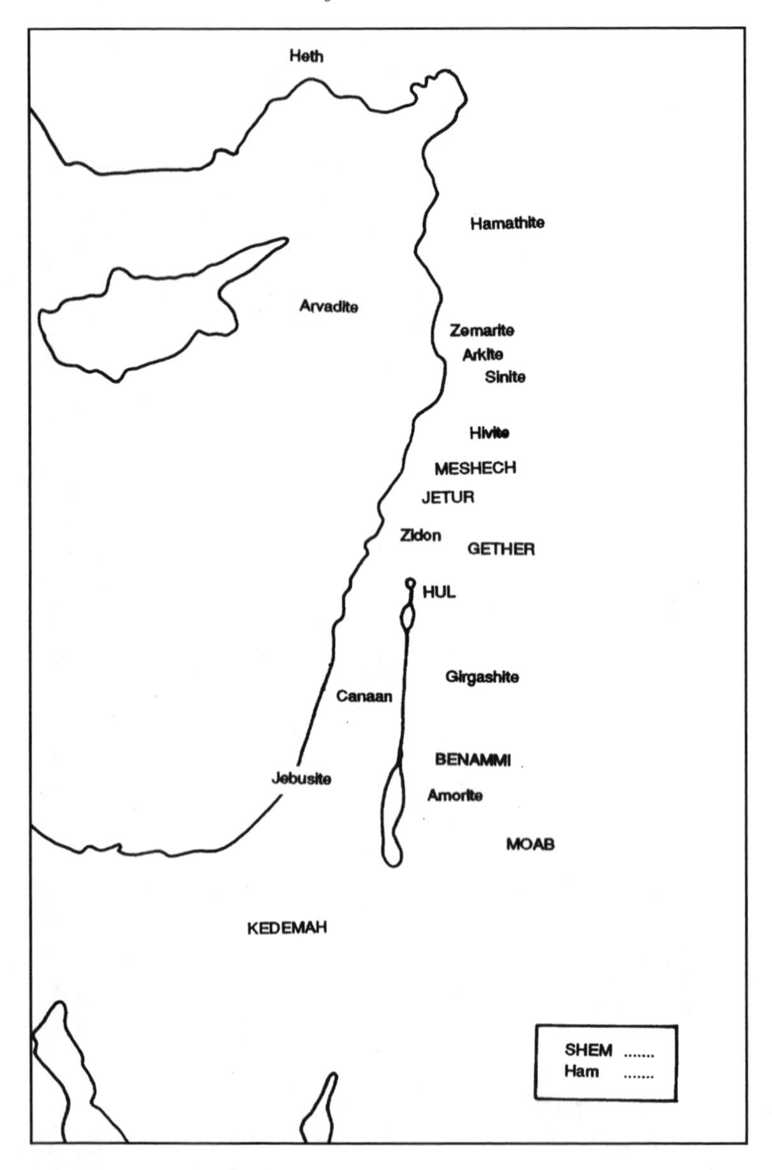

Map 4 The distribution of certain Semitic peoples throughout Palestine, Lebanon and Syria. Among them are certain Hamitic peoples. Again, these various areas of settlement are not necessarily contemporaneous.

Appendix 4

Surviving MSS of the early Welsh Chronicles

(based on Griscom's list, pp. 586–599. See Bibliography)

The National Library of Wales, Aberystwyth

1. Dingestow Court Manuscript – early 13th cent.
2. Peniarth MS. 44 = Hen. 315 (prev. 21) – early 13th cent.
3. Peniarth MS. 45 = Hen. 536 (prev. 29) – late 13th cent.
4. Peniarth MS. 46 = Hen. 27 – early 14th cent.
5. Peniarth MS. 21 = Hen. 50 (prev. 16) – early 14th cent.
6. Peniarth MS. 19 = Hen. 15 – c. 1400.
7. Peniarth MS. 22 = Hen. 318 – 1444.
8. Peniarth MS. 24 = Hen. 175 – 1477.
9. Peniarth MS. 23 = Hen. 313 – mid. 15th cent.
10. Peniarth MS. 25 = Hen. 305 – c. 1500.
11. Peniarth MS. 212 = Hen. 319 – c. 1565.
12. Peniarth MS. 168 = Hen. 437 – 1589–90.
13. Peniarth MS. 118 = Hen. 518 – late 16th cent.
14. Peniarth MS. 261 = Hen. 446 – 16th cent.
15. Peniarth MS. 260 = Hen. 442 – 16th cent.
16. Peniarth MS. 162 = Hen. 354 – late 16th cent.
17. Peniarth MS. 266 = Hen. 55 (prev. 3) – 1634.
18. Peniarth MS. 314 = Hen. 293 (prev. 87 and 21) – 1634–1641.
19. Peniarth MS. 264 = Hen. 272 (prev. 2, 55 and LX) – 1635–6.

20. Peniarth MS. 265 = Hen. 439 (prev. i, 72 and LIV) – 1641.
21. Peniarth MS. 270 = Hen. 530 – ????.
22. Llanstephan MS. 1 = Shirburn Castle MS. 113 C. 18 – early 13th cent.
23. Llanstephan MS. 5 = Shirburn Castle MS. 34 – early 14th cent.
24. Llanstephan MS. 188 – mid. 16th cent.
25. Llanstephan MS. 195 – c. 1570.
26. Llanstephan MS. 59 = Shirburn Castle C. 7 – late 16th cent.
27. Llanstephan MS. 129 = Shirburn Castle D. 17 – early 17th cent.
28. Llanstephan MS. 137 = Shirburn Castle D. 12 – c. 1640.
29. Llanstephan MS. 149 = Shirburn Castle D. 15. – c. 1700
30. Mostyn MS. 117 – late 13th cent.
31. Mostyn MS. 116 – early 14th cent.
32. Mostyn MS. 109 – 16th cent.
33. Mostyn MS. 159 – 1586–7.
34. Mostyn MS. 115 – 17th cent.
35. Mostyn MS. 211 – c. 1685.
36. Panton MS. 9 – c. 1760.
37. Panton MS. 68 – 18th cent.
38. *The Book of Basingwerk* MS. (alias *The Black Book of Basingwerk Abbey*) – 14th and 15th cents.
39. Additional MS. 13 – B = Williams MS. 216 – early 17th cent.
40. Additional MS. 11 – D = Williams MS. 213 – 1694.
41. Additional MS. 312 = Williams MS. 514 – early 18th cent.
42. Additional MS. 23 – B = Williams MS. 227 – c. 1775.

Free Public Library, Cardiff, Wales

43. Cardiff (Havod) MS. 1 – early 14th cent.
44. Cardiff (Havod) MS. 2 – 15th cent *'or earlier'*.
45. Cardiff (Havod) MS. 21 – 1641.
46. Cardiff MS. 21 = Phillipps 13720, part III – 1569.

47. Cardiff MS. 61 = (Tonn 21) – 1734.
48. Cardiff MS. 62 = (Tonn 22) – 1754.

Jesus College Library, Oxford

49. MS. CXI = 1, Hist. MSS. Com., *Report of MSS in the Welsh Lang* – c. 1380.
50. MS. CXLI = 6, Hist. MSS. Com., *Report of MSS in the Welsh Lang* – c. 1471.
51. MS. LXI = 8, Hist. MSS. Com., *Report of MSS in the Welsh Lang* (aka the *Tysilio* Chronicle) – late 15th cent.
52. MS. XXVIII = 19 Hist. MSS. Com. – 1695.

British Museum, London

53. Additional MS. 19,709 = MS. 14, Hist. MSS. Com. – early 14th cent.
54. Cotton, Cleopatra B. V., = MS. 15, Hist. MSS. Com. – 14th cent.
55. Additional MS. 14,903 = MS. 17, Hist. MSS. Com. – early 16th cent.
56. Additional MS. 15,566 = MS. 16, Hist. MSS. Com. – late 16th cent.
57. Additional MS. 14,872 = MS. 41, Hist. MSS. Com. – post 1632.
58. Additional MS. 15,003 – 18th cent.

The above list of chronicles that give the history of the early Britons, constitutes a rather large percentage of the total number of Welsh manuscripts that have come down to us from medieval times. Given that they are all catalogued in easily accessible collections, it is astonishing that even their very existence goes unmentioned by most scholars who are aware of them, and that British history prior to 55 BC remains a blank page. But perhaps their acknowledgement would lead the recorded history of the early Britons uncomfortably back to Genesis, and that is a concept that modernism simply could not accommodate.

Appendix 5

The Latin Text (and translation) of Nenniun 17 and 18

Cap. XVII

Aliud experimentum inueni de isto Bruto ex ueteribus libris ueterum nostrorum.

Tres filii Noe diuiserunt orbem in tres partes post Diluuium. Sem in Asia; Cham in Africa; Iafeth in Europa dilitauerunt terminos suos. Primus homo uenit ad Europam de genere Iafeth Alanus cum tribus filiis suis quorum nomina sunt Hessitio, Armeno, Negue. Hessitio autem habuit filios quattuor hi sunt Francus, Romanus, Britto, Albanus. Armenon autem habuit quinque filios, Gothus, Valagothus, Gebidus, Burgundus. Negue autem habuit tres filios, Wandalus, Saxo, Boguarus. Ab Hisitione autem ortae sunt quattuor gentes, Franci, Latini, Albani, et Britti. Ab Armenone autem quinque, Gothi, Walagothi, Gebidi, Burgundi, Langobardi. A Neguio uero quattuor, Boguarii, Vandali, Saxones, et Turingi. Istae autem gentes subdiuisae sunt per totam Europam. Alanus autem ut aiunt filius fuit Fetebir, filii Ougomun, filii Thoi, filii Boib, filii Simeon, filii Mair, filii Ethach, filii Aurthach, filii Ecthet, filii Oth, filii Abir, filii Rea, filii Ezra, filii Izrau, filii Baath, filii Iobaath, filii Iovan, filii Iafeth, filii Noe, filii Lamech, filii Matusalem, filii Enoch, filii Iareth, filii Malaleel, filii Cainan, filii Enos, filii Seth, filii Adam, filii Dei vivi. Hanc peritiam inueni ex traditione ueterum.

Cap XVIII

Qui incolae in primo fuerunt Brittanniae. Brittones a Bruto. Brutus filius Hisitionis, Hisition Alanei. Alaneus filius Reae Silviae, Rea Silvia filia Numae Pampilii, filii Ascanii, Ascanius filius Aeneae, filii Anchisae, filii Troi, filii Dardani, filii Elise, filii Iuuani, filii Iafeth. Iafeth uero habuit septem filios. Primus Gomer, a quo Galli; secundus Magog, a quo Scythas et Gothos; tertius Madai, a quo Medos; quartus Iuuan, a quo Graeci; quintus Tubal, a quo Hiberei et Hispani et Itali; sextus Mosoch, a quo Cappadoces; septimus Tiras, a quo Traces. Hi sunt filii Iafeth, filii Noe, filii Lamech.

Translation

Chapter Seventeen

I found another explanation concerning this Brutus in the ancient books of our elders:

After the Flood, the three sons of Noah divided the earth into three parts. Shem (settled) in Asia; Ham in Africa, (and) Japheth expanded his borders in Europe. Alanus, of the line of Japheth, (was) the first man who came to Europe with his three sons, whose names were Hessitio, Armenon and Negue. Now, Hessitio had four sons, Francus, Romanus, Britto (and) Albanus. Then Armenon had five sons, Gothus, Walagothus, Gepidus, Burgundus [note: the name Langobardus should have been given here]. (And) Negue had three sons, Wandalus, Saxo (and) Boguarus.

Four nations, then, are arisen from Hessitio: the Franks, the Latins, the Albans and the Britons. Then, from Armenon (come) five (nations): the Goths, the Valagoths, the Gepids, the Burgundians (and) the Lombards. (And) from Negue (come) four (nations): the Bavarians, the Vandals, the Saxons and the Thuringians. (And) these nations are subdivided throughout all Europe.

Alanus, it is said, was the son of Fetebir, (who was) the son of Ougomun, (who was) the son of Thous, (who was) the son of Boib, the son of Simeon, (who was) the son of Mair, the son of Ethach, (who was) the son of Aurthach, the son of Ecthet, (who was) the son of Oth, the son of Abir, (who was) the son of Rea, the son of Ezra, (who was) the son of Izrau, the son of Baath, (who was) the son of Iobaath, the son of Javan, (who was) the son of Japheth, the son of Noah, (who was) the son of Lamech, the son of Methuselah, (who was) the son of Enoch, the son of Jared, (who was) the son of Mahalaleel, the son of Cainan, (who was) the son of Enos, the son of Seth, (who was) the son of Adam, the child of the living God. I found this teaching in the tradition of the elders.

Chapter Eighteen

The first inhabitants of Britain were the Britons (so named) from Brutus. Brutus was the son of Hessitio. Hessitio (was the son of) Alanus. Alanus (was) the son of Rhea Silvia, (who was) the daughter of Numa Pompilius, the son of Ascanius. Ascanius (was) the son of Aeneas, the son of Anchises, (who was) the son of Trous, the son of Dardanus, (who was) the son of Elishah, the son of Javan, (who was) the son of Japheth.

Japheth, in fact, had seven sons, the first (being) Gomer, from whom (came) the Gauls. The second was Magog, from whom (came) the Scythians and the Goths. The third (son was) Madai, from whom (came) the Medes. The fourth (son was) Javan, from whom (came) the (Ionian) Greeks. (And) the fifth was Tubal, from whom (came) the Iberians, the Spanish and the Italians. The sixth (was) Meshech, from whom (came) the Cappadocians. (And) the seventh (son was) Tiras, from whom (came) the Thracians. These are the sons of Japheth, the son of Noah, (who was) the son of Lamech.

(My translation)

Appendix 6

The Molmutine Laws and Pagan Britain

Introduction

The following is an account of the law and society as they stood in ancient Britain during the centuries preceding the Roman invasion of 55 BC. It is based upon the surviving laws of king **Dyfnal Moel Myd** (Dunvallo Molmutius), who reigned in the 5th–4th centuries BC. The account, from pp. 20–24 of Flinders Petrie's paper, [1] bears repeated reading, for it reveals a level of culture and literacy amongst the early Britons that is quite unlike the popular image that has been cultivated in recent years by the modernist treatment of British history. It also speaks volumes for the existence of a king whom modernists have always said was a mythical figure, and it reveals our ancestors to have been a highly cultivated and civilised people, and not the illiterate painted savages of popular fame.

The Molmutine Laws and Pagan Britain

by Flinders Petrie

The condition of pagan Britain is remarkably preserved in the laws of Dyvnal Moelmud. That these laws are certainly long before the tenth century is proved by the gulf that exists between the state of society shown by them and that of the laws of Howel fixed to AD 914. The laws of Howel show a highly complex and detailed condition of law, and an elaborate royal court, with the rights of officials minutely fixed. In the laws of Moelmud there is very simple law, always subject to proved custom and to adaptation to circumstance; there is no royal court, and very few officials, with no defined claims. Moreover, the laws of Howel refer back to Moelmud. What takes the laws of Moelmud at least to Roman times is that they are purely Pagan, and the only Christian allusion is an addition to the forms of legal oath, saying that 'In subsequent times the form of oath was given by the Ten Commandments, the Gospel of St. John, and the blessed Cross' (no. 219). This stamps the previous oaths and the rest of the laws as of the pagan period, and therefore at least of the third century, as British bishops attended the Council of Arles in AD 314. How much farther back these laws may date, towards the traditional time of Moelmud, the fourth or seventh century BC, we cannot now enquire. Probably they were of gradual accretion; but apparently no part comes under the influence of Christian usage. We can, then, at least accept the picture of society here shown as being that of the Britons under the earlier part of the Roman dominion. Of the two series of legal triads, the short first series, 1–34, is here marked **A**;[2] the long series is simply numbered 1–248.[3] Skene agrees to the laws of Howel being of the tenth century, but never mentions those of Moelmud. Stephens asserts that the laws of Moelmud were certainly not composed earlier than the sixteenth century. What writer of that date would forge a consistent body of punitive tribal law, entirely pagan in character, and why any one should do so when the laws of Howel were celebrated and prized, are questions ignored by the easy assertion of a late date for which no reason is given.

First we may note the laws referring to the state of society. Wherever little children, dogs, and poultry are found, the place has a right to the privilege of the court and the sacred place (87). The fields were private property, but cultivated in common tillage (A 5). The wild land was tribal property, free for wood-cutting, hunting, and gathering acorns to feed pigs

(142); but it could not be taken into cultivation without consent of the lord and his court (101). Iron mines were common property; but the ore dug out was private (49). A permit was needed to shift the family wagon or booth; if done without permission, the mover lost all rights, like a criminal or foreigner (A 33). The only general movement allowed was that of the public shepherd of the township, or the chase of wild beasts by the public horn, or of bards spreading knowledge. But bankrupt men who had no kin or land were free to travel (A 28). Thus the organized society was held together.

The idea of the bonds of society was very strong. The mutual bonds of a social state are equal protection, tillage, and law (45). The duties of public help, which every person must render, are in invasion, the public cry of base deeds or murder, and fire (A 15). Society is disorganized by oppressive privilege, unjust decision in law, and negligence allowing regulations to be destroyed (31). The tribal bond is broken up by famine, earthquake, flood, or conquest, and the tribe must begin to form a new social state (A 32).

In more personal matters no arms might be shown in a convention of the country and lord, or convention of independence, or convention of the bards (58). The things indispensable to a free man were his tunic, harp and kettle. The indispensables of a vassal were his hearthstone, bill-hook and trough (239, 240). The property of which a man might not be deprived were his wife, children, clothes, arms, and implements of the privileged arts (53). The three ornaments of a tribe were a book, a harp, and a sword, and they could not be distrained by law (54). The hereditary owner of land could always reclaim it after sale by offering the value (93). This proves that strictly private ownership co-existed with tillage in common.

Government was not despotic, and the chief or king was hardly more than a spokesman. The chief was the oldest efficient man in the tribe (88, 165). The meeting of a country could be called by public proclamation, not only by the king or lord of the district, or the chief of a tribe, but also by a family representative (171). There were three privileged conventions

– first, that of the bards for sound instruction on virtue, wisdom, and hospitality, to record events, actions, and pedigrees, and proclaim laws; second, that of the country and lord for court of law; third, for independence, to establish harmony by mutual reason and agreement of country and country, prince and prince, vote and vote (59, 61). The reasons for taking the vote of the country were to enact or repeal a law, to give judgement when the law is insufficient, and by the privilege of the country to guard against illegal measures by opposing the offenders (161). The consent of the country was needed to abrogate the king's law, to dethrone the sovereign, and to teach new sciences and new regulations in the convention of the bards (63). The native rights of all freeborn men and women were the gift and free use of five acres of land (eight English acres), the carrying of arms, and a vote to a man at puberty, and to a woman when she marries (65). A woman also had the privilege that if she had a son by a foreigner against her consent, as when in the power of foreigners in any way, by tribal order or accident,

her son inherited as a free man, although a foreigner could not inherit privileges of free men for nine generations (116). Each generation of bondmen or foreigners that married a freeborn woman gained one degree of the nine necessary for freedom.

Law was but custom enforced. 'There are three pillars of the law: custom before record and tradition; the king through legal authority; and the decision of the country by vote where there has been neither custom nor law' (155). Three kinds of custom are to be maintained: first, the custom that sets the law aside; second, custom that excels law, but limited to local use; third, custom which excels law in the special circumstances, to be confirmed by the verdict of the country (28). Three things might supersede law: acts of the king to enforce truth or justice; privilege, which nothing can remove; and a contract with witnesses. The judge was to use his discretion widely; he must know the law, know the customs so that law may not injure them, and know the tendencies of his times and their consequences, leaving a wide opening for judge-made law (12).

The court consisted essentially of the king, or lord, to listen and declare what the sense of the law and its application is, the judge to hear the evidence and decide on what is proved of the facts, the clerk to write the pleadings (204, 210) and to destroy the record after the cause is finished (130). This entirely prevented a growth of law by precedents as in England.

Learning was greatly respected. Privilege of support was given to rank, to bards or teachers, and to orphans (A 12). The free man must support a wife, also a fighting man if he does not fight himself, and a family tutor (81). The family teacher was exempt from all manual work, bearing arms, or cultivation, like infants and the aged (55). The privileged arts, that give complete liberty, are bardism, metallurgy, and learning or literature. Those who profess these have an extra five acres of land besides their five acres as free men (68, 71). The smith, mason, and carpenter all had equal rights (73). No bondman was to learn the arts of freemen; if he did so he was free (69), but his sons reverted to bondage (70). Hereditary learning therefore kept the family free, before the nine generations of bondage were over.

The most remarkable part of the law was the respect to foreigners. A foreigner under the protection of the tribe must be assisted in travel (A 8). He was as a trader not to be oppressed or injured though speaking a barbarous tongue (78). The foreigner practising arts obtained the status of freeman in the third generation (70). He was to be allowed an advocate in law courts (209), protection and support from the taxes (209), and to be excused in case of capital crime, as ignorant (23). In case he was shipwrecked on the coast he had free maintainance (198, 199).

These laws give a remarkable view of a community with the greatest respect for weakness and misfortune, high rights for women, full consideration for foreigners, and great privilege for learning, for the arts, and the crafts. Social duty was strongly held, and the full power rested on the vote of every free man and woman, even to deposing the king. Arms were prohibited in civil assembly, and the harp was as necessary to a free man as his coat and his cooking-pot. The whole air is that of simple conditions and a free life, with much personal cultivation and sympathy in general conduct. It would be impossible to produce such a code from a savage or violent people, and this intimate view of their life is the best ground for judging of their qualities. That there was generally a well-organized peace kept in the country is shown by Caesar's statement that 'the number of the people is countless, and their buildings exceedingly numerous.'

Notes

1. Flinders Petrie, W.M. *Neglected British History*. Proc. Brit. Academy. 1917. Vol. VIII. pp. 1–28.
2. Probert, W. (trans). *The Ancient Laws of Cambria*. 1823. pp. 8–14.
3. *ibid.* pp. 15–87.

Appendix 7

The Genealogy of the early British Kings

The following genealogy shows the descent of the early British kings as it was traced down from Japheth, the son of Noah. The sources for this are Nennius 17 and 18 (see Appendix 5), covering from Japheth to Brutus; and Geoffrey of Monmouth who carries the story on from Anchises. To gain an idea of the time-scale involved, I have included the dates of each king's first year of reign as far as that can be calculated from internal and external sources. The Welsh chronicle agrees with Geoffrey of Monmouth almost exactly, although the names are obviously closer in the Welsh to the original early British forms than they are in Geoffrey. For ease, I have used here Geoffrey's latinised forms.

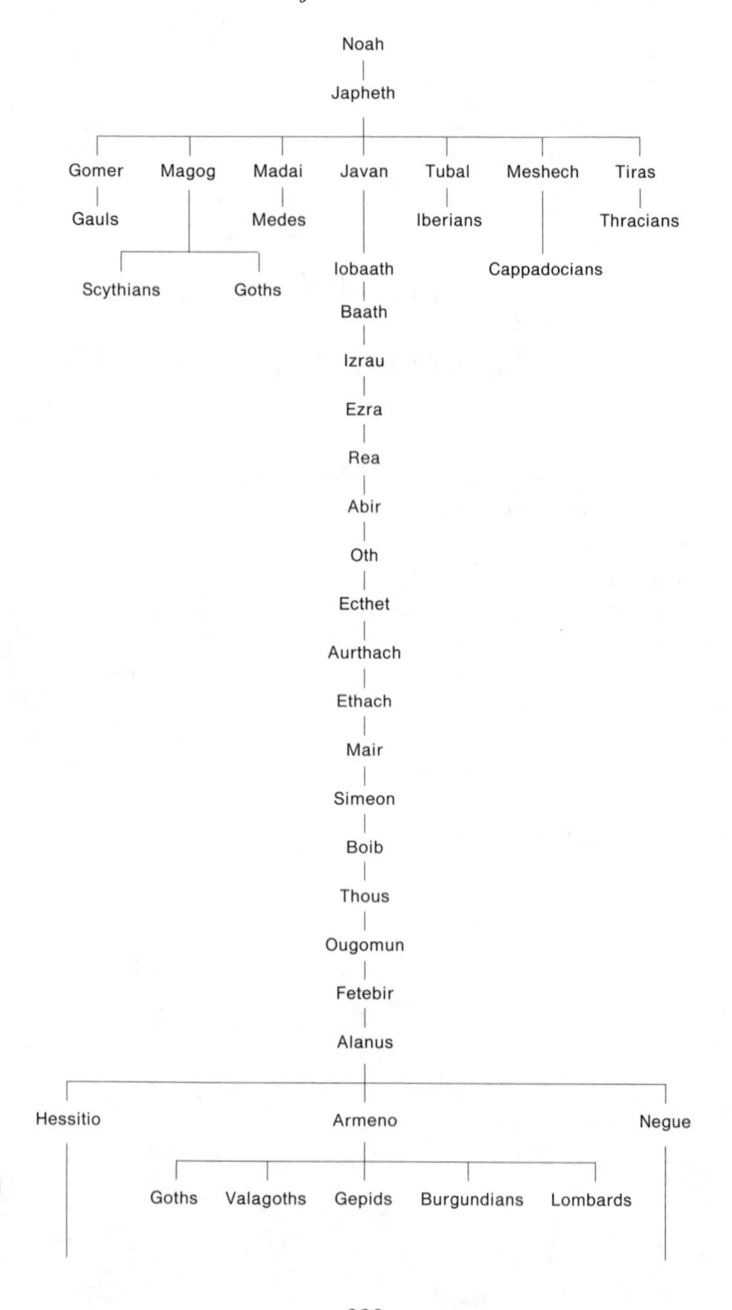
Noah
Japheth
Gomer
Magog
Madai
Javan
Tubal
Meshech
Tiras
Gauls
Medes
Iberians
Thracians
Scythians
Goths
Iobaath
Cappadocians
Baath
Izrau
Ezra
Rea
Abir
Oth
Ecthet
Aurthach
Ethach
Mair
Simeon
Boib
Thous
Ougomun
Fetebir
Alanus
Hessitio
Armeno
Negue
Goths
Valagoths
Gepids
Burgundians
Lombards

Appendix 7

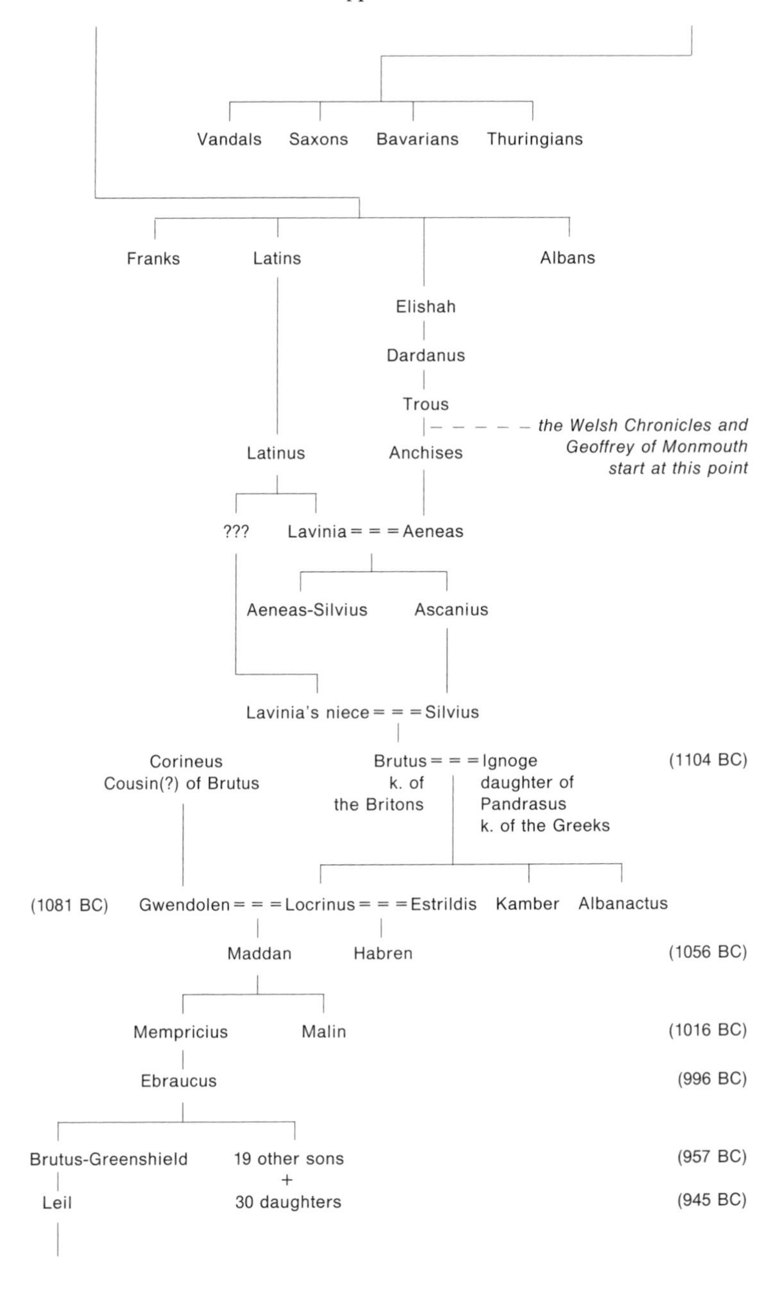

Vandals
Saxons
Bavarians
Thuringians
Franks
Latins
Albans
Elishah
Dardanus
Trous
the Welsh Chronicles and Geoffrey of Monmouth start at this point
Latinus
Anchises
???
Lavinia = = = Aeneas
Aeneas-Silvius
Ascanius
Lavinia's niece = = = Silvius
Corineus
Cousin(?) of Brutus
Brutus = = = Ignoge
k. of the Britons
daughter of Pandrasus k. of the Greeks
(1104 BC)
(1081 BC)
Gwendolen = = = Locrinus = = = Estrildis
Kamber
Albanactus
Maddan
Habren
(1056 BC)
Mempricius
Malin
(1016 BC)
Ebraucus
(996 BC)
Brutus-Greenshield
19 other sons + 30 daughters
(957 BC)
Leil
(945 BC)

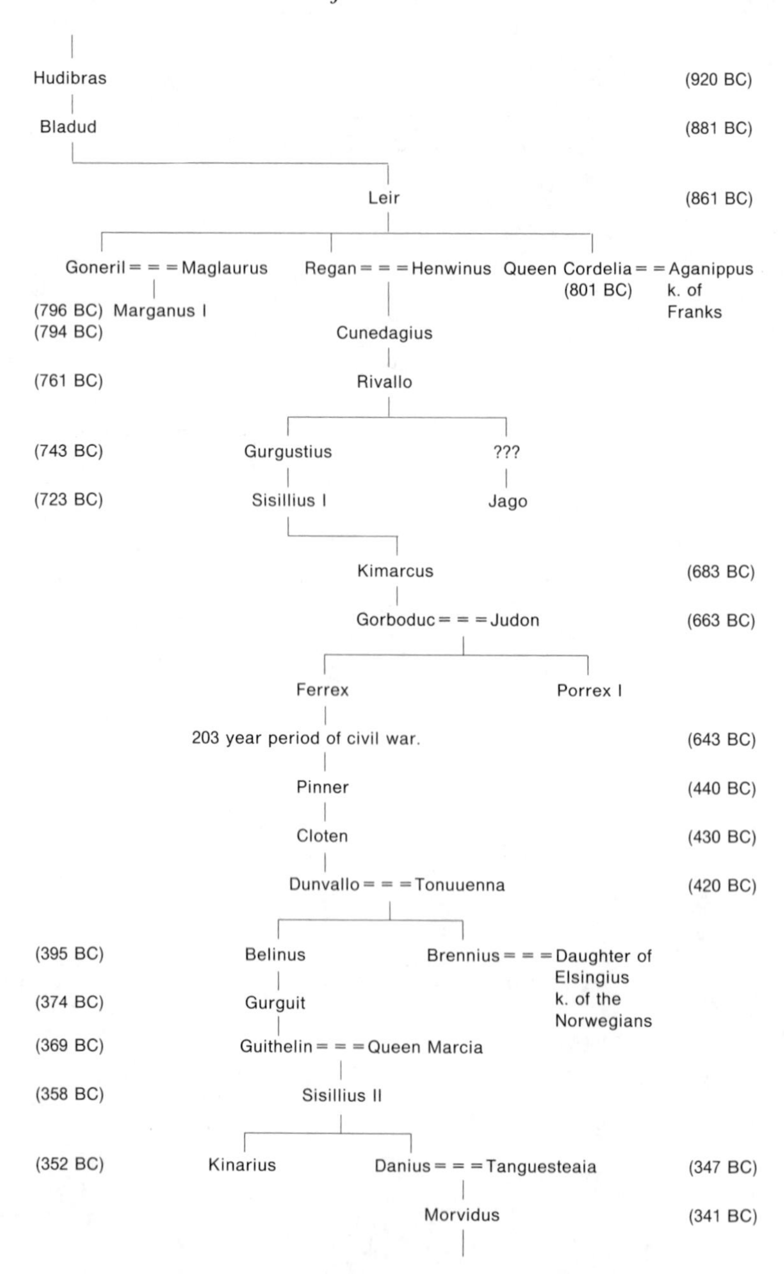
Hudibras
(920 BC)
Bladud
(881 BC)
Leir
(861 BC)
Goneril = = = Maglaurus
Regan = = = Henwinus
Queen Cordelia = = Aganippus k. of Franks
(801 BC)
(796 BC) Marganus I
(794 BC)
Cunedagius
(761 BC)
Rivallo
(743 BC)
Gurgustius
???
(723 BC)
Sisillius I
Jago
Kimarcus
(683 BC)
Gorboduc = = = Judon
(663 BC)
Ferrex
Porrex I
203 year period of civil war.
(643 BC)
Pinner
(440 BC)
Cloten
(430 BC)
Dunvallo = = = Tonuuenna
(420 BC)
(395 BC)
Belinus
Brennius = = = Daughter of Elsingius k. of the Norwegians
(374 BC)
Gurguit
(369 BC)
Guithelin = = = Queen Marcia
(358 BC)
Sisillius II
(352 BC)
Kinarius
Danius = = = Tanguesteaia
(347 BC)
Morvidus
(341 BC)

Appendix 7

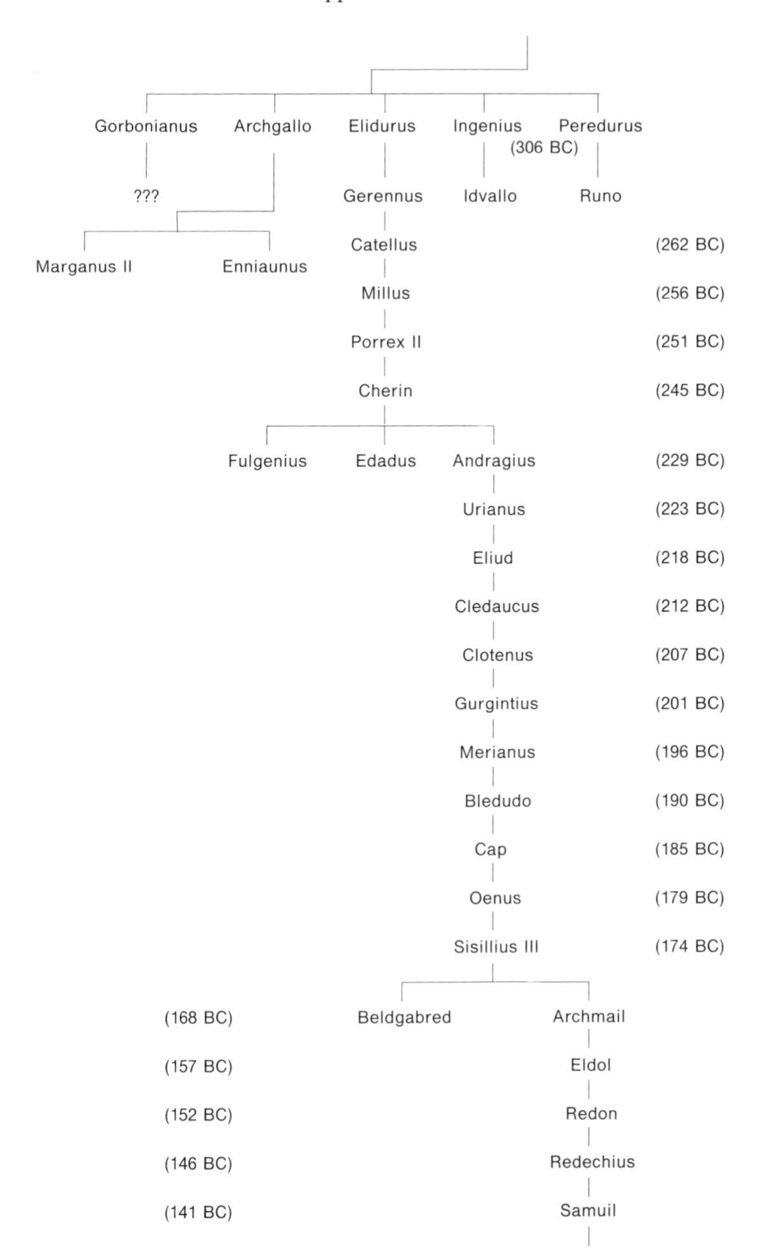

Gorbonianus
Archgallo
Elidurus
Ingenius
Peredurus
(306 BC)
???
Gerennus
Idvallo
Runo
Marganus II
Enniaunus
Catellus
(262 BC)
Millus
(256 BC)
Porrex II
(251 BC)
Cherin
(245 BC)
Fulgenius
Edadus
Andragius
(229 BC)
Urianus
(223 BC)
Eliud
(218 BC)
Cledaucus
(212 BC)
Clotenus
(207 BC)
Gurgintius
(201 BC)
Merianus
(196 BC)
Bledudo
(190 BC)
Cap
(185 BC)
Oenus
(179 BC)
Sisillius III
(174 BC)
(168 BC)
Beldgabred
Archmail
(157 BC)
Eldol
(152 BC)
Redon
(146 BC)
Redechius
(141 BC)
Samuil

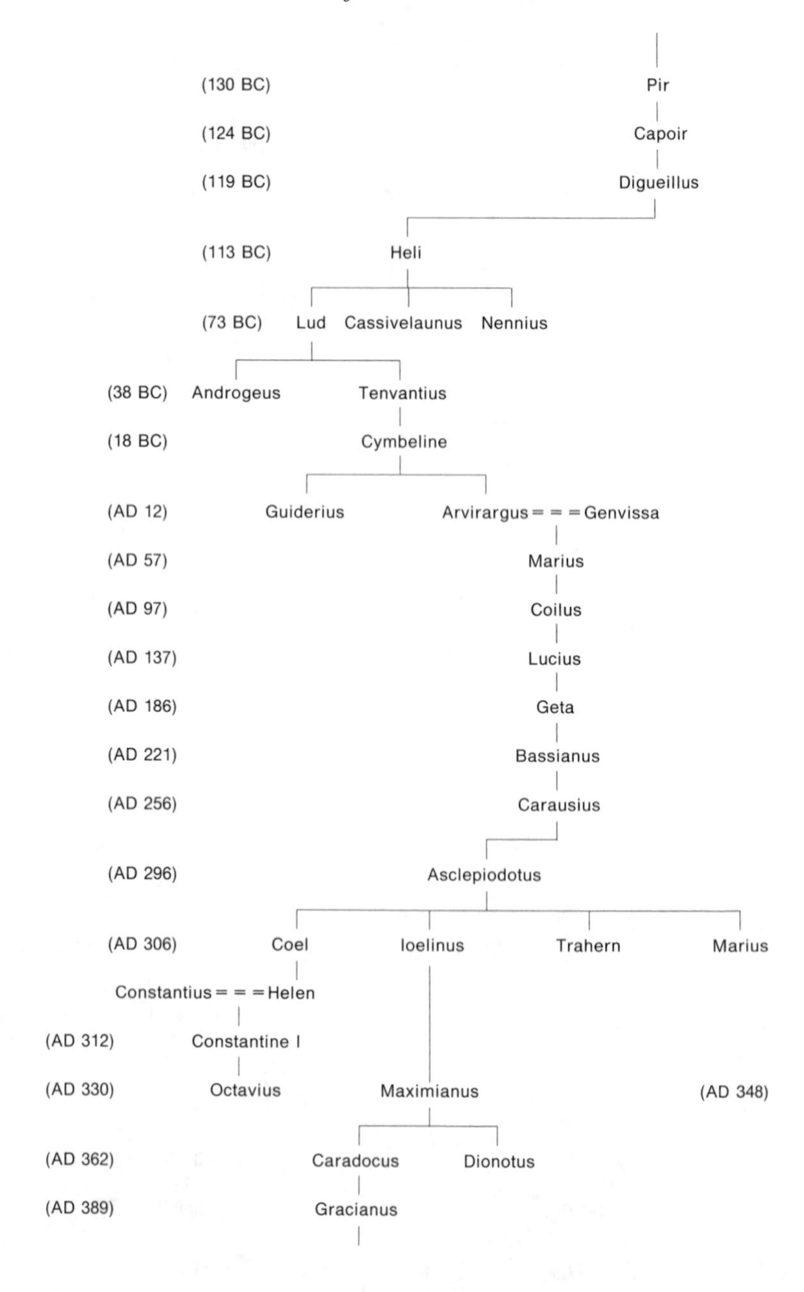
(130 BC) Pir
(124 BC) Capoir
(119 BC) Digueillus
(113 BC) Heli
(73 BC) Lud Cassivelaunus Nennius
(38 BC) Androgeus Tenvantius
(18 BC) Cymbeline
(AD 12) Guiderius Arvirargus = = = Genvissa
(AD 57) Marius
(AD 97) Coilus
(AD 137) Lucius
(AD 186) Geta
(AD 221) Bassianus
(AD 256) Carausius
(AD 296) Asclepiodotus
(AD 306) Coel Ioelinus Trahern Marius
Constantius = = = Helen
(AD 312) Constantine I
(AD 330) Octavius Maximianus (AD 348)
(AD 362) Caradocus Dionotus
(AD 389) Gracianus

Appendix 7

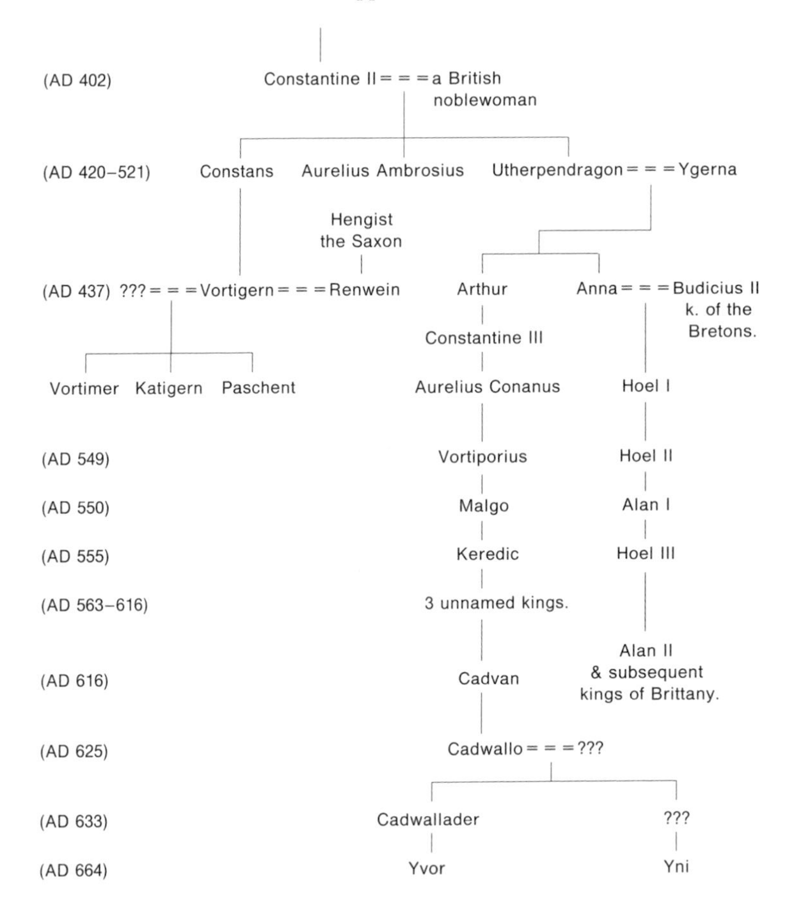

(AD 402)
Constantine II = = = a British noblewoman
(AD 420–521)
Constans
Aurelius Ambrosius
Utherpendragon = = = Ygerna
Hengist the Saxon
(AD 437)
??? = = = Vortigern = = = Renwein
Arthur
Anna = = = Budicius II k. of the Bretons.
Constantine III
Vortimer
Katigern
Paschent
Aurelius Conanus
Hoel I
(AD 549)
Vortiporius
Hoel II
(AD 550)
Malgo
Alan I
(AD 555)
Keredic
Hoel III
(AD 563–616)
3 unnamed kings.
Alan II & subsequent kings of Brittany.
(AD 616)
Cadvan
(AD 625)
Cadwallo = = = ???
(AD 633)
Cadwallader
???
(AD 664)
Yvor
Yni

Appendix 8

The Descent of the East Saxon Kings

The genealogy of the East Saxon kings (from whom the English county of Essex derives its name) was discovered comparatively recently. It was being used as part of the binding of an old book. However, it was happily retrieved and published by Sweet in *The Earliest English Texts.* (Oxford Univ. Press. 1885. p. 179). In the original document the genealogy is set out as follows, the letters appearing here in parentheses belonging to those small portions of the document that had been cut away when binding the book:

de regibus orientalium seaxonum

Offa sighering, sighere sigberhting, sigberht s(aweard)**ing, saweard saberhting, saberht sledding, sle**(dd) **aescwining, aescwine offing, offa bedcing, bedca sigefugling, sigefugl swaepping, swaeppa antsecging, ants**(ecg) **gesecging, gesecg seaxneting.**

item de regibus orientalium seaxonum

Swithred sigemunding, sigemund sigeharding, si(gehard) **sebbing, sebbe seaxreding, seaxred sab**(erhti)**ng, saberht sledding.**

item de regibus orientalium seoxo(num)

Sigered sigericing, sigeric selereding, selered sigeberhting, sigeberht sigeb(aldi)**ng, sigebald selerferthing, selerferth sigeferthing, seaxing, seaxa sledding.**

Appendix 8

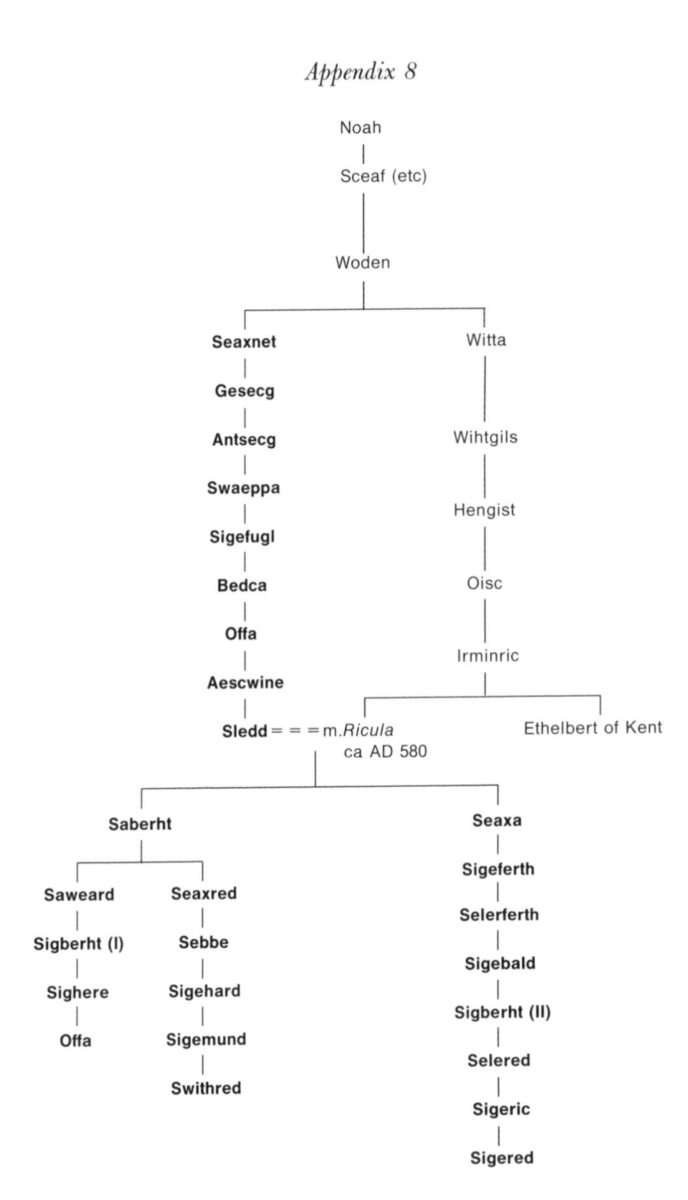

KEY

House of Essex – bold type
House of Kent – medium type (see chapter 7)
Male – roman type
Female – italic type

. . . all of which translates, in today's genealogical terms, into the above table of descent. The point most worthy of consideration here, however, is the method used by the early Saxons for safeguarding against omissions and accidental repeats (or 'scribal doublets' as they are known), the very things, in fact, that modernist scholars assure us render these lists untrustworthy. Although the system was not one hundred per cent foolproof (what system is?), it was nevertheless so simple, it was ingenious. As an exercise, try copying out the list as it is laid out in the original. While spelling mistakes may well occur, you will see that it is virtually impossible to omit a name or accidentally repeat it, for each name is written twice, once with the suffix **-ing** (which simply means **son of**), and once without it.

Indeed, not only the written record was secured against error by this method of recording, but oral transmission was made that much easier and more dependable by the poetic rhythm that was set up by reciting the names thus.

Appendix 9

The Historical Characters of *Beowulf*

Introduction

Virtually every edition of the *Beowulf* epic (and virtually every commentary on the poem), will take pains to assure the reader that what he is reading is **not** a historically accurate account of events or personages. *Beowulf* is described as a moral tale composed several centuries after the times of which it treats, a good yarn, and so on and so forth. What it does not do is embody real history. However, the best test for historicity that can be applied to any document from the past, be it chronicle, epic poem or prose narrative, is the test of its genealogies and personal names. Are the men and women mentioned in the work characters who are known to us from other contemporary sources? Can the genealogies be verified? If they can, then we are dealing with an account that we can rely on as history. If their information is demonstrably wrong or fictitious, and if it is seen to contradict other accepted historical sources, then clearly the rest of the matter can be dismissed as mere fiction. Thus, and in the light of the persistent modernist assertion that *Beowulf* is merely fiction, we shall examine the complex genealogies that are embodied within the poem in the sure knowledge that no compiler of fairy-stories ever went to such enormous lengths to add such circumstantial verisimilitude to his tale as we find in the *Beowulf*. The following evidence will speak for itself.

I have relied on Klaeber (3rd ed. see bibliography) for much of the information contained in the notes, and for the dates which, as he points out, are estimated as closely as the poem and its external corroborative sources will allow. The pivotal date on which most of the others depend, is AD 521, the year in which King Hygelac was slain by the Franks as depicted in Gregory of Tour's **Historiae Francorum**. However, having verified *Beowulf*'s extraordinary historical accuracy on almost all points of the narrative, even those minor insignificant and insubstantial points that only an authentic historical narrative can yield, Klaeber still denies the essential and historical authenticity of the narrative. It is a peculiar position in which many a modernist scholar has found himself.

THE DESCENT OF
THE GEATISH ROYAL HOUSE

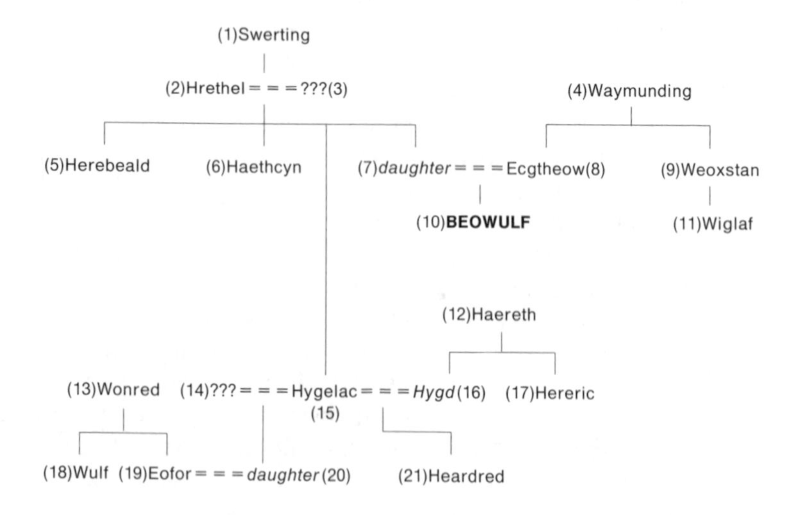

KEY

Male – roman type
Female – italic type

Notes on the Descent of the Geatish Royal House

1. ***Swerting:*** This is Hrethel's father-in-law's surname, not his forename. Swerting would have flourished from c. AD 425 onwards. He was defeated by Frotho, whom we met earlier killing a dragon (see chapter 11). Swerting planned to put Frotho to death, but in the ensuing battle both men slew each other. Swerting's daughter, unnamed, married Hrethel.
2. ***Hrethel:*** AD 445–503. Having reigned over the Geats of southern Sweden, Hrethel died of grief a year after his eldest son's tragic death (see 5 and 6).
3. ***?:*** Unknown.
4. ***Waymunding:*** This is the surname of Beowulf's grandfather. He would have lived during the latter half of the 5th century.
5. ***Herebeald:*** AD 470–502. He was killed by his younger brother Haethcyn in a hunting accident.
6. ***Haethcyn:*** AD 472–510. Haethcyn came to the throne in AD 503. From that time war broke out between the Geats and the neighbouring Swedes culminating in the famous Battle of Ravenswood (**Hrefnawudu**) in the year AD 510. Just before this battle, Haethcyn was killed by Ongentheow (see next table (1)) after having captured the Swedish queen.
7. ***Daughter:*** Unknown.
8. ***Ecgtheow:*** Beowulf's father, otherwise unknown.
9. ***Weoxstan:*** Paternal uncle to Beowulf, he surprisingly helped Onela gain the throne of Sweden (see next table (4)). He and his son, Wiglaf (11), are henceforth known as **Scylfingas**, or Swedes, to denote their treacherously aiding the Swedish king.
10. ***BEOWULF:*** AD 495–583. The subject of the epic that bears his name.
11. ***Wiglaf:*** Beowulf's cousin. Otherwise unknown from external sources, Beowulf adopted him as his heir. (See also Weoxstan 9.)
12. ***Haereth:*** Father of Queen Hygd.
13. ***Wonred:*** Father of Eofor and Wulf.
14. ***?:*** Unknown.

15. ***Hygelac:*** AD 475–521. The pivotal date, AD 521, and from which all other dates are here calculated, is provided by Gregory of Tour's *Historiae Francorum*, where he mentions Hygelac's raid on the Franks. During this raid, Hygelac was slain by Theodebert, the son of Theoderic, the Merovingian king of the Franks.
16. ***Hygd:*** Hygelac's queen.
17. ***Hereric:*** Queen Hygd's brother, he was uncle to prince Heardred.
18. ***Wulf:*** Eofor's elder brother.
19. ***Eofor:*** In the year AD 510, Eofor slew Ongentheow, king of the Swedes (see next table (1)).
20. ***Daughter:*** Unknown.
21. ***Heardred:*** AD 511–533. In AD 532, diplomatic relations between the Geats and the Swedes were ruptured by Heardred's granting asylum to Onela of Sweden's rebellious nephews. Heardred was killed the following year by Onela's forces.

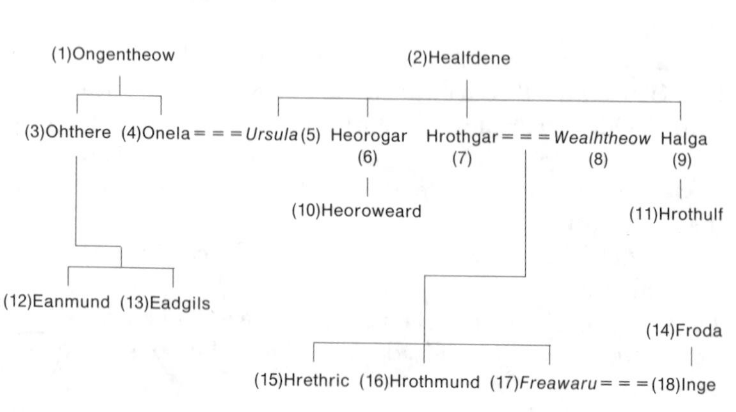

Notes on the Descent of the Swedish and Danish Royal Houses

1. ***Ongentheow:*** AD 450–510. King of Sweden, he has been identified as the Angeltheow of the early (pre-migration) Mercian genealogies (see table to chapter 7). In other early Nordic sources his name is also given as Angantyr and Egill. His queen was taken captive by Haethcyn and Hygelac (see previous table (6) and (14)), and he was killed in the ensuing battle of Ravenswood by Eofor and Wulf (see previous table (18) and (19)).
2. ***Healfdene:*** AD 445–498. Otherwise known as Halfdan, he is celebrated in other sources as the father of Hrothgar (Hróarr) and Halga (Helgi). According to the *Skjoldungasaga*, his mother was the daughter of Jomundus, king of Sweden. His seat of power, which Beowulf tells us was called Heorot, is today marked by the village of Lejre on the Danish island of Zealand.
3. ***Ohthere:*** AD 478–532. His name is rendered Ottar in early West Nordic sources. The burial mound containing his ashes is still known as Ottarshögen.
4. ***Onela:*** AD 480–535. Otherwise Ali in old West Nordic sources, namely the *Skáldskaparmal*; the *Ynglingasaga*; the *Ynglingatal*; and the *Skjoldungasaga*.
5. ***Ursula:*** Orig. Yrsa. In the *Hrolfssaga* and *Skjoldungasaga*, she is depicted as Healfdene's eldest child, not his youngest as given in the *Beowulf*.
6. ***Heorogar:*** AD 470–500. According to the *Beowulf* epic, he died within two years of inheriting his father's crown at 28 years of age. His is one of only two names of the Danish royal house that are not attested in other records (see also 16).
7. ***Hrothgar:*** AD 473–525. Otherwise Hróarr, he was king of Denmark.
8. ***Wealhtheow:*** She was a descendant of the Helmingas, and was renowned for her tactful and diplomatic ways. Intriguingly, her name means Celtic Servant.

9. ***Halga:*** AD 475–503. He is known as Helgi in other Scandinavian sources and as Halgi Hundingsbani in the Eddic poems.
10. ***Heoroweard:*** Born AD 490. Heoroweard did not inherit the crown on his father Heorogar's death. This may have been due to his minority, (he was 10 when his father died), although other young lads have taken the crown at even earlier ages. Lines 2155 ff of *Beowulf* may hold the clue to this. His father refused to pass on to him the royal standard, helmet, sword and breastplate, an extraordinary act that normally denotes that the son has lost his father's respect. How he lost it we are left to imagine.
11. ***Hrothulf:*** AD 495–545. Renowned in other Scandinavian records as the son of Halga, he was, according to the *Skjoldungasaga* (cap. XII) and the *Ynglingasaga* (cap. XXIX), orphaned as a boy of 8. But he was adopted by Hrothgar and his queen at the Danish royal court. He was counted as one of the **suhtergefaederan** (close relatives of the king) and he occupied the seat of honour next to Hrothgar. However, he later attempted (AD 525) to usurp the throne from his cousins Hrethric and Hrothmund (see 15 and 16).
12. ***Eanmund:*** AD 503–533. He was known as Eymundr in the *Hyndluljoth* (cap. XV) and as Aun in the *Ynglingasaga*. Saxo latinised his name as Homothus. He was slain by Weoxstan (see previous table (9)).
13. ***Eadgils:*** Born AD 510. He became king in AD 535, and was known as Athils in other Nordic sources.
14. ***Froda:*** King of the Heathobard's (a Danish people), his lineage (not given in the *Beowulf*) is of great interest to us. We have already seen how the pre-Christian Saxons, Irish and early Britons all traced their royal descents through various lines from Japheth. Froda's line is likewise given as beginning with Japhet (see chapter 8).
15. ***Hrethric:*** Born AD 499. Known in other records (the *Bjarkamal* and Saxo [ii]) as Hroerekr and Roricus respectively, he was slain by Hrothulf (see 11) in AD 525.
16. ***Hrothmund:*** Born AD 500. His is one of only two

names in this genealogy that cannot be verified from other surviving sources (see also 6).

17. ***Freawaru:*** Born AD 501. She married Ingeld of Sweden in AD 518.

18. ***Ingeld:*** Identical with Ingjaldr illrathi of *Ynglingasaga* fame, his prowess was sung for ages in the halls of Scandinavia. Indeed, his fame is referred to in a somewhat indignant letter written in AD 797 by Alcuin to bishop Speratus of Lindisfarne: *'Quid enim Hinieldus cum Christo?'* – What has Ingeld to do with Christ? This was written in rebuke of the monks of Lindisfarne who loved to hear the old pagan sagas retold in cloisters. Yet it is to such monks that we owe the often clandestine preservation of works like the *Beowulf* and the old pagan genealogies, which have in turn yielded such vital information concerning our pre-Christian forebears' unexpected knowledge of the Genesis patriarchs. Ingeld himself married Hrothgar's daughter, Freawaru, in the year AD 518. In the *Langfethgatal* (roll of ancestors) he is listed as Ingialdr Starkadar fostri.

Comment

It is very obvious indeed from the above information that in *Beowulf* we are not dealing with a Christian-inspired fiction in spite of everything that has been said about the poem by the modernist school of thought. All the characters in the epic have their places set very firmly indeed within the pagan pre-Christian framework of the recorded histories of Denmark and Sweden, and we note an astonishing accuracy throughout the *Beowulf* epic whenever it deals with these characters and their often very complex relationships with one another. That is not the kind of thing that arises by chance or fiction. But further to this, and crucial to our study, are the graphic zoological depictions that appear in the poem of the creatures that these historical characters had to deal with. These depictions are listed in the following Appendix.

Appendix 10

Zoological applied terms in the *Beowulf* Epic

Saxon term	Literal meaning	Line	Creature denoted
1. aelwiht	alien monster	1500	Grendel (female)
2. atol aglaeca	the terrifying ugly one	732	Grendel (male)
3. andsaca	adversary	1682	Grendel (male)
4. angenga	solitary walker	449	Grendel (male)
5. atol	terrible	165	Grendel (male)
6. atelic	horrible	784	Grendel (male)
7. attorsceatha	venomous foe	2839	Flying reptile
8. brimwylf	she-wolf of the lake	1506	Grendel (female)
9. cwealm cuma	death visitor	792	Grendel (male)
10. daedfruma	evildoer	2090	Grendel (male)
11. deathscua	death shadow	160	Grendel (male)
12. deofl	devil	2088	Grendel (male)
13. draca	dragon	2290	Flying reptile
14. eacen craeftig	exceedingly powerful	3051	Flying reptile
15. ealdorgewinna	life enemy	2903	Flying reptile
16. ellengaest	powerful demon	86	Grendel (male)
17. ellorgaest	alien spirit	807	Grendel (male)
18. ent	giant	2717	Flying reptile
19. feond	fiend, enemy	101	Grendel (male)
20. feondscatha	dire foe	554	Grendel (male)
21. feorhbealu	life destruction	2077	Grendel (male)
22. ferhthgenithla	deadly foe	2881	Flying reptile
23. fifelcyn	race of monsters	104	Grendel (species)
24. gastbona	soul slayer	177	Grendel (male)

Saxon term	Literal meaning	Line	Creature denoted
25. geoscaftgast	demon sent by fate	1266	Grendel (male)
26. gesaca	adversary	1773	Grendel (male)
27. graedig	greedy, ravenous	121	Grendel (male)
28. grimlic	fierce, terrible	3041	Flying reptile
29. gromheort	hostile hearted	1682	Grendel (female)
30. grundwyrgen	hellish monster	1518	Grendel (male)
31. gryrefah	terr. variegated colouring	3041	Flying reptile
32. guthsceatha	enemy, destroyer	2318	Flying reptile
33. haethstapa	heath stalker	1368	Stag
34. heorowearh	accursed outcast	1267	Grendel (male)
35. hordweard	treasure guardian	2293	Flying reptile
36. hringboga	coiled (or wrapped) creature	2561	Flying reptile
37. idese inlicness	the likeness of a woman	1351	Grendel (female)
38. inwitgaest	malicious foe	2670	Flying reptile
39. lathgeteona	loathly spoiler	974	Grendel (male)
40. ligdraca	fire dragon	2333	Flying reptile
41. ligegesa	fire terror	2780	Flying reptile
42. lyftfloga	air flier	2315	Flying rept. spec.
43. manfordaedla	wicked destroyer	563	Sea monster
44. manscatha	wicked ravager	712	Grendel (male)
45. mearcstapa	march stalker	103	Grendel (male)
46. meredeor	sea beast	558	Sea monster
47. muthbona	mouth slayer	2079	Grendel (male)
48. nearofah	cruelly hostile	2317	Flying reptile
49. nicor	water monster	845	Lake monster
50. nihtbealu	night evil	193	Grendel (male)
51. nithdraca	hostile dragon	2273	Flying reptile
52. nithgaest	malicious foe	2699	Flying reptile
53. orcneas	monsters	112	Monsters general
54. saedeor	sea beast	1510	Sea monster
55. saedraca	sea dragon	1426	Sea monster
56. sceadugenga	walker in darkness	703	Grendel (male)
57. scinna	demon	939	Grendel (male)
58. scucca	demon	939	Grendel (male)
59. scynscatha	hostile demon	707	Grendel (male)
60. searogrim	fierce in battle	594	Grendel (male)

Saxon term	Literal meaning	Line	Creature denoted
61. theodsceatha	waster of peoples	2278	Flying reptile
62. thyrs	giant	426	Grendel (male)
63. weres waestmum	the shape of a man	1352	Grendel (male)
64. widfloga	wide flyer	2346	Flying reptile
65. wiht unhaelo	unholy monster	120	Grendel (male)
66. wildeor	wild beast	1430	Lake monster
67. wohbogan	coiled (or wrapped) creature	2827	Flying reptile
68. wrecend	avenger	1256	Grendel (female)
69. wyrm	serpent	1430	Lake monster
70. wyrmcynn	race of serpents	1425	Monster species
71. ythgewinnes	wave-thrasher	1434	Lake monster

Appendix 11

From Japheth to Brutus

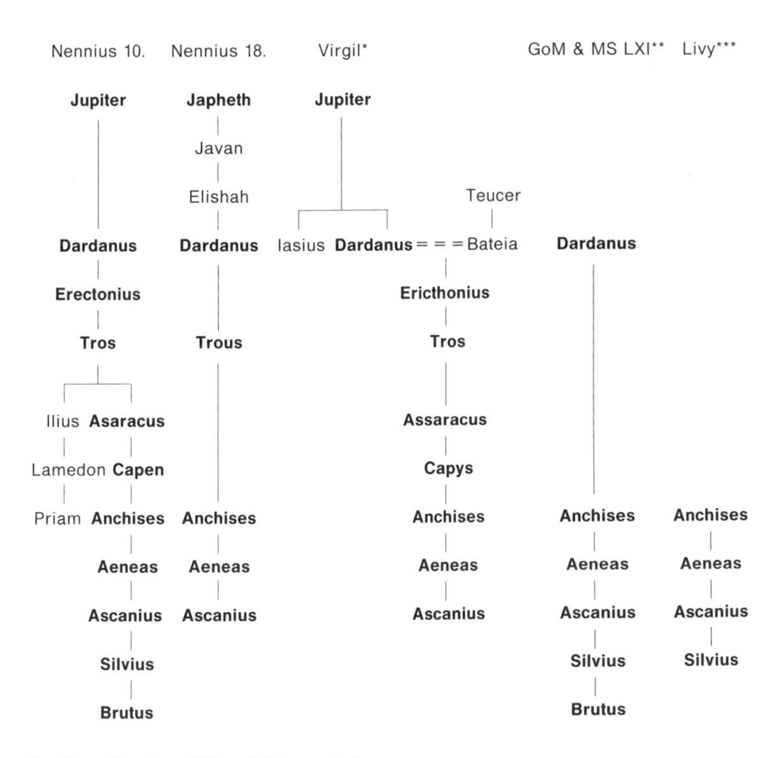

* From *The Aeneid* (see bibliography).
** Geoffrey of Monmouth's *History of the Kings of Britain* (see bibliography) and **Jesus College MS LXI**, the so-called *Tysilio Chronicle*.
*** From *The Early History of Rome* (see bibliography).

Note

In the above table, I have brought together the genealogies contained in no less than five diverse and ancient sources which show the descent of certain early patriarchs. Three of those sources begin with the same original, namely Japheth, otherwise remembered as Jupiter amongst the ancient and pagan Latin races, thus demonstrating beyond any reasonable doubt that Japheth was synonymous with Jupiter. And two of them end with Brutus, the eponymous founder of the early Britons. All of the sources differ from one another in many and various points, which rules out inter-dependency or copying. However, they also agree on many independent points, which demonstrates the historicity of the patriarchs listed. If it were at all possible to cite a comparable case where such ancient patriarchs are commonly listed amongst such diverse and independent sources, there can be little doubt that their historicity would be accepted without question amongst modern scholars. After all, the historicity of many other characters from the ancient world is accepted on much less evidence than this. Indeed, their historicity is accepted, more often than not, merely upon the single appearance of a name, without any other corroborative evidence being required. And yet the above genealogies that present the historian with such uniquely comprehensive and corroborative evidence are commonly listed as myth and fable. Perhaps the reason for this is better pondered upon than stated.

Appendix 12

The Descent from Japheth of the Miautso People of China

I have constructed the following patriarchal genealogy from the translation by Edgar Truax[1] of the oral traditions of the Miautso people of China. They were yet another early people who regarded themselves as being descended from Japheth, and who remembered some of the other early patriarchs whose names likewise appear in the Genesis record. They were found to already possess this knowledge in the form of ancient couplets when they were encountered for the first time by Christian missionaries. Moreover, they were in possession of surprisingly accurate recollections of the Creation and the Flood, and some of the close detail of their accounts coincides almost identically with the Genesis record. Having originally settled in what is now the Kiangsi province of China, from where they were later driven out by the Chinese, they claim that they are not themselves of Chinese stock, and this is borne out by their insistence that they are descended from Japheth. i.e. of Indo-European descent. The oral traditions in which the descent of the Miautso has been preserved, owe their purity to the fact that they have been recited faithfully and in full at funerals, weddings and other public occasions since time immemorial.

THE DESCENT OF THE MIAUTSO PEOPLE OF CHINA

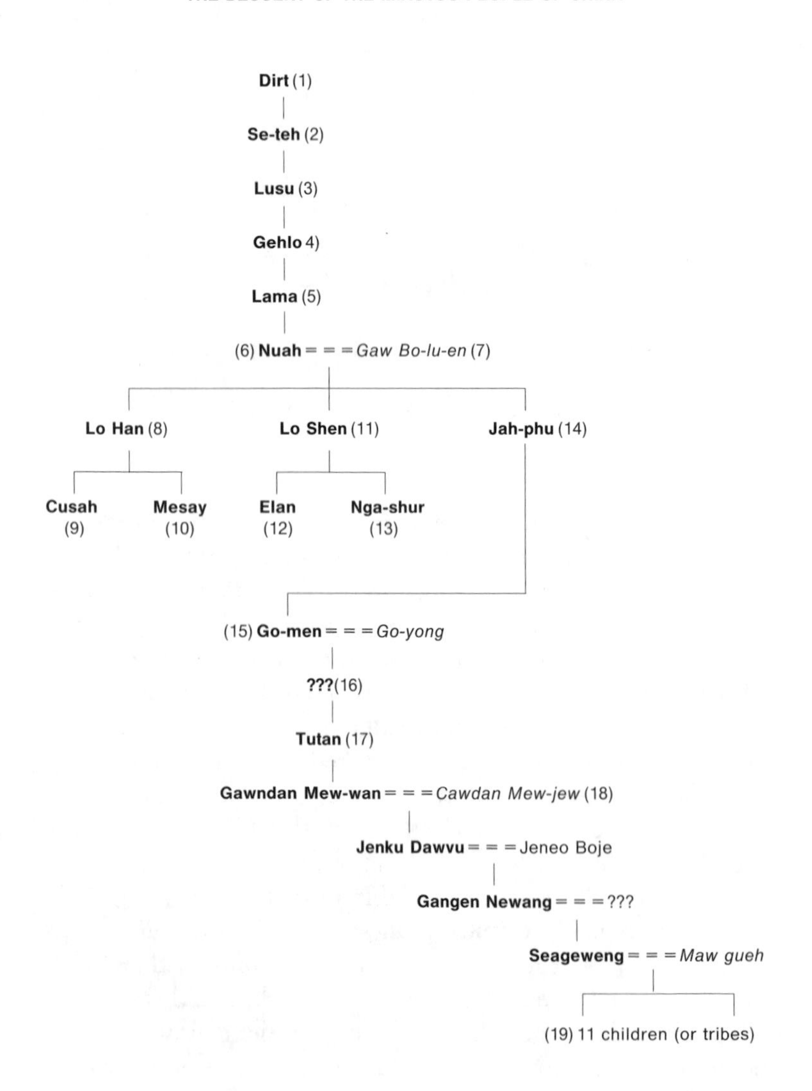

KEY

Male – bold type
Female – italic type

Notes on the Descent of the Miautso People of China

1. ***Dirt:*** This is Truax's English rendering of the original name, not a transposition. It is clearly meant to portray Adam, the version of whose name in the Miautso language (as in Hebrew, Akkadian and so on), means earth or clay, the substance from which he was created.

2. ***Se-teh:*** The Biblical Seth.

3. ***Lusu:*** The names in the book of the Generations of Adam (Genesis 5) that immediately follow that of Seth are: Enos, Cainan, Mahalaleel, Jared, Enoch and Methuselah. The name Lusu may conceivably be identified as a corruption of one of the elements of Mahalaleel. Otherwise, it is unidentifiable.

4. ***Gehlo:*** A corruption, perhaps, of the final element of Methuselah's name. Otherwise, it is unidentifiable.

5. ***Lama:*** The Biblical Lamech.

6. ***Nuah:*** Noah. In the Miautso account, Nuah was a righteous man who was commanded by God to build a great ark. The release of the dove from the ark is mentioned amidst a graphic and somewhat horrifying depiction of the Flood itself and the eventual drying out of the land.

7. ***Gaw Bo-lu-en:*** Apart from certain Jewish traditions, this is an interesting and rare naming of Noah's wife. Genesis, of course, does not give her name.

8. ***Lo Han:*** The Biblical Ham. The descent of the following identifiable patriarchs is given along with a graphic account of Babel and the confusion of tongues. It is then told how the nations spread out from Babel and encircled the globe. This is a surprising preservation of ancient knowledge, for the Miautso, at the time of their first encounter with missionaries, had no concept of the earth being round.

9. ***Cusah:*** The Biblical Cush.

10. ***Mesay:*** The Biblical Mizraim.

11. ***Lo Shen:*** The Biblical Shem.

12. ***Elan:*** The Biblical Elam.

13. ***Nga-shur:*** The Biblical Asshur.

14. ***Jah-phu:*** The Biblical Japheth.

15. ***Go-men:*** The Biblical Gomer.

16. ***???:*** An unnamed patriarch.

17. ***Tutan:*** This was an adopted name.

18. The following list of patriarchs and matriarchs indicate the seriousness with which the Miautso kept their pedigrees in common with many other early peoples.

19. According to the Miautso themselves, of these eleven children or tribes, five formed the Miautso nation, and six intermarried with the invading Chinese.

Note

1. Truax, E. *Genesis According to the Miao People*. Impact Article. April 1991. Institute for Creation Research. PO Box 2667. El Cajon. California 92021. USA.

Appendix 13

Britain's First Christian

> 'The wars and persecutions which followed the first preaching of the gospel in Britain have destroyed all certain records of Christianity in these early times.'
>
> (Churton, E. *The Early English Church.* London. 1841. p. 3)

The above comment, made over 150 years ago, is typical of the mistaken assumption under which scholars have laboured for centuries. The records of this island's earliest Church, far from having been destroyed or lost, are in fact to be found in the Welsh documents known as the Triads. The fact that no notice has been taken of them down the centuries is due entirely to the prejudice that has been lain upon anything of Welsh origin since the Augustine-inspired massacre of the Welsh clergy at Bangor in the early 7th century. To read some books these days, one could easily be misled into thinking that Augustine himself was practically the first Christian to land on these shores, the 'Lucius' mission to Rome of the late 2nd century and the Celtic Church in general receiving minimal notice.

Modern scholarship, when dealing with the earliest appearances of the Christian faith in Britain, will usually set up straw-men, personified in the late Saxon-cum-Norman legends of Joseph of Arimathea and of St Paul's allegedly landing here, only to knock them down again with the erroneous observation that nothing can be certainly known before Augustine's day. Otherwise, all is legend and insubstantial myth. But is it? As is often the case, the original records carry a somewhat different story. Flinders Petrie tells us about it:

> 'The Lucius question next arises. To judge of this we must look at the whole of the statements about the rise of the British Church. We must carefully keep to the authorities, as confusion has arisen by modern authors making arbitrary identifications of the east British or London family of Casswallon with the west British or Silurian family of Caradog. The actual statements of the triads name two generations before Caradog (Caratacus) and three after him – Llyr, Bran, Caradog, Cyllin, Coel, Lleirwg. From triads 18 and 35, Bran was seven years a hostage in Rome for his son Caradog – implying that Caradog was sent back to rule in Britain. The seven years, therefore, would be from AD 51 to 58. From Rome he "brought the faith of Christ to the Cambrians". Looking at the Epistle to the Romans, written AD 58, the obvious strength of Christianity then, its hold in Caesar's household, where Bran was a hostage, and its political position under Nero, there is nothing in the least improbable in a British hostage in Rome being among converts by AD 58. In triad 62, Lleirwg, the great-grandson of Caradog, "first gave lands and the privilege of the country (i.e. position of native free-men) to those who first dedicated themselves to the faith of Christ", and he founded the first archbishopric, that of Llandav. This would be about AD 130 to 160. Three generations for such a spread of influence from one of the royal family is certainly not too short a time.
>
> Next comes the account in Tysilio [i.e. Jesus College MS LXI] and the Liber Pontificalis, that Lles (Lucius) sent to Eleutherius, "soon after his entrance upon the pontificate", or about AD 180, for missioners from Rome. If the west British rulers had already started official Christianity a generation or two earlier, there is

nothing unlikely in this movement. That Christianity was firmly established in even remote parts of Britain at the close of the second century is shown by Tertullian stating that "the Britons in parts inaccessible to the Romans, Christ has truly subdued".[1] Collateral with this is the great importance of the Gallic Church under Irenaeus AD 180. The later stage, of the British bishops in AD 314 attending the Council of Arles, brings the development into the full course of ecclesiastical history. In this growth thus recorded there is not a single stage that is historically inconsistent or improbable. Further agreeing with this is the genealogy of Vortigern in Nennius (49), where, amid purely British names, Paul occurs at about AD 175.'

Note

1. *Adv. Iud.*, p. 189, edit. 1664.

Flinders Petrie made just one mistake here in that he misinterpreted the genealogy of Vortigern as being given in **de**scending order in the original Latin of Nennius, when in fact it is given in **a**scending order. In other words, Paul did not live **before** Vortigern (who flourished ca AD 450) but **after** him, probably around the year AD 600:

Nennius chapter 49

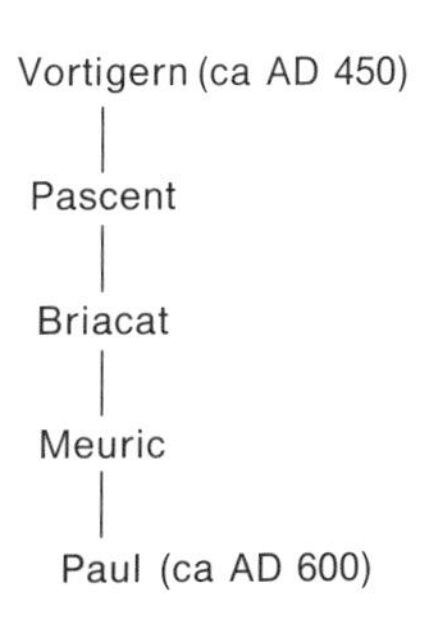

* See Appendix 7.

The mistake is surprising, for Nennius specifically states that this genealogy is 'traced backwards to the beginning' (*Haec est genealogia illius quae ad initium retro recurrit*), i.e. in ascending order, rather than forwards to the end in descending order. But in everything else, Flinders Petrie is perfectly correct. It is unequivocally stated in the early records that the man who first brought the Christian faith to these shores was none other than Bran, the father of Caratacus (Caradog) who, with his family, was taken to Rome in chains and paraded before the Senate by the Emperor Claudius with the view to their immediate and summary execution. Caratacus (or, more usually, Caractacus), however, gave his famous speech of defiance that earned him instead the Senate's applause, a state pension and apartments in the Imperial Palace. And here conventional history loses sight of him. But the triads add to our knowledge. They tell us that, in perfect accord with previous Roman practice, Caratacus was allowed home to rule as a puppet king, but his family were kept behind as surety for his good behaviour. Whilst detained for seven years in Caesar's household, his father Bran was converted to Christ, and when allowed to return to Britain in AD 58, the very year of Paul's epistle to the Romans, he brought the Christian faith with him. It is difficult to imagine a more straightforward, uncomplicated and entirely feasible account, and we can only wonder why it has been ignored all these years.

Appendix 14

The Irish Chronicles and the end of the Ice Age

One of the questions often raised concerning the early post-Flood history of Europe, is that of the Ice Age, the impression being no doubt that the Ice Age poses some kind of a problem for the biblical model. Few creationists would question the historical reality of the so-called Ice Age, although we would certainly question the vast span of time allotted to it under the evolutionary scheme of things. In other words, it is something that would have lasted only a few centuries, perhaps even a thousand years or more, rather than the hundreds of thousands of years proposed by others. But of added interest to us in this present study is the fact that the receding of the ice sheets over northern Europe seems to have been witnessed by some of its earliest colonists who have left intriguing records behind them.

Nennius, for example, in the 13th chapter of his *Historia Brittonum*, has preserved a fascinating account of an unexpected encounter with an iceberg by some early colonists of Ireland. Having arrived from the warm Mediterranean basin via the Spanish peninsula at an unspecified date, and being entirely unfamiliar with ice at sea, at the end of their first year in Ireland they looked out at sea and saw what they described as a 'tower of glass' (*... conspiciunt turrim uitream in medio mare*). Moreover, upon the tower they could see what they took to be men, but could get no reply from them when they shouted (... *et homines conspiciebant et quaerebant loqui ad illos nunquam respondebant*). They therefore launched an attack upon the tower. Some of their boats were wrecked on the ice, while some men who had managed to land upon it were washed off by the heavy seas and drowned (... *et demersi sunt*).

The creatures on the ice that had looked like 'men' at a distance, were probably seals. But added to this intriguing account (icebergs have always been a rare sight off the coast of Ireland since those early days), we have the following detail that can be dated with fair precision. It appears in the Irish *Annals of Clonmacnoise*, translated into English in the year 1627 by Conell Mageoghagan, where firstly we are told that during Partholan's coming to Ireland (15th century BC) he counted 'but three laughs [lochs or lakes] and nyne Rivers in the Kingdom'.[1] But then, during the later second colonisation of Ireland, we are told that 'Many Laughs and Rivers broke out in their time'.[2]

Lakes and rivers don't just suddenly 'break out' in a short period of time without a source of water that is truly vast. So it would seem, therefore, that we are given in the early Irish records an intriguing glimpse into the melting of the north European ice-sheets which occurred some short time after the 15th century BC. Given Ussher's chronology for the year of the Flood, 2348 BC, and assuming that the ice covered Europe soon after the receding of the Flood waters, that would allow about a thousand years for the Ice Age. The Britons didn't settle under Brutus in these islands until some three hundred years later (ca 1104 BC), which is doubtless why their records contain no allusions to ice or a sudden burgeoning of rivers and lakes as do the earlier Irish accounts.

Notes

1. Mageoghagan, C. 1627. *The Annals of Clonmacnoise.* Printed in Dublin at the University Press. 1896. (Murphy ed.). p. 13.
2. *ibid.* p. 15.

Bibliography

Alexander, Marc. 1982. *British Folklore, Myths and Legends.* Weidenfeld & Nicholson. London.

Alexander, Michael. 1973. *Beowulf.* Penguin Classics. London.

Ashe, G. 1990. *Mythology of the British Isles.* Methuen. London.

Bord, J. and C. 1987. *Ancient Mysteries of Britain.* Paladin. London.

Bowden, Malcolm. 1982. *The Rise of the Evolution Fraud.* Sovereign Publications. Bromley (PO Box 88, Bromley, Kent BR2 9PF).

Brewer, E.C. 1894. *Dictionary of Phrase and Fable.* enlarged ed.

Caie, G.D. 1989. *Beowulf.* Longman (York Notes Series). Harlow.

Campbell, J. 1982. *The Anglo-Saxons.* Penguin Books. London.

Caradoc of Llancarvan. (?). *Jesus College MS LXI.* Bodleian Library.

Comay, J. 1972. *Who's Who in the Old Testament.* Weidenfeld & Nicholson. London.

Cottrell, Leonard. 1958. *The Great Invasion.* Evans Bros. London.

Creation Ex Nihilo Technical Journal. Creation Science Foundation. PO Box 6302. Acacia Ridge DC. Queensland 4109. Australia.

Cusack, C.F. 1868. *The Illustrated History of Ireland.* Since published in facsimile by Bracken Books. London. 1987.

Dhorme, P. *Les Peuples Issus de Japhet, d'après le Chapitre X de la Genèse.* Syria. XIII. pp. 28–49.

Dickins, B. *The Genealogical Preface to the Anglo-Saxon Chronicles.* Univ. Cambridge Mus. of Archaeology Occasional Papers. No. 11.

Dumville, D.N. *The Anglian Collection of Royal Genealogies and Regnal Lists.* Anglo-Saxon England. 5: 23–50.

Ellis, P.B. 1978. *Caesar's Invasion of Britain.* Orbis. London.

Flinders Petrie, W.M. 1917. *Neglected British History*. Proc. Brit. Academy. Vol. VIII. pp. 1–28.
Garmonsway, G.N. 1990. *The Anglo-Saxon Chronicle*. Everyman. London.
Griscom, Acton. 1929. *Geoffrey of Monmouth's Historia Regum Britanniae*. Longman, Green & Co. London.
Handford, S.A. and Gardner, J.F. 1982. *Caesar: The Conquest of Gaul*. Penguin Classics. London.
Himmelfarb, G. 1959. *Darwin and the Darwinian Revolution*. Chatto and Windus. London.
Hislop, A. 1959. *The Two Babylons*. Loiseaux Bros. New Jersey.
Hodgen, M. 1971. *Early Anthropology in the Sixteenth and Seventeenth Centuries*. Univ. Pennsylvania. Philadelphia.
Interpreter's Dictionary of the Bible. 1962. 4 vols and Supplementary. Abingdon Press. New York.
Johns, G. and T.1989. *The Mabinogion*. Everyman's Library. J.M. Dent & Sons Ltd. London.
Jones, Canon Robert Ellis. 1929. *Untitled Literal Translation of Jesus College MS LXI* (now at the Bodleian Library, Oxford). See Griscom pp. 217–536.
Keating, G. 1634. *The History of Ireland*. Dublin. 1902–14.
Keller, W. 1974. *The Bible as History*. Hodder & Stoughton. London.
Klaeber, Fr. 1950. *Beowulf and the Fight at Finnsburg*. 3rd ed. D.C. Heath & Co. Boston.
MacFirbis. 1650. *The Book of Genealogies*. Dublin.
Mackie, J.D. 1985. *A History of Scotland*. Dorset Press. New York.
Magoun, F.P. *King Aethelwulf's Biblical Ancestors*. Modern Language Review. 46: 249–50.
Manley Pope. 1862. *A History of the Kings of Ancient Britain*. Simpkin, Marshall & Co. London.
Morris, John. 1980. *Nennius: British History and the Welsh Annals*. Phillimore. Chichester.
Morris, John. 1977. *The Age of Arthur*. Volumes 1–3. Phillimore. Chichester.
New Bible Dictionary. Inter-varsity Press. London. 1972.
Norton and Sackville. 1992. 'Gorboduc' in *Two Tudor Tragedies*. Penguin Classics. London.
O'Brien, M.A. 1962. *Corpus Genealogarium Hiberniae*. Dublin.
O'Clery Book of Genealogies, The. Analecta Hibernica. 18. Dublin. 1915.

Palgrave, Sir Francis. 1876. *History of the Anglo-Saxons*. William Tegg & Co. Since published in facsimile by Bracken Books. London. 1989.
Plummer, C. 1892. *Two Saxon Chronicles Parallel*. (British Library).
Poole, Matthew. 1685. *Commentary on the Holy Bible*. 3 vols. Since published in facsimile by Banner of Truth Trust. London. 1962.
Probert, W. 1823. *Ancient Laws of Cambria*. London.
Ralegh, Sir Walter. 1628. *The Historie of the World in Five Bookes*. Walter Burre. London.
Roberts, Peter. 1811. *Chronicle of the Kings*. (Sole remaining copy held at Bodleian Library. Shelfmark Douce T., 301).
Ronan C. 1983. *The Cambridge Illustrated History of the World's Science*. Newnes. Cambridge.
Salway, Peter. *Roman Britain*. Clarendon Press. Oxford. 1981.
Savage, A. 1982. *The Anglo-Saxon Chronicles*. Macmillan. London.
Sélincourt, Aubrey de. 1960. *Livy: The Early History of Rome*. Penguin Classics. London.
Sherley-Price, Leo. 1985. *Bede: A History of the English Church and People*. Dorset Press. New York. Also available in Penguin Classics.
Simpson, J. 1980. *British Dragons*. B.T. Batsford Ltd.
Sisam, K. *Anglo-Saxon Royal Genealogies*. Proc. of Brit. Academy. 39: 287–348.
Smith, G. 1876. *The Chaldean Account of Genesis*. Sampson Low. London.
Stenton, Sir Frank. 1985. *Anglo-Saxon England*. Clarendon Press. Oxford.
Stevenson, W.H. 1904. *Asser's Life of King Alfred*. Oxford.
Stowe, John. 1614. *The Annales or Generall Chronicle of England*. Thomas Adams. London. (Copy held at Croydon Reference Library).
Sweet. 1885. *The Earliest English Texts*. Oxford Univ. Press.
Tatlock, J.. P. 1950. *The Legendary History of Britain: Geoffrey of Monmouth's Historia Regum Britanniae and its Early Vernacular Versions*. Univ. Calif. Press.
Thompson, Aaron. 1718. *The British History Translated into English from the Latin of Geoffrey of Monmouth*. London (Guildhall Hall Library).
Thorpe, Lewis. 1966. *Geoffrey of Monmouth: The History of the Kings of Britain*. Penguin Classics. London.

Thorpe, Lewis. tr. 1974. *Gregory of Tours: The History of the Franks.* Penguin Classics. London.
Topsell, E. 1608. *The History of Four-Footed Beasts and Serpents.* London. Also printed by G. Sawbridge, T. Williams & T. Johnson. London. 1658.
Unger, M. 1954. *Archaeology and the Old Testament.* Zondervan. Michigan.
Wade-Evans, A.W. 1938. *Nennius's History of the Britons.* SPCK.
West, David. 1990. *Virgil: The Aeneid.* Penguin Classics. London.
Westwood, Jennifer. 1985. *Albion: A Guide to Legendary Britain.* Granada. London.
Whiston, William. 1981. *Josephus: Complete Works.* Pickering & Inglis. London.
Whitlock, R. 1983. *Here Be Dragons.* George Allen & Unwin. Boston.
Wright. (ed.). 1841–5. *Reliquae Antiquae.* Copy held at London's Guildhall Library, Aldermanbury.